Saffron Walden (Edwin Smith)

towards a NEW society

Published in association with
NEW SOCIETY
Series editor: PAUL BARKER
(Editor of NEW SOCIETY)

NICHOLAS TAYLOR

the village in the city

TEMPLE SMITH·LONDON

First published in Great Britain in 1973
by Maurice Temple Smith Ltd
37 Great Russell Street London WC1

ISBN 0 8511 7011 0 paperback, 08511 7012 9 cased

Book designed by Craig Dodd
Printed by Ebenezer Baylis & Son Ltd
The Trinity Press, Worcester, and London

This series is published in association with New
Society; but the opinions expressed are the responsibility of the author and do not commit the magazine
as such in any way.

Contents

1

Without a City Wall

Pundits still pontificate about 'Town and Country Planning' on the unwarranted assumption that people live either in the town or in the country. Yet in fact most of us in the industrially developed countries live in suburbs, and enjoy it; and for Englishmen in particular there is nothing new in this. Thanks to the encircling sea, 'Which serves it in the office of a wall or as a moat defensive to a house', the pattern of settlements has for many centuries differed radically from that in the war-torn countries of the Continent. Instead of a compact walled mass with formal piazzas and inevitable avenues, the typical English market town such as Lavenham or Chipping Campden has grown gradually as a rambling comfortable sprawl of cottages and workshops and farmyards, responding freely to the logic of local geography, local climate, and local family life.

There was in fact an instinctive rightness in the landscape of the English cottage long before anyone thought of calling it 'picturesque' or reproducing it for quaint effect. In real life, as against Renaissance myth, it is the client who demands and defines the basic form of his settlement and the architect who merely responds and refines it. When the inhabitants of Umbria and Tuscany betook themselves to spectacular hilltops, it was not for the sake of the view (not until the fourteenth century did an adventurous poet, Petrarch, climb a mountain for that), nor was it to satisfy a sculptural delight in the picturesque arrangement of building masses on hillsides (for that one has to wait for the sensibility of the English eighteenth-century landscapists, beginning with Vanbrugh). All along they had a far, far more pressing reason — the need to protect themselves and their families and their stored crops from the armed assaults of their neighbours.

This was equally true in England for a time in the mid-twelfth century, when the barons roamed the land at will in King Stephen's reign and thus gave at least a temporary relevance to the imported Norman notion of the walled town. But once Henry II had firmly established lasting peace, it was only on the half-conquered Celtic fringe, and in certain strategic border counties, that Westminster found it necessary to hold down a rebellious peasantry with systematic walled *bastides* on the Continental model: Conway, Caernarvon, Stirling, Derry — the walls of the last-named still in use for their original purpose. On the South Coast there was also a special need to fortify certain ports against French raiders: Rye, Winchelsea, Southampton, Portsmouth. But elsewhere in England the random ribbon-like growth of suburban houses was able to proceed naturally, without fear of defencelessness, even where the Normans had at first built walls.

Such extramural freedom, out of reach of the earliest byelaws, did on occasions have its seamy side, as Chaucer suggests:

> Where dwelle ye? If it to telle be.
> In the suburbes of a town, quod he,
> Lurkynge in hernes and in lanes blynde,
> Where-as thise robbours and thise theves, by
>   kynde,
> Holden hir pryvee, fereful residence...

Such evils certainly accompanied the immediate purlieus of London's city gates, particularly the markets and inns of Smithfield and Southwark. But a good deal of anti-suburban prejudice was motivated simply by the commercial jealousy of the guilds who found to their chagrin that fellow-craftsmen, by escaping outside the financial demands of paying rates or maintaining price-rings, were able to produce a more competitive product — a logic of low over-heads which is still the main selling point of the Loca-tion of Offices Bureau today, in persuading business-men to decentralise from London. Given the foetid stench of the medieval alleyway an escape to purer country air was in any case only commonsense.

By the time of Leland's tours around 1540, even the Welsh town of Tenby, heavily fortified and pre-serving to this day an almost intact *enceinte*, had already sprouted outside its main North Gate 'a pretti suburbe'. By the seventeenth century 'suburban' was

8

a common adjective for an uncommonly attractive way of life. Defoe, for example, in describing the spa of Epsom fifteen miles outside London, wrote in 1724 that 'the greatest of the Men, I mean of this Grave sort, may be supposed to be Men of Business, who are at London upon Business all the Day, and moving to their lodgings at Night, make the Families, generally speaking, rather provide Suppers than Dinners: for 'tis very frequent for the Trading part of the Company to place their families here, and take their Horses every Morning to London . . . and be at Epsom again at Night.' A generation before the railway William Cobbett was already observing that, fifty miles from London, 'Great parcels of stockjobbers stay at Brighton. They skip backwards and forwards on the coaches and actually carry on stockjobbing in Change Alley though they reside in Brighton.'

On the Continent by contrast, with land warfare on an ever-ascending scale of violence right up to the Berlin Airlift in 1948, it is not surprising that there has been continuing pressure for the herding together of people into tightly knit towns and cities, girt by walls. Such enforced togetherness behind the sentry-guarded gate has admittedly not been without its compensations in community life: man is an almost infinitely adaptable creature and even in prison camps is capable, as at Stalag Luft III and Changi Jail in the last war, of developing a highly elaborate and even exhilarating diversity of organised community life. Not surprisingly, therefore, when confined behind the precipitous cliffs and walls of a hill city, the Italian farmers and peasants, led by the commercial entrepreneurs who profited from their products, were capable of developing a constricted but in some respects extremely satisfying way of life, centred on those sunlit piazzas and pavement cafés. In central Italy the spatial forms of enclosure by buildings, in the form of piazza and loggia, are a particular response to the opportunities of the local climate, in which it is a pleasure for large parts of the year to sit out in public in the open air. Such places of public assembly can be delightful, and we have nothing in

England that remotely matches the best of them — witness the squalid maelstrom of traffic around the road islands of Piccadilly Circus or Parliament Square.

But the problems of the hill-city start just at the point at which those of London begin to be satisfied, the point where the tourist leaves the central squares and begins to explore the private world of side-streets and alleyways and enclosed courtyards where the mass of the population lives. Whereas in London there is, even close to the central area, a vast unvisited sequence of intimate single-family cottages with tree-shaded gardens, in the equally unvisited back yards of the average central Italian hill-city it is easy to grasp amidst the congestion and the stench why the city fathers of the *comune* are Communist.

I remember Nikolaus Pevsner telling me how a young Italian architect, whom he had just been taking on a tour of those few isolated examples in London of monumental architecture that begin to match up to the best in Europe (Greenwich...Greenwich... Greenwich...) had kept insisting on stopping the car instead in perfectly ordinary spec builders' avenues and drives and crescents of the 1920s, exclaiming at their so exquisite design. Yet it is, I suppose, symbolic of our recent national tendencies to self-denigration that the only book available which describes, however briefly, the really remarkable feature of London — the high average quality of the conventional suburban house — is not by an English critic but by a Danish architect, Professor Steen-Eiler Rasmussen: *London, the Unique City* (1935).

Yet sixty years ago, after all, in the generation of Unwin and Lutyens and Ebenezer Howard's garden cities, the pre-eminence of the 'English house' was as unquestioned amongst the progressive architects of Europe as the 'English garden' had been a hundred years earlier. In 1897—1903 the Government of Prussia actually sent the critic Hermann Muthesius as a special ambassador to the Court of St James to report upon it (which he did, naturally in three volumes, in *Das Englische Haus* of 1904—5). Today, at a time when our social sensibility has been gradually extended from the individual house-and-garden to the total environment of the community, the same proud position, in the same picturesque tradition, is enjoyed by the English New Towns which attract thousands of international visitors every year to study the best answer yet found for modern industrial society.

Not that one would be aware of that from reading English architectural journals: for, perhaps partly because of unrelated psychological problems connected with the decline of Britain's imperial power in the world, there has been since the mid-1950s a quite remarkable and unreasonable loss of confidence in their own local traditions amongst English architects and architectural critics. This is all the sadder because, in spite of the vicissitudes of English architecture between the wars, a successful reconciliation had eventually been achieved between the English Garden City tradition and the international Modern Movement (the latter filtered to us via the Sweden of Sven Markelius and Backström & Reinius). This *modus vivendi* was triumphantly demonstrated in the first New Towns, where several of the leading figures were not surprisingly specialists in English landscape garden design, including Sir Frederick Gibberd (architect-planner of Harlow), Geoffrey Jellicoe (consultant planner for Hemel Hempstead) and Peter Shepheard (deputy chief architect at Stevenage). In his Reith Lectures in 1955 Sir Nikolaus Pevsner was thus able optimistically to chronicle 'The Englishness of English Art' as a continuing growth from the medieval village to the eighteenth century landscape to the postwar New Town.

Yet by that date some of the younger architects, addicted as they were to the Gaullist rhetoric of Le Corbusier, were already beginning to react violently against the supposed evil of 'cosiness' in the lowly terrace houses of Harlow and Stevenage — a sneer that admittedly had some point given to it by the much less imaginative architecture of such places as Bracknell or Crawley, and the apparent 'levelling down' of the Welfare State implied by the monotonous uniformity of some estates. But the attack rapidly became a more aesthetical and less rational one against modesty and prettiness as such: 'Swedish charm' actually became a sarcastic catchphrase of abuse amongst those who hated the 'escapism' of the 1951 Festival of Britain and pinned their colours instead to Alison and Peter Smithson's New Brutalism, with its compound of exposed Miesian steelwork and exposed Corbusian concrete.

In principle there was indeed much to commend in Brutalism as a reactionary movement of tough-mindedness that, like Butterfield's and Philip Webb's a century before, turned sharply away from the inoffensively synthetic and back to the crude peasant origins of the vernacular, with a puritanical aversion to anything but raw materials in their naked state. The Smithsons themselves, furthermore, with their pioneering interest in the Pop Art of domestic trivia (the exhibition 'Parallel of Life and Art' in 1953), had always had a much more tolerant attitude towards the genuine vernacular of everyday life than most of their colleagues in the Team-X group did. Their fascination with aspects of suburban imagery — the 'peasant commuter' — comes out well in the self-conscious banality of their pitched-roofed house for Derek Sugden at Watford in 1955, which they justified at the time in admirably pragmatic and subjective terms: 'On the whole the English still resist really large windows and are happiest with the Tudor cottage. This is probably because the Tudor cottage looks as if it would protect you from the outside, and feels as if it fits you on the inside. The bald glass window has against it six months' glare of a flat grey sky . . . The distribution of the windows in the Sugden house deliberately allows the brickwork to flow together and ultimately coalesce with the roof to form a solid mass resulting in that appearance of all-round protection which was once characteristic of English popular architecture so expressive of our climate.'

Yet only a year before those same Smithsons had completed their determinedly *un*popular and *un*-

protected steel-and-glass school at Hunstanton. Similar split-mindedness could be seen at the same time in Le Corbusier himself: in the very year (1952) that he completed the appallingly aggressive splendour of the Unité flats — a high-rise slab of rough concrete isolated in the fields outside Marseilles — and began the equally aggressive public buildings stranded in the empty centre of his new town of Chandigarh, he made a brief but brilliant dash into the intimacies of the suburbs in designing the Maisons Jaoul at Neuilly-sur-Seine, a pair of red-brick villas with arched roofs set informally in a leafy garden in western Paris. They were in a rough peasant manner which Corbusier himself had previewed nearby in the little garden pavilion (or *petite maison de weekend*) at Boulogne-sur-Seine in 1935, amazingly reminiscent in its geometry of Lutyens's Deanery Garden entrance court of 1900. The Jaoul style was paralleled too in the early fifties by the brick-copper-timber vernacular of Alvar Aalto in Finland, where the planning philosophy from Saarinen's Helsinki Plan of 1916 onwards had been closely related to the English garden suburb. Meanwhile in the States the octogenarian Frank Lloyd Wright was as usual enjoying the last laugh of *plus ça change*... for it was precisely the reaction of a a commuter in his rustic brick-and-timber home against the synthetic smoothness of his machine-made workplace that Wright had been catering for in Chicago ever since the early 1890s (and his disciples subsequently on the West Coast too), in an American tradition going back to H. H. Richardson and through him owing much to the English influence of Norman Shaw.

Yet the new hand-crafted modern vernacular of the fifties, successfully adapted as it was to suburban circumstances in places as far apart as Melbourne and Oslo, had surprisingly little effect in England, in spite of the enthusiastic projects for pitch-roofed 'rural housing' sent in by the Smithsons and their friends to the CIAM architectural congress in 1955. The private market was insufficiently enterprising to move away from gingerbread-tiled fireplaces and Crittall's steel windows, apart from the occasional individual house for an aesthete such as John Voelcker's for Humphrey Lyttleton — and that had difficulty with planning permission. The delightful split-pitch-roofed estate cottages of whitewashed brick at Rush-brooke in Suffolk designed for Lord Rothschild in pure 'rural housing' style by Richard Llewelyn-Davies and John Weeks were a freak in England, where once they would have been in the mainstream, and they had an immediate effect only at the single new town to be started under the Tory Government in the fifties, Sir Hugh Wilson's Cumbernauld in Scotland, where the similarly white-walled local vernacular of 'harling' in rough plaster gave the cue. Yet even Cumbernauld, situated as it was in a faraway country of which English architects know little, did not have any widespread influence in its turn until 'high density, low-rise' got under way in the sixties.

Meanwhile English local authorities, and a whole generation of local authority architects, had reso-lutely turned their backs on the individual cottage and gone hell-for-leather for the standardised flat. At the normal outer-suburban density of 50—70 people to the acre (rather less in fact than the two-storey houses of Cumbernauld at 77) borough after borough went for a standard four-storey maisonette block in a sea of communal lawn, with a communal staircase up to a narrow communal access balcony. At higher densities, even as little as 90, architects rapidly espoused the so-called 'mixed development' of high-rise slabs amongst lower maisonettes and houses, beyond which logically lay the cul-de-sac of the iso-lated tower, the so-called 'point block', where families with young children could be stranded on high without compunction. At first the point block had mild features of pink brick — a wolf in Swedish clothing — as in Gibberd's The Lawn at Harlow or the LCC's Alton East estate at Roehampton. But at the Alton West estate of 1955—8, the mailed fist of Corbusian concrete, *béton brut* as at the Unité, burst out above the trees in a fine revolutionary gesture;

and, in a way that Corb himself had never managed (not having pliant local authorities at his command), the young team of LCC architects were able to give built reality to his prewar vision in *La Cité Radieuse* of towers-in-a-park.

Whereas the Unité itself was an isolated failure — the only block to be built of the dozen or more that Corb had planned — its aesthetic image, in a cut-price version without the communal laundries or libraries or nurseries, was salvaged by official architects in England as a massive practical prescription for reconstructing hundreds of acres of Victorian suburb. At least at Roehampton there was a genuine park — three parks, in fact, of eighteenth century country houses converted into colleges — and the density was barely 100. But, back in the inner suburbs, with a zoned density of 136 or more, the same point blocks and high slabs were made to rise, Phoenix-like, out of the ashes of East End bombed sites, and often on street corners hemmed in by existing dwellings. Into these castles-in-the-air were stacked the thousands of council tenants, who had no choice in the market but to acquiesce in the judgment of elected committees and their professional advisers. The manifest social drawbacks of such blocks were all too easily unperceived through spectacles misted over by the sheer political beauty of utopia rising heroically out of ruin; and when the drawbacks did become apparent, the crudest could in any case be blamed by architects upon the Philistinism of such totem figures of professional jealousy as borough engineers and package dealers (meaning those building firms who provided their own 'free' architectural service).

But the social disadvantages of point blocks are no less oppressive, and sometimes seem to be even more so, when the elevations are styled up like fun. In any case the intellectual and emotional enthusiasm for towers in the fifties emphatically did not come from borough engineers and package dealers, who as usual jumped only on the back of the bandwaggon when the risks became conventionally or commercially acceptable; it came from architects, and it came in the context of an irrational hate of 'suburban sprawl' and an equally irrational passion for all things 'urban' — 'urbanism', 'urbanity', 'urban values', 'urban cluster', 'urban grain' — extrapolated aesthetically not from the humdrum English market town but from the romantically fortified Mediterranean hill city, with its piazzas, patios and kasbahs. However remote it might be from the needs and experience of council tenants, the San Gimigniano image was irresistibly attractive to those architectural students who had not been abroad since 1939 and were bored by the drabness of postwar rationing.

There was some intellectual ballast for the new Grand Tour in the writings of Rudolf Wittkower on Palladio and of the South African architect Martienssen on the Acropolis, but camera-toting architects were lured primarily by aesthetics — by the wonderfully clear 'image quality' of Mediterranean communities on walled-up hilltops. It was a wonderful summer escape from the wide-open expanses of bare mud on postwar building sites in winter. In 1953 Pevsner's fellow-editor at the *Architectural Review*, J. M. Richards, launched a bitter attack on what he called the 'prairie planning' of the New Towns, carefully springing it before those prairies had had a chance to sprout and bloom in the way that Letchworth and Welwyn had; and meanwhile even Pevsner himself canonised Roehampton, with all its inherited Georgian oaks, as being in the true apostolic succession of the Picturesque. It was a brilliantly unfair comparison: for what happened when the slabs and towers were dumped instead within the dusty wastes of slum clearance in Camberwell or Hackney? It was left to the professional perspectivists of 'artist's impressions' to disguise the wind-blown litter of the lift-halls with evocative sketches of striped awnings over pavement cafés. The sunlit hillsides of Umbria and Andalusia were oddly hard to reproduce on bleak slopes outside Leeds or Glasgow. Even at Cumbernauld, where Sir Hugh Wilson had proved that the essential two-storey cottage house could be built

satisfactorily in steeply banked terraces at a density

half as great again as the 'prairies' of Harlow or Stevenage, the Mediterranean fantasy was allowed to take over in placing the town centre at the summit of the hilltop site — a choice of site, of course, with real practical disadvantages in the Scottish climate, given that there was no need to choose it for military defence. Sir Hugh publicly claimed the 'hill city' image of Cumbernauld as one of its great virtues compared with earlier, cosier new towns; and he gave carte blanche to one of his assistants, Geoffrey Copcutt, in designing the dirty, windy megalith of piled-up shopping ledges, which now crushes into insignificance the mothers who push their babies up endless ramps to get to it.

Perhaps the most breathtakingly seductive of all the dream books from the new Grand Tour, a kind of high-class architectural equivalent of the girlie magazine, was *The Italian Townscape*, originally published as a special issue of the *Architectural Review* in 1962, being both written and photographed by that magazine's proprietor, H. de Cronin Hastings, under the pseudonym Ivor de Wolfe. It is a lyrical, almost ecstatic sequence of black-and-white photographs — very black, very white and usually devoid of people — accompanied by a no less poetic text which makes the unscholarly assertion that the ordinary streets and piazzas of the hill cities were, to their uttermost details, consciously designed, the implication being that architects in England should go and do likewise. Yet even the most arrogant of Italian Renaissance aesthetes claimed preeminence for the artist-architect only in the design of certain monumental groups of buildings; whereas *The Italian Townscape* implied that, whatever the ordinary man or woman or community might desire, the artist-architect was entitled to manipulate the minutest details of the shape of things to create his own private ideal environment. That this is what de Cronin Hastings was getting at is proved by his second Ivor de Wolfe book, *Civilia*, again published first in the *Architectural Review* (June 1971). It consists of a proposal for a major new city at Hartshill, just north of Nuneaton in the Mid-

The new hill city? The 31-storey towers of Red Road, Balornock, crown the exurban spoilheaps east of Glasgow. (Marilyn Stafford)

lands, in an area of colliery spoilheaps, turned over-
night into instant Tuscan hillsides — the urban image
being composed out of photographic collages of all de
Cronin Hastings's favourite modern buildings, the
nose of one being joined to the legs of another, like
that children's party game played with cut-outs of fat
women and thin men. The result is a truly mind-
blowing nightmare, which could be dismissed as a
mere frivol if it were not all too typically indicative of
the kind of secret world of illusion which so many
architects and architectural critics nurture within
them, in defiance of the real world of people. De
Cronin Hastings does not, of course, live in a hill-city
himself (or on a colliery spoilheap); he lives in a nice
comfortable farmhouse in the Sussex stockbroker
belt near Petworth. *Civilia* is not intended for him —
it is intended for the rest of us, and particularly for
the great mass of council tenants who have no control
over the environment in which the architect-planners
put them. It is an apotheosis of the dishonesty of
fashionable architects, who sit all day at their drawing
boards in County Hall designing harsh piazzas for
Battersea and Bermondsey, and then at 4.51 p.m.
sharp descend to the tube train, roaring out under the
forgotten redevelopment areas for which they are
responsible, until they come to the surface at their
own cosy creeper-hung suburban cottages in Hampstead and Wimbledon.

The reality of the Italian townscape — in Italy — is
somewhat different from the photographs. At Venice,
where the corset of self-defence was drawn (even
more tightly than by walls) by the waters of the
lagoon, the neighbourhood hierarchy around the
campi and *campielli* does indeed represent a triumph
of man's ability to overcome his circumstances and
make some kind of organisational sense out of what
might otherwise be a disease-infested mob in a
swamp. Anyone, however, who has visited Venice as I
have at the end of January will realise that in
Northern Italy there is another side to the picture: in
the drizzle of an Adriatic mist, hardly a soul sits outside, and one becomes depressingly conscious, as per-

haps one does not during the summer, of the appalling decay of this once splendid community, because of its inability to adapt to the demands of family life. On one of the days that I was there in January 1969, the annual census figures came out, showing that during the previous year another 2,000 people had left old Venice, leaving it with a population of 108,000 — and it was not difficult to work out what would happen if this steady annual decrease was not arrested. Yet the population of the total *Comune di Venezia* had risen to 269,000. Where were the other 161,000 living? The answer lay shrouded beneath the pall of industrial smoke hanging over the mainland side of the lagoon, just across the causeway from the old city: there lay the oil refineries, the chemical factories and the motor car production lines of the suburbs of Mestre, Marghera and Santa Margherita, Italy's third largest industrial complex after Milan and Turin. Few visiting architects and planners seem to realise that the city which they so much admire has been deserted by the majority of its inhabitants for sound functional and economic reasons — that the suburbanites who now fill as many as 17 per cent of the jobs in the old city have good grounds for preferring even the polluted air of Mestre as a setting for family life, rather than the crumbling canalside palazzi, which must look for salvation instead to tourists and students. The tragedy is that there is no Northern Italian tradition of peacetime suburban design (hence the excitement in South London of Professor Pevsner's friend), so the major part of new Venice consists of jerry-built multi-storey flats deposited aimlessly in a marshy waste.

The raw failure to adapt is no less alarming in the suburbs of Paris. The draconian powers of the Gaullist Governments have certainly succeeded in conserving the scale of the central avenues and boulevards laid out in the last golden age of self-defence by Baron Haussmann, who, within an encirclement of new nineteenth century ramparts, was able nicely to calculate the length of street that could be commanded by the breech-loading rifle. Outside the historic centre, however — outside the areas where the leaders of community still live — all hell has been let loose in the last ten years. Enormous suburbs of high-rise flats now surround the Communist strongholds of Saint-Denis to the north and Belleville to the east, and the middle-class neighbourhoods around Sceaux and Orly to the south; time and again one has the sensation that one could be anywhere in the scenery of some Eastern European propaganda film. The dominance of the Beaux-Arts conventions of formal composition in design, originally worked out for the communal life of city centres, has led to an arrangement of uniform ten-storey blocks in an absolutely rigid symmetry which defies both the contours of the landscape and the individual personalities and private life of the people living there.

It is a hideous irony that, in the Gadarene spasm of industrialised (or prefabricated) building which has carried the ideals of Roehampton into the sixties and seventies, British local authorities have imported from the continent, and often from Paris, the worst vices of anti-suburban high-rise flats (for example, in the Balency system of construction used in London's 'new town' at Thamesmead); yet the planners of Greater Paris's first new city of Cergy-Pontoise have invited an English firm of architect-planners, Shankland, Cox and Associates, to advise them how to establish a viable and humane tradition of low-rise suburban houses. In May 1971, furthermore, it was announced that the first neighbourhood of houses-for-sale at Cergy-Pontoise had been entrusted, after an open design competition with forty entrants, to an English firm of building contractors, Higgs & Hill, with Clive Pascall and Peter Watson as architects and Leslie Bilsby, the former joint chief of Span, as the Paris-based director-in-charge; the houses are in Span's usual terraced rows around courtyards, but with such Parisian adaptations as larger kitchens and more sophisticated mechanical services.

There is no point in being falsely modest about the domestic life which the majority of English people are now able to enjoy in suburban houses, just as there is no point in avoiding criticism of those things like Piccadilly Circus, which we do extremely badly. Our merits and defects are exactly the opposite of those on the Continent, and, to say it once again, they relate to an historical development, not merely economically and socially but also psychologically, which has been strikingly different from that of the Continental countries. Whereas in France and Italy, from Roman times and even from Magna Graecia, power has traditionally lain in the cities, in England power has almost always lain principally in the countryside and on the land. It has always been the businessman's first ambition, having made his pile, to escape from the city and establish his family as hereditary landowners of a country estate. The Romans, it is true, built some symmetrical cities, but most of these crumbled away, for the Saxons preferred irregular villages. The two Saxon royal palaces which have been excavated in the last ten years, at Yeading in Northumberland and Cheddar in Somerset, have revealed not the grand, formal, symmetrical courtyards that the Continental cities inherited from their Roman governors (the British equivalent, the palace of Cogidubnus at Fishbourne which Barry Cunliffe has excavated, was significantly abandoned by the Saxons) but an apparently random conglomeration of large timber huts. This tradition of building in timber the Saxons brought with them from the German forests, where the Romans had never succeeded for long in imposing any kind of formal authority.

Because architectural historians have tended to be brainwashed into the assumption that the classical Graeco-Roman ideal of beauty, based on perfect proportions and formal symmetry, is the highest (or only) kind of beauty, the apparently random settlements of the Saxons have been regarded only as vernacular fodder for the archaeologist interested in the primitive. But their layout was not random in the sense of being without meaning; it was based on the functional requirements of those who lived in them, and thus in some senses was *more* sophisticated than the Graeco-Roman tradition of imposing a symmetrical facade, which can indeed be without meaning when it has little relationship to the human beings who have to live behind it. The Saxons showed a healthy disrespect for the rigid grid-plan of the Roman forts, and in a Roman grid-city such as Chichester or Winchester they freely bent the lattice to suit their own convenience, so that visually there now remains little impression of straight lines and right angles. At Chester they squatted upon the Roman ruins to such purpose that by the later Middle Ages there had evolved in the Rows a two-storey shopping centre so sophisticated and flexible that it has only been seen elsewhere since its revival by Sir Donald Gibson in the rebuilding of Coventry after the last war. The upper walkways of the Rows gave a separate front door to each house over its retailing floor, thus preserving privacy for those who lived over their businesses; and the timber framing gave a 'modern' flexibility, it being easy to knock holes in wattle-and-daub walls without disturbing the basic structure of oak. It is this kind of gently accommodating humanism that is so attractive in Saxon manuscripts compared with the fierce formalism of the Normans.

The basic Saxon dwelling was (and has been ever since) the timber-framed one-room cottage, and it still seems a marvel of commonsense with its fixed structure of 'crucks' or 'forks' made from curved tree trunks, interwoven with an anything-but-fixed envelope of wattle-and-daub walls which could be pushed outwards, away from the family hearth, to form the specialised outbuildings of kitchen or larder or cowshed or loo. These multiple 'outshots', giving each family the freedom to extend its home in the way that it wanted it and giving each residence its distinctively different character, can still be seen each week in the advertisements for home extensions and garden sheds on the back page of the *Radio Times*. The ability to alter and adapt one's own home to one's own desires is a fundamental freedom for Englishmen and woe betide the council committee

who ignore it. Almost equally rooted is the psychological necessity of the pitched roof, the triangle of
crucks or forks, as a symbol of family affection and
security. 'Fork' is after all an anatomical word, and
'cruck' is the same as 'crotch' — the point being that
the home is to the family what the body is to the
individual. It is no wonder that English people feel so
strongly threatened by the flat roofs of modern architects and compare them to 'desert forts' and 'block-
houses' — an attitude that would be incomprehen-
sible in a Mediterranean hill-village where the roof is a
place for sitting out in the evening sun. But to the
Englishman, in his colder climate, the cosy pitched
roof is a sacrament of family love — and the Abbey
National Building Society's admen knew what they
were doing when they drew that young couple holding a pitched roof over their heads as an umbrella.

Not that the Normans shared such sentiments at
first: although they also came originally from scattered villages in the forests of Scandinavia, they had
developed themselves into a fighting force so highly
disciplined that they were able not only to assimilate
the Roman tradition of building fortified cities, but
actually to elaborate upon it. Maurice Beresford illustrates many examples on the Celtic borders of the
standard three-tier system which evolved: the baron's
keep and inner bailey in the centre, then the outer
bailey where his troops were quartered and goods
could be stored in time of trouble, and finally the
fortified town wall, with its gates and battlements,
which encircled the local population. Edward I's *bastides* at Conway and Caernarvon in North Wales,
Winchelsea in Sussex and Montpazier near Bordeaux,
have indeed the same kind of military discipline and
architectural coherence which one enjoys in Central
Italy — except that, typically, Winchelsea is now only
a tiny village within the ramparts, with rolling Sussex
farmland covering the site of the streets and only the
hedgerows echoing the grid.

It is a comment on the dictatorial mentality en-
gendered in young architects by their teachers that an
architectural coherence of this military kind is still

24

seen by so many of them as a sensible solution for mid-twentieth-century communities. Yet even in the late twelfth century Norman barons were already becoming sublimated into English farmers, and their vassals were beginning to chafe against the previous barracks mentality. A prime example of this is Old Sarum in Wiltshire, a fortified town occupying an old Roman site on a promontory of windswept chalk downland. The Bishop, his Chapter and their cathedral, packed closely as they were within the precincts of the royal castle, began increasingly to resent an atmosphere of imprisonment by the garrison, while at the same time the lack of water and the inconvenient access up steep hills were making the townsmen restive. The troubles of King John and the minority of Henry III were seized as an opportunity for mass escape; and in a Papal Bill of 1219, Pope Honorius II gave his authority: 'Let us descend joyfully to the plains, where the valley abounds in corn, where the fields are beautiful and where there is freedom from oppression.' The following year a new cathedral was begun at the foot of the downs in the lush meadowland where five rivers meet — the Cathedral of New Sarum, or Salisbury. Next to it the Bishop planned a model city, still on a grid plan but very spaciously disposed so that each square block, called a 'chequer', contained within it a delightful 'soft centre' of green gardens and walled yards: and its particularly significant feature was that it never had a fortified wall around it, but only a ditch, sufficient merely to keep out vagrants.

Thenceforth the later medieval English town became an increasingly peaceful and liberated sprawl. Those towns which had inherited fortified walls from the Roman and Norman conquerors gradually allowed them to fall into disrepair. Prosperous merchants saw no reason why they should pay for gates and battlements which were not needed; while 'market towns' which had never had walls were, as we have noticed, not much more than enlarged villages. It is a matter perhaps more of status than of truth to

call a place like Lavenham or Chipping Campden a

'town', when it is in effect a single street with a few
small offshoots; and it is highly significant that many
of the residences of the principal merchants, such as
Grevel's House at Chipping Campden or Corpus
Christi Guildhall at Lavenham, were designed on the
principle not of the town house, flat-fronted and
tightly formal, but of the manor house, irregularly
projecting and comfortably asymmetrical. Even at
cities such as York, which were near enough to the
marauding Scots for the walls to be kept in good
order, the houses of the prosperous classes began to
spread out into the open fields outside the walls.
Some of the most beautiful streets in England are to
be found in the ribbon development of such medieval
suburbs, but in our recent fashion for 'urbanity',
planners have often been allowed, or encouraged, to
ignore them.

We have in fact tended to have a disastrously one-
eyed view of our cities: in saying 'York' we have
tended to mean only that part of York which lies
within the medieval walls, whereas in fact three-
quarters of the city is eighteenth, nineteenth and
twentieth century suburb, including such delicious
spots as the Victorian riverside village of Clifton and
Sir Raymond Unwin's model settlement of New Earswick for the Rowntrees. In preparing his recent Conservation Plan for York, Viscount Esher was specifically prevented from considering any beyond the
walls — even though the city engineer's pseudo-
boulevard of a ring road would sever the historic
suburb of merchants' houses called Bootham. In
saying 'Cambridge', we have similarly tended to mean
only that little bit of medieval town that is inter-
twined with the colleges between the King's Ditch
and the river, whereas in fact seven-eighths (or even
nine-tenths) of the city is eighteenth, nineteenth and
twentieth century suburb, ranging from the mansard-
roofed cottage terraces of Orchard Street to the
Edwardian retreats for dons designed by Baillie Scott
in Storey's Way. When we say 'Oxford', few of us
think of the multi-coloured Gothic villas of North
Oxford, and even fewer of the pink brick postwar

cottages of Cowley — even if Cowley is where very many citizens of Oxford live and work. Of course Cowley may not seem particularly worthy of admiration as an environment; and that is in part precisely because a one-eyed emphasis on the ancient centre has led to a concentration of financial and technical resources there, and a corresponding neglect of the rest of the city. But even if the 'sprawl' of Cowley may not at first sight seem attractive to those who peer at it from outside, we can be fairly certain that those actually living there do find beauties in it, if only in the flowers blooming in back gardens or the bay windows giving views across the road to friends and neighbours. By contrast those Italian hill cities which seem most seductive to the tourist usually offer few back gardens and few outward-looking views, the piling up of humanity within their walls permitting all too few of the more relaxed feelings of family life to be given expression. As for Mestre and Marghera, which are in effect the Cowley of Venice, who can deny their inferiority to their English counterpart?

Now it may seem perverse or self-consciously paradoxical to press the virtues of Cowley, a name which, in an élitist society whose highest expression is Oxford, has so often been held up to contempt as the lowest of proletarian lump. Yet at the very least it must be admitted that it is in just such 'monotonous sprawl' that the majority of our fellow citizens not only live but prefer to live. I have rarely met an architect who designed a council estate as a hill city who did not himself live in a low density suburb. Indeed, Mr Ernö Goldfinger's carefully publicised stay of a week at the top of the twenty-six storey tower block of flats which he designed for GLC tenants beside the Blackwall Tunnel in East London, far from proving that such towers are suitable for family life, only served to highlight the fact that Mr Goldfinger otherwise lives in Hampstead.

This is a book about where people actually live, and about where they would like to live if given the chance — not in some fortified tourist hotspot on the edge of the Apennines (or even in the mountains of Wales) but in a semi-detached house with a garden in a nineteenth or twentieth century suburb. To the planner commuting to work from his own suburb, who sees other people's suburbs only from the top of the railway viaduct, such places may seem featureless and monotonous and sprawling and dull — and all the other words that have been used for the past generation or two in the architectural schools to denigrate the way of life of ordinary people. But as someone who lives in one of those suburbs and who spends much of his time there politically, knocking on people's doors and hearing their views about their neighbourhood (which they are not slow to give), I find that within these quiet suburban villages there is a way of life which in its freedom, diversity and individuality — the ability of ordinary families to do their own thing — is more sophisticated than either the Tuscan piazza or the Oxford quad. There are of course good English suburbs and much less good English suburbs; but, rather than dismissing their defects wholesale as 'sprawl' (with the implication that there is really nothing that can be done about them except to pull them down and start again from scratch with a pristine hill city), we should be asking instead: *How can we do them better?* If a man asks you for a rather philistine kind of fig, you do not satisfy him by pressing upon him a beautiful architect-designed thistle. You need instead to find out more about that fig: why was it needed, what kind of satisfaction was it hoped to give, and how can it be more perfectly ripened?

At the public enquiry held in 1947 into the proposal to site the brick stack of Sir Giles Gilbert Scott's Bankside power station in a position where it would seriously conflict (as it does) with views of St Paul's, the late Sir Patrick Abercrombie, pressed by counsel to say why he still persisted in criticising the design of so eminent an architect, stated: 'I would not wish to have my bath in my drawing room, *even if it were* designed by Sir Giles Gilbert Scott.' Similarly — call me philistine if you will — I would not

wish to bring up my children in a flat on the six-
teenth floor, even if all fifteen floors below me had
been individually designed by Sir Basil Spence or Sir
Robert Matthew or some genius in the GLC Architect's Department, and even if the piazza at the foot
of the lift-shaft had been enlivened by the most exquisite collage of *Architectural Review* cobbles and
bollards.

The question remains: can we design better
suburbs, with architectural forms which positively
encourage and enhance the kind of family life which
is traditional to such places? To answer this, we must
turn to more recent history, and examine the evolution of the small English suburban house — detached,
semi-detached or terraced — which was initially
middle-class but is ultimately classless.

2

A House for Everyman

The peculiar flavour of the bourgeois 'English house' stems paradoxically from its aristocratic upbringing. It is not so much the 'Englishman's castle' as the 'Englishman's manor house'. Once the landowner no longer required the castle wall for self-defence, he was free to develop the comfortable, practical, undogmatic relationship between hall and porch, hall and kitchen, hall and solar, solar and bedchamber, which had been gradually rationalised out of the Saxon irregularities of Cheddar and Yeading. The limbs of the house extended informally in each direction so that they enclosed sheltered yards and gardens. When Augustus Welby Pugin argued for the Gothic Revival in *The True Principles of Christian Architecture* (1841), it was not the sacerdotalist rantings of the Catholic convert, or the neo-feudal fantasies of the 'art-architect' of the Houses of Parliament, which attracted middle-of-the-road practical men such as Gilbert Scott to the medievalist cause; it was rather the unanswerable functionalist case, after two centuries of Renaissance formalism, for reviving the simple manorial arrangement of asymmetrically disposed walls and windows, roofs and chimneys, which Pugin put into practice immediately in small suburban schools and presbyteries and convents. In such modest buildings it was less of a Gothic Revival and more of a Vernacular Revival, within which such Pugin disciples as Butterfield and Street were able without flinching to accommodate such up-to-date conveniences as the Georgian sash window and the cast-iron verandah.

In rejecting the aristocratic artifices of the Grecian portico and the Romantic battlement, and in returning to the vernacular of the manorial farmhouse, the radically minded Victorians succeeded in exactly capturing the aspiration of back-to-the-soil which is basic to most suburban Englishmen — landowning made democratic, every man his own manor house, even if there do have to be as many as twenty of them to each acre. As F.L.M. Thompson has demonstrated, the majority of the Victorian middle classes were far more subservient to the aims of the landed

aristocracy, and for far longer, than one might suspect from the sweeping myths of Whig historians —
the Industrial Revolution, the Rise of the Middle
Classes, the Railway Age and so on. Even though the
population of England and Wales increased from less
than 9 million in 1801 to almost 18 million in 1851
and on to 32½ million in 1901, the aristocracy did
not lose its hold on the main centres of power until
the agricultural slump of the 1870s. It continued to
call the tune in politics and in culture, while industrial *nouveaux riches* from humble backgrounds
remained ill-educated and unsure of their taste. Not
until their children and grandchildren had been
systematically disciplined in the newly founded or
re-founded public schools did the families of commerce acquire a smooth professional polish of their
own — and architecturally this relates exactly to the
brick Dutch villas of the so-called Queen Anne style
of the 1870s. Even then they retained the same fundamental ambition, possessed by every English
merchant since the Middle Ages, of using their wealth
to settle their families on country estates, which
could be handed on to future generations. It may
have gradually become less and less a country estate
and more and more a suburban villa — and eventually
a semi-detached or even a so-called 'town house' —
but the aspiration of the owner-occupier, to own not
only his own house but the earth and trees and
flowers around it has remained constant, even after
the virtual disappearance of the hereditary principle.

But let no one be misled by such phrases as Gothic
Revival (or a few years later Queen Anne or neo-
Georgian) into imagining that the Victorian rediscovery of the vernacular involved a literal imitation of
past epochs, even if such propagandists as Pugin and
the Ecclesiologists insisted that this was what they
were doing. The stylistic propaganda was really only
an appeal to authority — in the way that Protestant
reformers appealed to the Early Christian Church or
Oxford Tractarians to medieval Catholicism. English
radicalism has perennially conjured up a picture of
some pristine utopia, Eden before the Fall, to which

society should be returned, and in the nineteenth century such fantasy was central to the protest against the new evils of industrial laissez-faire. Pugin's 'Town of 1440' (in the famous illustrated comparison with the 'Town of 1840' appended to the second edition of his *Contrasts*), Ruskin's chapter on the Nature of Gothic in *The Stones of Venice*, Morris's *Dream of John Ball* and *News from Nowhere* — prima facie these were all black reactionary attempts to drive England back into a past age. But not one of these visionary utopias had ever actually existed, and thus, under the guise of 'revival', their authors were in fact being highly original and inventive. This kind of imaginary step backwards in order to take two real steps forwards is the essence of evolutionary rather than revolutionary progress and so, although Victorian Gothic was quite different from any Gothic that the world had ever seen before, it was at the same time an integral part of the English domestic tradition; and Norman Shaw's vernacular classicism of the 1870s has appropriately been dubbed 'Domestic Revival'. Conversely, whilst Muthesius's *Englische Haus* of the nineties had clear roots in the medieval tradition of manorial hall and solar, the kind of environment it sheltered and enclosed was distinctively Victorian not only in being free from dung and geared up with the latest mod. con. (Norman Shaw's dramatically Wagnerian château of Cragside, for example, was the first country house to have electric light) but also in having a totally different relationship with the surrounding countryside. In this respect the Gothic Revival owed everything to the eighteenth century, not the thirteenth.

The English picturesque tradition of landscape gardening came to maturity in the 1730s in the works of William Kent, who, in Horace Walpole's immortal words, 'leapt the fence and saw all nature was a garden'. Like all such leaps, however, it did not happen quite as quickly as that, and Kent owed a great deal to his immediate predecessors: to the garden which the poet Alexander Pope had created for himself from 1718 on the banks of the Thames at

Twickenham; to the ideas of 'associational' aesthetics (based not merely on the proportions of things seen but on the emotional associations aroused by them) put forward from 1709 by Joseph Addison in *The Spectator*; and especially to the remarkable landscape gardening exploits of Sir John Vanbrugh at Castle Howard and Claremont. It is difficult at this distance of time to appreciate the profound change of human attitudes involved in 'leaping the fence'. For the medieval villager, outside the manorial moat and the three big fields there lay in wait the unfriendly attentions of vagrants and robbers, and also such terrors as wolves and bears; it was natural for the squire to ride out into the woods to hunt, but that was all. By the fifteenth century, when mansions were semi-fortified and brick-walled (Oxburgh and Herstmonceux) or totally unfortified (Cothay and Cotehele), it became fashionable, largely under the civilising influence of the monasteries, to lay out a small pleasure garden (or pleasaunce) immediately next to the house. These were highly artificial in the intricate geometrical patterns of their flower beds (as can be seen, restored on the grand scale, at Villandry on the Loire) and they were in deliberate and direct contrast with the wildness of the surrounding landscape; from them developed the highly elaborate Italian and Dutch gardens which were planted round Elizabethan and Carolean country houses.

The late seventeenth century house of the Dutch type, brought back from the Continent by the Court of Charles II after its exile and conventionally (though wrongly) associated with the name of Wren, was architecturally as well as horticulturally a total defiance of nature, with its prim, upstanding doll's house silhouette and its patterned garden of trim box hedges. It was in reaction to such houses that Vanbrugh and Bridgeman began to break up the formality of the planting and extend the pleasure garden into the forest without any clear break (the sunken wall known as the ha-ha was a device for keeping cattle out of the purlieus of the house while preserving the illusion of a continuous landscape). Such devices were

B

not merely aesthetic but expressed a fundamental change in the attitude of landowners to their property, culminating in the great movement for agricultural improvement at the end of the eighteenth century, which had a much more widespread effect on the environment than any inventions of industry until the railways. There was an increasing tendency among the landed aristocrats to cultivate every acre of their estates, thus creating the tame man-made landscape of hedgerows and copses which two hundred years later is taken for granted as 'natural'; and this was done (*pace* Marx) not so much for crudely economic reasons — F. L. M. Thompson indicates how small the financial returns usually were — but much more for reasons of family pride. It became a positive pleasure for the landowner, and increasingly his wife as well, to ride through his estate and simply enjoy the sensation of owning it all; this was undoubtedly the feeling of Mr and Mrs Andrews in Gainsborough's picture, depicted sitting on a wrought iron park bench, painted green, just like those which are used today in countless *public* parks — neatly making the point that, only seventy years later, Sir Joseph Paxton, head gardener to the Duke of Devonshire, was employed at Birkenhead Park to transfer to the municipal domain of public pleasure the qualities of landscape which hitherto had been enjoyed only by the private grandee.

It is impossible to exaggerate the enlargement of human personality made possible by this taming of nature. There had already been tentative excursions out into the landscape from the Elizabethan country houses — the 'standings', for example, from which the ladies watched the progress of the hunt, or the gazebos, which at Montacute stand out overlooking the landscape at the corners of the garden terrace — but in the eighteenth century these first stirrings became rapidly absorbed into an exuberant and widespread exodus, represented architecturally by legions of subtly sited temples and grottoes and belvedere towers. At Stowe, where a Vanbrugh-Bridgeman landscape was remodelled and extended around 1735 by

Kent and Gibbs, with Lancelot Brown as head gardener (before he went public as 'Capability'), the trees and temples and inherited thirteenth century church were all transformed into three-dimensional objects in space, the landscapist having now learnt to study the kinetic effects of being able to walk freely in all directions (instead of being restricted to the straight-sided parallax of avenues, as in the seventeenth century gardens on the Versailles pattern). Stowe was the seat of the Grenvilles, the leaders politically of the Whig Party, and among the park ornaments there is a Temple of British Worthies (by Kent) which exhibits busts of democratic heroes from Alfred the Great to Hampden and Milton (the Milton of *Areopagitica*); and there is no doubt, as Nikolaus Pevsner was the first to point out, that in the mid-eighteenth century the new freedom of movement through nature was seen as having a political symbolism — the secular freedoms guaranteed by the English Revolution of 1688. This exaltation of Liberty was naturally felt even more strongly by the Victorian creators of public parks; in the 1890s, for example, Octavia Hill, the housing reformer and co-founder of the National Trust, campaigned vigorously for the public purchase of suburban hilltops for the recreation of the common people, in the belief (paralleled by Frank Lloyd Wright) that hills should be built round, not on.

This changed attitude towards nature led to equally profound changes in the house, with the increasing tendencies towards the asymmetrical and the informal, which became known as the Picturesque. Here again there has been overmuch emphasis on the specifically aesthetic decisions by architects, particularly the adoption of the stylistic detail of Gothic by Vanbrugh at Greenwich or by Kent at Esher. Much more important was the demand from the client, spurred on by the many amateur architects of his own social class, for a layout of his home which would relate him and his family more intimately to the surrounding landscape. By means of the bay window, with its projection of the interior of the house out into the landscape, and the verandah or balcony with its reception of the landscape inwards into the house, the square brick box of the external walls was increasingly folded and facetted, and the next generation of landscape architects after Brown, led by Humphry Repton, added complicated mixtures of semi-internal, semi-external space in such things as cloisters, arbours, pergolas, conservatories and French windows.

From his country estate the aristocrat came up to London briefly for the Season, during which he lived at his own town house or at one he had rented. Insofar as there has been a specifically urban architecture in England, to rival the piazzas of the Continent, it lies in the fashionable squares and crescents of Bloomsbury and Belgravia — a form of architecture with which English architects were rarely at ease. In 1712, on the north side of Grosvenor Square, Edward Shepherd applied for the first time to a row of identical narrow houses the theatrical dress, endlessly repeated over the next century, of a single palace facade, with the illusion of a Palladian corps-de-logis flanked by pavilions. The Woods began to deviate from it in their Circus and Royal Crescent at Bath by using a repetitive sequence of giant columns in order to emphasize logically the equal vertical divisions into separate houses. Further articulation of the individual house came with the addition of a projecting porch to each front door, as in George Basevi's Belgrave Square of 1825 and Thurloe Square of the 1830s; and this monotonous flickering rhythm was taken up as the mid-Victorian norm for the Italianate stucco terraces of Pimlico, Bayswater and South Kensington.

Such urbanism was given a further lease of life in the 1850s by the influence of Haussmann's Paris, but Parisian frills, as in C. J. Richardson's Queen's Gate houses, were usually shaved off by Protestant probity and self-restraint. The Anglo-American clergyman Moncure D. Conway in his *Travels in South Kensington* (1882), directly attributed the 'ugliness' of the endless anonymous terraces around him to Puritanism; although he admitted that *inside* each house one could be fairly certain of finding good music, English, French and German literature, and 'pictures of noble men and heroic deeds', adding that 'Between all that and a fine outside they have chosen the better part.' Not until the Queen Anne of the seventies did the individual middle-class villa, by outwardly expressing such private domestic culture, at last undermine the hold of the palace-terrace in Inner London; on the western edge of Earls Court, Philbeach Gardens was still being built up in the old style in 1884. It was in tall inconvenient terrace houses of this kind, where the wretched servants commuted between their work-rooms in the basement and their bedrooms in the attic (five storeys up), that John Galsworthy's Forsytes were living in *A Man of Property*, set in 1886. Galsworthy, as the son of a property developer knew what he was talking about: his father had built the last of the Regents Park 'palaces', Cambridge Terrace (designed in 1875 by Archer & Green in the same Haussmannesque Second Empire style as their Café Royal in Regent Street); and the retreat in the Surrey hills to which Soames Forsyte tried to escape was in fact based upon Coombe Hill near Kingston, where the big brick Gothic mansions built by Galsworthy senior can still be seen.

For most suburbians (a seventeenth century word which, as Dyos says, is greatly preferable to 'suburbanites') the choice between town and country was not so stark. Country landowners on the edge of London began to discover that houses were profitable as crops on their fields, and naturally they looked to the country village, rather than to the town, in order to establish the right relationship between the new suburbs and the existing landscape. As early as 1795 there was a plan (admittedly unexecuted) for the Eyre Estate at St John's Wood, where a compromise between the detached house and terrace was negotiated in the form of semi-detached houses; at about the same time, the South-East London builder-architect Michael Searles achieved a similar effect in his Paragons at Blackheath and New Kent Road, where the paired houses were connected up by elegant single-storey colonnades. Certainly semi-detached houses were being built by landowners in country villages by that date — M. W. Barley illustrates a fine example at Holbeach, Lincolnshire of 1793 — and they were a firm suburban favourite after 1815.

But the 'semi' was essentially only one expression of the continuous and consistent development for several generations of that basic form of middle-class house: the villa. Ever since the later Middle Ages merchants had been increasingly moving out to surrounding villages, still keeping on their 'house over the shop' in the city but commuting to it by carriage after weekends spent in the country with the family (as Defoe noticed at Epsom). The first distinctive bourgeois forms of merchant house were, not surprisingly, Dutch; for while Central Europe tore itself apart in religious conflict in the early seventeenth century, the merchants of the Netherlands had succeeded in establishing a brief hegemony of bourgeois culture as well as commerce, the like of which was not seen again until the nineteenth century. What is now called Kew Palace, because of its absorption into a Crown estate, is a typical example of the 'Dutch house' of the 1630s, with shaped gables of moulded brick, built in this case for a merchant of Dutch birth, Samuel Fortrey. After the Restoration the Court of Charles II brought back a second and stricter Dutch uniform in the hip-roofed brick box; merchant-commissioned examples of it close to London include Hugh May's Eltham Lodge and Edward Stanton's Denham Place.

But when the pace of the suburban exodus began to increase rapidly in the early eighteenth century, it was once again the aristocracy who set the example for the merchants to follow. Under the English system of primogeniture, younger sons and other close relations inherited little property and only modest allowances, and thus they needed a smaller kind of house that was nevertheless recognisably of good family. For them a perfect formula became available in the Palladian villa, as foreshadowed by Inigo Jones in his little house for James I's queen in the back garden of the royal palace at Greenwich. In Italy the reason for the small size and compact layout of the Venetian villas had been quite different — indeed the exact opposite of English customs — in that the aristocratic families lived in the cities and camped out in the countryside only in the summer, so that the villa was an occasional residence, not the permanent family seat. The Earl of Burlington, the aristocrat who was responsible almost single-handed for the victory of Palladio's style in England, attached a small Palladian villa as a kind of entertainment suite next to his country house at Chiswick; so successful was it that eventually the old house was demolished and the villa left on its own. Over the next three generations the banks of the Thames around Richmond and Twickenham and Putney became lined with these pocket-sized country houses which rarely had attached to them more than fifty acres. As Marcus Binney has shown, they were built for an increasingly varied range of people, and were in fact a fulcrum for social mobility. Binney quotes travellers from Europe in the eighteenth century who appreciated the unique quality, socially as much as architecturally, of this suburban landscape of Thames-side villas. At Twickenham, for example, there were the villas of Pope the poet (1718), of the Countess of Suffolk (the King's mistress) (1725) and of the gossip and author Horace Walpole (1748); and engravings of the river bank and the village common show a happy jostle of villas built for lawyers, merchants, artists, doctors, dowagers and 'younger sons'. More obviously than the freely composed landscape garden, the freely associated dwellings of different people of different classes were an expression of the distinctively English tradition of liberalism or Whiggery, which held such a powerful appeal for those visitors, such as Voltaire, who were opposed to the Catholic autocracies of Europe. The suburban village became a living parable of free thought and free trade.

For some merchants the Thames-side villa was merely a stepping stone to the acquisition of some greater property in the countryside; but increasingly the supply of full-scale country estates for the *nouveaux riches* began, by its very nature, to be insufficient to meet demand. Thus the villa, instead of being merely a second London house or the house of a younger son or a stepping stone to higher things, became a social necessity as a family seat in itself. Marcus Binney has picked out Sir Robert Taylor, himself a City of London mason of humble origins, as the architect who did most to develop a pattern of aristocratic villa suitable for the London merchant and his family. Asgill House at Richmond (1760) is typical of his handling of the square Palladian block, pushing out the confines of the sheer stone envelope into canted bay windows and other projections, and enclosing an intricate interpenetration of curved rooms of different sizes. But Taylor was aesthetically a rather stodgy second-generation Palladian and his massive architecture hardly integrates with the surrounding landscape.

At Strawberry Hill, by contrast, which was itself a small Palladian villa before Horace Walpole transformed it, there was a very happy mingling of tracery and foliage. Even if Walpole was not the pioneer of Gothic that Eastlake claimed him to be — much the finest Gothic country house of the 1750s is in fact Arbury in Warwickshire, where George Eliot's father was the agent — there is no question that Strawberry Hill fascinated contemporary men of taste; and the reason was, I think, that Walpole in his intricate fantasy demonstrated that it was possible to create on a riverside plot a miniature park which induced quite as satisfying a sense of proud ownership as the broad acres of the shires. It was a triumph of *illusion*. Unfortunately, after over a hundred years of architectural moralising about Truthfulness and Honest Expression of Structure, it is difficult for architects today to appreciate that aspect of their trade which makes it an art of illusion; yet I am convinced that the essence of successful domestic design in crowded surroundings lies precisely in providing an artificial impression of a broader space, a prouder seclusion and a lusher scenery than would actually exist without architectural intervention.

For the suburban villa the great masters of the art were Humphry Repton and his partner between 1796 and 1803, John Nash, a former Taylor assistant. Nash was commissioned to design suburban villas in Dulwich, Surbiton, Bromley, Kingston and Southgate, all on pocket-handkerchief sites (by aristocratic standards). In the great landscaped parks by Kent and Brown the intention had been to flatter the aristocrat's new-found pride in ownership by landscaping his hillsides in such a way that, as he looked out from drawing room bay or bedroom balcony, he could feel a satisfying sensation of 'mine, all mine'. The problem for Nash and Repton was that their suburban clients were going to look out upon hillsides which were not theirs at all, so the primary aim of architect and landscapist had to be, by artifices of orientation and planting, to give an illusion of 'mine, all mine' that was no less satisfying than the real thing. So successfully did Repton make the small suburban house seem to be the centre of ancestral acres that a paradoxical reaction was stimulated from some of the aristocracy; on their secondary estates they had no wish to repeat the inconvenient magnificence, with hundreds of servants, of their main seat, so it began to be fashionable to make them look instead like the villas of the bourgeois. The Duke of Bedford, for example, in 1812 built on his Tavistock Estate a charming Gothic house for himself called Endsleigh Cottage (significant name), the spreading verandahed architecture by Sir Jeffry Wyatville being set in the midst of a vast sylvan landscape by Repton along the Tamar.

For more confined sites, the Red Books in whch Repton presented his schemes to his clients in the form of pairs of illustrations (Before and After) are full of ingenious devices for screening or hiding the unsightly. For example, for the Royal Fort, a fine Rococo villa on the slopes of Clifton, he suggested a thick belt of trees to hide the newly built Bristol streets on the opposite hill, thus preserving the precious sense of rural seclusion. The architect

William Cowburn has pointed out that, when an architect today is asked to lay out a housing estate in the landscaped grounds of some demolished country house, his first reaction — so strong are the powerful moral arguments for community life brought to bear upon him in his education — is to treat a surviving feature such as an artificial lake as the centrepiece of a 'communal space', round which he will then range the terrace houses in such a way that they all overlook each other across it. The speculative builder, on the other hand, in the true suburban tradition of Repton and Nash, will want the houses arranged precisely so that they do not overlook each other, but instead give each householder a secluded view, down his own private garden, at the end of which the lake appears, by illusion, to be an extension of his own personal property. As a Socialist I can see nothing wrong in thus making the prerogative of the landowners the right of everyman, and if a little illusion helps the effect, so be it.

What makes Nash in particular the 'father of the suburb' is that he brought these devices of illusion to play upon the problem of creating complete housing estates. He was not the absolute pioneer of this: throughout the eighteenth century the aristocracy had increasingly been expressing their pride of overship, not to mention their increasing knowledge of the management of an improved agricultural economy, by housing their tenants in model villages of estate cottages. There is a vital book yet to be written about these new villages, surely the most important single source of the modern English garden suburbs and new towns. In his otherwise excellent book on the history of the garden cities (entitled *The Search for Environment*) Walter Creese traces their heredity back only to the industrial model villages of the mid-Victorian era such as Saltaire and Akroydon, not even mentioning Robert Owen's much earlier New Lanark. But as so often in the pre-1870 period, such newly enriched entrepreneurs as Sir Titus Salt and Colonel Akroyd were only copying, within the industrial environment, what their aristocratic superiors had already achieved in the rural environment. In fact Akroyd's workers knew only too well the feudal associations of the style of Gothic-cum-Elizabethan cottage which Sir Gilbert Scott had designed for them (1859); as the Colonel put it in his memoirs, 'The dormer windows were supposed to resemble the style of almshouses, and the independent workmen who formed the building association positively refused to accept this feature of the Gothic, which to their minds was degrading.'

Initially the Georgian model village tended merely to be a rather more organised assembly of the ordinary local vernacular cottage, designed as well as constructed by the ordinary local mason: such things did not yet fall within the purview of the architect, who at that time was employed mainly for country houses and public buildings. Examples of this purely vernacular phase are the mansard-roofed cottages of white plaster erected for the Earl of Suffolk at Audley End and the brown stone village square at Blanchland in Northumberland, planned by the Earl of Crewe's Trustees in 1752 within the precinct of the former abbey. But quite soon architects began to be involved in more menial buildings: Isaac Ware in his *Complete Body of Architecture* of 1756 and Roger Morris in his *Select Architecture* 1755 were among the first to illustrate and discuss farm buildings as well as lodges and follies. Then followed one or two classical villages of considerable pretension particularly Harewood in Yorkshire, designed in 1760 for Edwin Lascelles by the eminent local architect John Carr as a kind of forecourt to the park gates, and Lowther in Westmorland, designed in very formal squares and crescents for the Earl of Lonsdale, probably by Robert Adam's brother James (c. 1765–73). James Wyatt's Westport is in Ireland which, partly because of conscious Protestant colonisation, received far more aristocratic village planning than the rest of the British Isles; and other fine examples, such as Savannah, Georgia, survive in the thirteen colonies across the Atlantic.

But such classical villages soon came to seem inappropriately urban for the natural landscape around them. The first major example of a Picturesque model village was probably Milton Abbas in Dorset, the strange story of which epitomizes the paradoxes and contradictions out of which the English garden suburb was born. The abbey church today seems the epitome of Cistercian seclusion in its steep wooded valley, but it was in fact a Benedictine foundation, set in the usual way in the centre of a small market town. The Earl of Dorchester was frankly bored with having a town sitting out on the lawns in front of his mansion, the remodelled abbot's house, so in 1774 he decided to shift the entire settlement; and it was bodily removed half a mile down the valley and up a little cleft to one side. There Sir William Chambers and Capability Brown designed a single long street, complete with church, pub, shop and almshouses. Such enforced resettlement seems incredibly remote from our present democratic way of doing things (whatever Chairmen of Planning Committees might like to do in their dreams); yet in its actual appearance, Milton Abbas looks, equally incredibly, up-to-date. The prim little detached houses, with their white plastered walls and thatched roofs, their long back gardens and their swathe of communal lawn in front, all perfectly related to the sheltering contours of the hills, look like nothing so much as a twentieth century garden suburb at its best, an obvious product of egalitarianism — though admittedly each front door originally gave access to two dwellings (for reasons of scale, Chambers concealed their semi-detachedness). Nonetheless the Earl did so well for his tenants that with one sweep of his arm he seems to have out-Welwyned Welwyn a century and a half in advance.

Nash moved closer still to the modern suburb in the miniature garden village he designed in 1811 at Henbury just outside Bristol, known as Blaise Hamlet. This was only marginally less aristocratic than Milton Abbas in origin, being intended for the old retainers of a Quaker banker, J. S. Harford, who had already built for himself the pseudo-baronial Blaise Castle.

Approached mysteriously from the main road along a

Forcibly transplanted out of the Earl of Dorchester's park, the Georgian model village of Milton Abbas is nonetheless a delectable prototype for the middle-class suburb. (Edwin Smith)

narrow pathway between hedges, the Hamlet in fact has only eight dwellings, but Nash gives the illusion of a much larger community by placing them irregularly around a village green, intricately moulding the lawn into little hillocks round a focal sundial on a pillar, and artfully, almost frantically, varying the composition and materials of the thatched-roof cottages. Yet the style of architecture is no less ahead of its time than Milton: it is clearly identifiable to mid-twentieth-century eyes as the 'Teahouse Tudor' of innumerable roadside pull-ins alongside prewar arterial roads — what Reyner Banham has called 'joke oak'. The main difference perhaps is that it is extremely well-built, with handmade panels of flint and weatherboarding, and spectacularly crazy clusters of brick chimneys. It is an environment which depends above all upon its intricacy of scale and the individuality of each dwelling. Nash did not actually invent this particular cottage style; since the early 1790s there had been a steady stream of architectural pattern books by architects such as Lugar and Papworth, giving suggestions for the design of picturesque cottages which could then be taken up, with or without the aid of an architect, by the owners of estates or their agents.

The agent was a comparative newcomer to the country village. As agricultural improvements became increasingly complicated to administer, it became normal for the larger landowners to hand over administration to a professional agent, sometimes known as steward or bailiff. There was already one other professional man supposedly residing in the village, the parson, and although it had become the practice in many places for him to be a pluralistic absentee, there were already some pioneers among the clergy who insisted on the pastoral necessity of living amongst their flock. At the same time the larger villages, particularly those with benevolent landowners, began to receive medical care from a resident doctor. Consequently, what might be called embryo middle-class villas began to be built, for the agent, the parson and the doctor; and another which was often no larger was the dower house, where the landowner's widowed mother ended her days.

It is over thirty-five years since Sir John Summerson, in his biography of Nash, spotted the supreme significance stylistically of the small Shropshire house called Cronkhill which Nash designed in 1802. It was the pioneering example of the 'Italian farmhouse' style of villa which was to become the principal semi-aristocratic form of middle-class house for the first generation of Victorians. Nash derived this idealised painterly vision of the semi-fortified Tuscan farm from the paintings of Poussin and particularly Claude Lorrain. These painters' more obviously architectural temples and mausolea had already been directly imitated in landscapes such as Stourhead; but the 1790s saw the publication in engravings of a number of paintings by Claude of much less formal Italian vernacular buildings which were in the collection of the architectural writer Richard Payne Knight at Downton Castle (not far from Cronkhill), one of these being the spitting image of Nash's design. But the crucial claim for Cronkhill as a suburban prototype is functional, that it was an agent's house, built for Mr Walford, who administered the Earl of Berwick's Attingham estate.

So once again this was not a case of an architect deciding on his own that a particular change of style was required; it was because he was asked by his client to provide a new kind of dwelling that he then had to devise an appropriate architectural expression for it — in sociologist's terms, a new life-style. The advantage of the Italian farmhouse — or *Villa Rustica* as it was called in the influential pattern book of that name produced by Charles Parker in 1832 — was that it combined the aristocratic snobbism of the classical with the substantial economies in ornament of the astylar (without columns) and the asymmetrical. Although Cronkhill is planned oddly, with the dining room and kitchen at opposite ends, it has nonetheless a clear functional expression externally of the three main spaces within, drawing room, dining room and study (although the elliptical tower does not cover all the dining room and its top storey with portholes does not contain a room at all). This kind of house, reproduced in pattern books by Papworth, Robinson and Parker, can be seen individually in almost every Early Victorian suburb, but it also formed the basic unit for the earliest planned housing estates for the middle classes, which broke away from the Georgian square-and-crescent formula in favour of the detached and the semi-detached.

Once again Nash was the pioneer, and on a site of the utmost prominence, at Regents Park. This vast speculation, planned and organised by Nash on behalf of George IV, has been renowned in the past mainly for its clever siting of the single-palace type of Georgian terrace so that a series of them overlook a landscaped park which in true suburban style gives each resident the impression, as he looks out of his front windows, that he owns it. But far more original was Nash's attempt to provide a range of different types of house appropriate to the life-styles of different social classes. At one extreme there were isolated large-scale villas set in the midst of the park, while at the other extreme there were working-class terraced cottages surrounding a market place beside the basin of the new Regents Canal. On either side of the canal, just north of the market, Nash laid out (from about 1824) Park Village West and Park Village East, which were completed by his adopted son Sir James Pennethorne. These consist of wholly delightful groupings of Cronkhill-type villas, in the case of Park Village West around an irregularly looped crescent. Several houses are semi-detached, and the range of stylistic influences is very wide, Tudor and Jacobean motifs being interwoven into the Italianate fabric, particularly mullioned bay windows.

The same kind of estate was repeated from 1829 at Calverley Park in Tunbridge Wells by one of Nash's young assistants at Regents Park, Decimus Burton; his Tuscan villas, again of an astonishing variety, are set back within their own private gardens, but also enjoy splendid views out over a communal park towards the Wealden hills. Italian villas were specially popular at seaside resorts (no doubt for being reminiscent of the Riviera): for example, the Queens Park scheme at Brighton by Sir Charles Barry, and the Gervis estate at Bournemouth by the normally Gothic church architect Benjamin Ferrey. The grandstand kind of villas can still be seen perfectly at the precipitous Early Victorian seaside resort of Ventnor in the Isle of Wight; as Messrs Ward Lock's Red Guide admirably puts it, 'The town, in fact, is built on the principle of a theatre, so that the occupant of every seat, no matter how far back or removed, shall have a full view of the stage, which in this case is the sea... The houses rise in terraces, one above the other, and all alike have open balconies, wide windows, and the indispensable south aspect.'

The Tuscan villa, however rustic, was still reminiscent of the formal manners of aristocratic classicism, in that it had stylistic tricks of console-bracketed eaves and round-arched loggias which were clearly not rooted in any English vernacular. The decisive moves towards a styleless, classless cottage for the twentieth century suburb came rather surprisingly from the Church, and specifically via the Oxford Movement; for the Movement's ritualistic return to Catholicism was of less lasting impact than its pastoral revitalising of the ordinary parochial system. The Bishop of Oxford himself, Samuel Wilberforce, who sympathised with the pastoral zeal of the High Churchmen, set himself the task of providing 'a gentleman for every parish' — that is to say a resident clergyman who would teach as well as preach. For his vast sprawling diocese, covering Oxfordshire, Berkshire and Buckinghamshire, this meant an immense building programme of parsonages and church schools; and in 1852 he appointed as his diocesan architect George Edmund Street, then aged twenty-eight and prominent as a layman in the pioneering Tractarian parish of Wantage.

There were already models from which Street could develop a domestic vernacular. In the pattern books by Papworth (1818) and Goodwin (1830) designs had appeared in the Georgian Picturesque tradition for Tudor parsonages, executed in flimsy stucco to simulate medieval stonework; but these 'shams' had soon been put to flight by the functionalist principles of honesty in structural expression which Pugin advocated in *The True Principles of Christian Architecture*. At the Bishop's House in Birmingham, for example, built in 1841—2, Pugin scooped out a U-shaped courtyard on a corner site backing onto a factory, the whole of the rear elevation of the house being windowless; on the other three sides, each main room was given its own clear external expression towards street and courtyard by means of oriel windows and tall chimneys, these simple elements being pulled together without extraneous Gothic ornament into a tight asymmetrical composition of bare red brick. As *The Ecclesiologist* (the Oxford Movement's architectural journal) remarked, when criticising an over-elaborate design by Street for a church on a steep triangular site at Hobart in Tasmania: 'We would remind Mr Street that the true picturesque follows upon the sternest utility.' Street himself followed these principles of high thinking and plain living in his multitude of small domestic buildings for Wilberforce's diocese in the early fifties. Denchworth School, near Wantage, for example, where Thomas Hardy's sister was the schoolmistress, has sharp detailing in local stone, one of the chimney-breasts at first floor level forming a neat canopy to the entrance doorway underneath. The way in which windows, chimneys and high-pitched roof are tied together by broad areas of plain wall surface closely foreshadows William Morris's Red House at Bexley-heath, designed by Philip Webb.

Webb and Morris, both graduates of Street's Oxford office, were not in fact the great 'pioneers of the Modern Movement' which they have been held up to be by Pevsner, following Muthesius; they were simply the best young practitioners of a clearly recognisable architectural vocabularly for the middle-class house which had been evolved in the 1850s from building types which previously had been narrowly ecclesiastical in purpose. Red House was not the first such building to be built wholly in red brick — there were already the excellent small vicarages and schools by William Butterfield near York (Hensall, Cowick and Pollington) not to mention a whole village of red brick cottages designed by Butterfield for Viscount Downe at Baldersby St James in the same county. Nor was it the first such house to be built for a secular client: there was already the delectable rough stone house in the main street of St Columb Major, Cornwall, called Penmellyn, designed by Street's friend William White; and there was also Butterfield's brick house at Baldersby for Viscount Downe's agent.

Less fluent but more truly original than Street, Butterfield was a major influence on the Vernacular Revival of younger architects such as Webb. Beginning with his clergy house and choir school at All Saints, Margaret Street (designed 1849—50), which had a three-sided courtyard clearly derived from Pugin's at Birmingham, he had boldly combined pointed relieving arches from the Gothic with the rectilinear sash windows of the Georgians. This mixture was devised not just for functional convenience but also for visual continuity with the vernacular tradition, which had always been prepared unsentimentally to absorb practical inventions within the Gothic matrix. Webb used similar sash windows at Red House — also some unexpected circular portholes for the upstairs corridors — and, ignoring his colleague Morris's narrow medievalism, he began in his third house, the gaunt whinstone Arisaig near Inverness (1864), to work out a new synthesis of vernacular forms, overtly classical as well as Gothic. In his red brick studio house in Holland Park for Val Prinsep in the same year, Webb established a prototype, albeit still Butterfieldian Gothic, for the picturesque artist's houses in which Norman Shaw was soon to specialise; and four years later for another painter, George Boyce, at 35 Glebe Place, Chelsea, he introduced into a London street what was in effect a comfortable Early Georgian farmhouse. The impact of its symmetrical brick entrance wing was recalled many years later by Webb's connoisseur friend Fred White (who

in 1887 was Shaw's client for the neo-Georgian paragon of 170 Queen's Gate): 'It revealed to me some of
the secrets of those by-streets of Westminster which I
had known from childhood. Its simple, quiet, brick
walls with windows, not holes, marked by four inch
white frames crossed by solid sash bars, taught me to
think of the eighteenth century with respect.' By
dividing up his sash windows in the Georgian way
into small panes with astragals, Webb had given the
building an intricate and human scale instead of the
usual gaping expanses of plate glass.

It is not surprising that painters were the most
prominent clients for the revived vernacular: they had
been aware of the qualities of the real thing for much
longer than the architects had. It was Webb's fellow-
partner in Morris's craft business, Ford Madox
Brown, who in 1852—4 had perfectly portrayed the
landscape of the Victorian suburb in *An English
Autumn Afternoon*; in this painting he had evidently
discovered for himself that the garden hedges and
dovecots of villas in Hampstead were as valid in terms
of man-made landscape as the traditional cottage
gardens of the country village.

In terms of actual architecture, just as Nash had
followed in the wake of Claude, so Webb and Shaw
were able to draw upon the minutely tactile appreciation of cottages and their materials which had been
shown by the previous generation's East Anglian landscape painters, Constable, Crome and particularly
Cotman.

The Norwich School showed cottages as they really
were, with a serious understanding of the reality of
local materials and the ways in which they were put
together by bricklayers and carpenters, totally different from the slaphappy collage effects which had
amused Nash at Blaise Hamlet. Cotman's disciples
included the art teacher J. D. Harding, one of whose
instructional books was an early possession of
Webb's. Harding personally gave lessons both to John
Ruskin, whose drawings of vernacular architecture in
Continental towns were far more remarkable than his
archaeological reproductions of Venetian palaces, and

also to the architect George Devey, who in the fifties was able to inject into the conventions of the Tudor-bethan country house the new painterly sensitivity towards materials. Devey's grouped cottages for Lord de l'Isle and Dudley in front of the church at Penshurst in Kent (dated 1850) form a 'model village' which the coach loads of tourists each summer enjoy as medieval (it being better than the genuine thing): there is a texture of hand-tooled surfaces, the product of the 'direct labour' of estate workers under the agent, which is worthy of William Morris's Arts and Crafts Movement more than a generation later. The landscape architect at Penshurst was William Andrews Nesfield, and his son, William Eden Nesfield, then aged fifteen, must have been enormously impressed by Devey's work. When the younger Nesfield and Norman Shaw set up in practice together in 1862 in a partnership that lasted six years, it was Nesfield who took the lead in two small jobs for his father: first he adopted the 'authentic' half-timber of Devey in a lodge at Regent's Park (1864) (he did the same in a group of estate cottages at Crewe a few months later) and then he designed a lodge at Kew Gardens (1866) in the crisp seventeenth century Dutch brickwork that became known as 'Queen Anne'. This style also, in its more picturesque vein of shaped gables, was derived from Devey, from the remodelling of the main part of Betteshanger Manor in 1861; but in Nesfield's lodge, with its symmetry and its hipped roof, the effect was nearer to Wren himself, the main influence almost certainly being Wellington College, Berkshire, designed in 1856 by John Shaw (no relation to Norman) for whom Nesfield's father had again been the landscape architect.

Holland was a natural source of inspiration to Victorian aesthetes for replacing the dull uniformity of the stucco terrace by an individual expression of each bourgeois family; for, as we have seen, it was Holland which had in the seventeenth century first invented a Northern European bourgeois culture, complete with such painterly trimmings as the still life, the genre scene and the paintings of cattle. In 1869 and 1871 the National Gallery acquired Pieter de Hoogh's two delicious paintings of houses in Delft, all of red brick with tile-paved courtyards, scrolly ironwork, white painted window frames and small inlaid panels of sculpture, providing the pattern in every respect for the purest 'Queen Anne' style of Norman Shaw, beginning in 1873 with Lowther Lodge in Kensington Gore, commissioned by Lady Wensleydale for her daughter Mrs Lowther.

It was a style not merely bourgeois, but feminine, being neatly domesticated in a manner appropriate to a generation which was at last giving women an opportunity to express themselves culturally. It is not surprising that Basil Champneys adopted it, also in 1873, for Cambridge's second women's college, Newnham, and that Elizabeth Garrett Anderson later adopted it, with J. M. Brydon as architect, for her hospitals. If the all-male clubhouse in Barry-Italianate is the fashionable Early Victorian stereotype in architecture, the feminine Queen Anne villa with red walls, white shutters and pretty wallpapers (not to mention blue-and-white china and colour-printed children's books illustrated by Kate Greenaway or Mrs Allingham) is the equivalent environmental cliché for the Late Victorian emancipation of women. It seems certain that the Aesthetic Movement — the wider effect of the Domestic Revival on the applied arts — was basically motivated by women, and by man's increasing appreciation of them, not only as 'stunners' but as intellectual equals. Not only did many of the houses of Shaw and Voysey and Lutyens have a woman as client (even where a husband was paying the bill); there was also an increasing participation by women in creative work, girls having attended the Female School of Design (and its successor at South Kensington) since 1841. There was a spate of books on interior design written for women by women (such as Mrs Orrinsmith and Mrs Haweis); and when Minton's established their Art Pottery Studios in South Kensington in 1871, they hoped to attract 'especially women' to design for them. There was an unusually permissive attitude towards women in the

The Late Victorian suburb, with its busy private yards of red brick and tile, owes much to the inspiration of seventeenth-century Holland. Pieter de Hooch's Courtyard of a House in Delft (1658) was bought by the National Gallery in 1871. (National Gallery)

Chelsea set around Rossetti, who was responsible more than anyone else for the aesthetic preferences, Japanese as well as Dutch, which Whistler learnt from him. The elopement in 1869 of the architect of Whistler's house, E. W. Godwin, with the actress Ellen Terry, was a significant incident: the house they built for themselves at Fallows Green, near Harpenden, became a total expression of the new bourgeois environment, complete with the unmarried mother and the two children (Gordon and Ellen Craig) dressed in kimonos.

There was above all a new secularism in the air, nowhere better displayed than in the new London Board Schools, set up under the Education Act of 1870; their first architects, E. R. Robson and J. J. Stevenson, consciously adopted the new Dutch style, both to distinguish the nonsectarian state school from the Church or Chapel, and to provide a humane and intimate environment, a kind of super-domesticity, in slum areas where such values were hard to come by in the actual homes.

The name 'Queen Anne' seems to have come from the title of Thackeray's novel *Henry Esmond, or The Adventures of an Officer in the Reign of Queen Anne*, the point being that the author had himself commissioned (in 1860–1) a curious red brick house in Kensington, 2 Palace Gate, in a jejune mixture of Italianate, Dutch and Early Georgian. The style's first mature appearance in a London street was The Red House, Bayswater Road, designed for himself by J. J. Stevenson, in an intentional scarlet clash with his stucco neighbours which infuriated the older generation. But the Movement's architectural leader was unquestionably Norman Shaw, certainly from 1873, the date of Lowther Lodge and also of New Zealand Chambers, in which the gay domesticity of Queen Anne was injected into the solemn counting houses of the City. Shaw, who had succeeded Philip Webb in Street's office, was the kind of brilliant extrovert who invents little himself but synthesises the ideas of others much more fluently than they could have done; he was no secular saint of architectural honesty like Webb, but on the contrary exploited to the utmost the painterly art of illusion in counterpoint to the utility of vernacular craftsmanship. In such roads as Chelsea Embankment and Melbury Road in Kensington, Shaw's bourgeois houses for artists still stand out boldly, bright red and very individual in total contrast to the anonymous sub-aristocratic terrace; and this type of house was turned by his younger rival, Sir Ernest George, into a coherent townscape in the Harrington Gardens/Collingham Gardens part of Earls Court (where one of the new residents was W. S. Gilbert).

Shaw had also developed a more rustic manner, derived from Devey and Nesfield, for the Surrey and Sussex hillsides, beginning with Glen Andred at Groombridge, built in 1866–7 for the influential Royal Academician, E. W. Cooke; there, on a steep Wealden escarpment, Shaw placed a simple tilehung farmhouse, with an elaborate romantic landscape of yellow sandstone boulders and lush evergreens similar to those in Cooke's own paintings. This kind of house, which Shaw turned out in great quantities in the seventies and eighties, established a basic formula for the stockbroker belt which has never since been supplanted. It responded to the desperate need of the middle classes to escape from the squalor of the Victorian cities and refresh themselves, if only at weekends, amidst natural scenery. Such architecture has often been accused of being escapist, and indeed it was, in the sense that escape into the countryside is one of the fundamental needs of modern man. Camille Pissarro understood this when he settled at South Norwood in 1870–1 and invented the main elements of impressionist landscape painting amid the commuter villages of South East London: his paintings of St Stephen's Church, Sydenham Hill, and 'La Route de Sydenham' (Lawrie Park Avenue) show the leafiness of the hillsides, and that of 'Penge Station' the freshness and primitive charm of the suburban adventure, where cheap workmen's tickets were shortly to enable clerks and mechanics to join the stockbrokers and lawyers in attractive mixed communities.

Shaw developed far more elaborately the Regency convention of the bay window and the verandah, using hidden steel joints (and he saw no point in revealing them) to support ever wider spans, so that interior and exterior could become a continuous landscaped experience. The landscape had become as important as the buildings in creating the new super-rural environment of the 1870s. The irascible propagandist William Robinson, ignored alike by architectural historians and *DNB*, almost single-handedly invented the main feature of the small suburban garden ever since, the herbaceous border, as part of his rediscovery of the English cottage garden and the English wild flower; at the Royal Horticultural Society's gardens at Kew he had been in charge of cataloguing the native botany. He directed mass publicity at the middle classes, pro-vernacular and anti-formal, in his magazines *The Garden* and *Gardening Illustrated* and in his books *The Wild Garden* and above all *The English Flower Garden*.

One of the contributors to Robinson's magazines and to *The English Flower Garden* was Miss Gertrude Jekyll (1843–1932), born and brought up in the Surrey stockbroker belt and typical of the lady art students of South Kensington in the sixties. Afflicted by myopia, she had had to give up her painting and carving in favour of gardening. 'Planting ground,' as she put it 'is painting a landscape with living things.' Miss Jekyll had in fact been profoundly influenced by an amateur painter of genius, Hercules Brabazon, the Sussex squire who formed a direct link between Turner and the English Impressionists of the nineties, but the oddity of her myopia is that it almost certainly made her see the 'drifts of colour', in which she mixed her plants, in a much more impressionistic blur than anyone else did. Nonetheless she had the wit (and the classically trained intellect) to realise that, like patriotism, English wild flowers were not enough; whereas Robinson cultivated the robust philistinism of a Little Englander, Miss Jekyll infused into her Surrey woodland at Munstead the exotic cuttings from her travels in the Mediterranean. The result was a kind of super-Surrey garden, with the heightened naturalism demanded for their emotional balance by those who had escaped from the heightened artificiality of the industrial city. To give architectural form to this vision she had as her protégé Shaw's and Webb's most brilliant disciple, Sir Edwin Lutyens, who combined with her wild planting his elemental sense of classical geometry. He satisfied the demands of his feminine clients in their role as hostesses by developing a highly sophisticated environment for the suburban country weekend, the layout of his houses being carefully organised in such a way that large public corridors and staircases connected recessed inglenooks and bay windows, suitable for private conversations. With his brilliant intuitive respect for *genius loci*, he carried on from Norman Shaw in responding to the need in our temperate climate for semi-internal, semi-external spaces, such as verandahs, loggias, terraces, pergolas and summer houses — the Jekyll garden being a natural extension of this whole domestic environment.

No one is now building the large country house of the Shaw or Lutyens kind, with its implicit platoon of servants; but its intricate relationship of spaces, internal and external, public and private, artificial and natural, can be extremely instructive to the present-day town planner, faced with the problem in the same suburban situations of creating pleasant places not for one family but for many. Groups of smaller modern houses can have a similar scale in the landscape to the large Edwardian villa, and there is in such enforced proximity an even greater need to scoop out human places for private conversation and communion with nature.

Shaw and Lutyens were themselves given pioneering opportunities to give effect to these town planning implications of their country house practice — Shaw in 1877, when he took over as architect of a planned middle-class suburban village between the West London suburbs of Chiswick and Acton, called Bedford Park. Bedford Park deserves its plaudits as 'the first of the garden suburbs', even though it owes so much to the model villages of the countryside and to the earlier planned suburbs of Nash. But whereas Nash's Italianate farmhouses were a miniaturised aristocracy in style, Shaw's villas, detached or semi-detached, were nothing but bourgeois. Immediately next to the viaduct of the District Line railway, he arranged round a village green a significantly secular-looking church, an arty pub, a row of generously glazed shops and the tree-lined entrance to radiating avenues of red-brick, Dutch-gabled houses, self-consciously evoking the atmosphere of some mythical early seventeenth century village.

Bedford Park had its absurdities, in terms of people rather than places, in that the aesthetes of South Kensington gravitated towards it in a herd. Yeats's parents, Chesterton's parents, Pissarro's son Lucien, the architect Voysey, the playwright Pinero, were among the early residents. Yeats wrote: 'We went to live in a house like those we had seen in pictures and even met people dressed like people in the story-books... the strangeness of it all made us feel that we were living among toys.' But the essence of the place was nonetheless commonsense and convenience: 'neither mansions nor mews, but comfortable dwellings fitted for persons wishing to live within 30 minutes of the town,' reported the *Daily News* in 1881, adding that 'The charm of the scene has been greatly enhanced by the loving tenderness with which every possible tree has been preserved' — all of them planted by a Kew curator, who had happened to own the land thirty years earlier. Every house (most of them semi-detached) became an independent object in a free-flowing landscape, with the same kinetic effects that we noted at Stowe a hundred and fifty years earlier; the Anglo-American artist Edwin Abbey said he 'felt as though he were walking through a watercolour', and Bedford Park naturally appealed to the Impressionist brush of Pissarro *père*. 'The peculiar characteristic of these streets,' said *Chambers' Journal*, 'is the utter absence of that stiffness which always seems to attend the chilly, regular and hideous house-rows of our other suburbs.'

The relaxed, unpuritanical attitude to community development of Shaw and his patron Jonathan Carr was something entirely new; previous philanthropic enterprises, however admirably motivated, had in their street layout been hung up on the rigid geometry of the Utilitarian reformers, from Jeremy Bentham downwards, who inspired what Sir Raymond Unwin called 'the paving, lighting and cleansing enthusiasm of the nineteenth century'. The health reformers such as Chadwick and Simon were quite right to concentrate first on exterminating the worst abuses of the medieval and Georgian rookeries that in London had lain just outside the City boundaries in Clerkenwell, Holborn and Southwark; the introduction of main drainage, the elimination of epidemics and the rooting out of the more noisome backyard industries were all essential preliminaries to a better family life. What makes it difficult, however, for us today to do justice to the Utilitarians is that, when in borough after borough their idealistic policies were adopted by realistic councillors and engineers, their methods of establishing a threshold for the good life came to be exploited instead as a substitute for the good life: the minimum standards stated in the byelaws were enforced as the maximum as well — in fact as the only standards. The result was mile upon mile of the so-called 'byelaw streets', rigidly uniform in their standard distances of seventy feet between frontages, of twenty or thirty yards between lamp posts and of three or four feet of brick between windows (so as to maintain the requisite percentage of fire-protective external walling). So dominant did health considerations (in the narrow physical sense of health) become that, when a national government-subsidised housing programme was at last established by Lloyd George in 1919 he placed it under the Minister of Health, and there it remained until 1951, when Harold Macmillan became the first Minister of Housing. (It is often forgotten that Nye Bevan, when he was brilliantly establishing the National Health Service, was also responsible for the nation's housing;

61

and it is just as well for his reputation that it is forgotten.)

Yet, as we shall see in the following chapters, even the byelaw street, in spite of its depressing standardisation, did have definite merits, house by house, not the least of them being solid construction. It is invariably byelaw districts which are now being designated as General Improvement Areas, precisely because their two-storey family houses are potentially so flexible. Excellent examples of such districts are the three in London begun between 1872 and 1881 by the Artizans', Labourers' and General Dwellings Company, the earliest being Shaftesbury Park in Battersea. In effect the byelaw house was a *reductio ad minimum* of the traditional two-storey cottage of the English villages. Instinctively there was nothing wrong with it, so long as overcrowding was not allowed to make it coalesce into the Siamese twin of the back-to-back. Unfashionable as the byelaw suburbs may always have been, and fiercely criticised since as 'monotonous sprawl', they nonetheless permitted a development of family life, in the privacy of back yards and back gardens, which is absolutely the opposite of monotonous.

No, the real evil of the byelaws environmentally was not the byelaw street, but the byelaw mentality of treating means as ends — which soon led 'realistic' administrators to propound 'solutions' for the 'housing problem' which were not related to the instinctive family life of the village cottage at all. I am referring of course to what were then called tenements but are now called apartments or flats; and I am referring to a frame of mind which in 1973 is still predominant in some of the upper reaches of our town halls. In Scottish cities, confined behind fortified walls until after the crushing of the '45, the tenement had become the traditional dwelling for all classes; so in that sense it was natural for the pioneer of the philanthropic industrial village, Robert Owen, to build his mill village of New Lanark on the upper Clyde in the form of long rows of four-storey tenement blocks running parallel with the river bank. But although the immediate proximity there of unspoilt countryside is attractive, as it also is in the valleys of Derbyshire or South Wales, one can only regard the architecture of New Lanark as ominous. The four-storey stone terraces may be dressed up with nice Georgian proportions and even an incidental cupola, but as places for family life they are grim and inflexible. Owen's proposals of 1819—20 for Villages of Unity and Cooperation have in fact been much admired by modern architects for the way in which they uncannily foreshadowed the worst aspects of forced communalism. Besides the multi-storey flats, each settlement had a full range of 'communal facilities': an Institute for the Formation of Character, dormitories for the surplus children of larger families, a communal kitchen and messrooms, a lecture room and chapel together with a school, an infirmary, and acres of open tree-planted landscape — just like a postwar Comprehensive Development Area.

Philanthropic housing began in London in the late 1840s under the sponsorship of Albert the Prince Consort through such bodies as the Society for Improving the Condition of the Labouring Classes. Their two-storey flats at the Great Exhibition of 1851 — re-erected since as the park-keeper's cottage at Kennington Park — were in a cosy Jacobethan style with shaped gables, projecting bays and big balconies; but the Society's architect, Henry Roberts, adopted elsewhere the conventional Scottish formula of the four-storey aristocratic-Italianate town house, simply dividing it up horizontally and clapping onto its backside the exposed ledges of the access balconies, issuing forth from a communal staircase. However charming the segmental arcades which link up the balconies of Roberts's Parnell House in Bloomsbury it was but a short step to the much larger scale of dehumanised stacking in the philanthropic barracks of the next generation: Baroness Burdett-Coutts's Gothic tenements around Columbia Market in Bethnal Green (designed in 1860 by Henry Darbishire), the even more minimal-Gothic of Sir Sydney Waterlow's Improved Industrial Model Dwellings Company (the first

63

in Shoreditch of 1863), and the stylelessly imper-
meable Peabody Buildings built from 1864 by the
Boston financier's massive Trust (with Darbishire
again the architect). Waterlow, Lord Mayor and print-
ing magnate, known as 'Philanthropy-and-Five-per-
Cent', actually earned nine per cent from his biggest
estate in Bethnal Green ('FOR 1027 FAMILIES', as
the gable wall still proudly advertises to passing
main-line trains); but then one must remember that at
that time industrial investments often paid dividends
of fifty per cent or more, so nine per cent represented
a real sacrifice for an ambitious capitalist. Furthermore, in resenting as we must the grimness of these
grey brick canyons, we have to admit that they have
proved surprisingly flexible: the Peabody Fund have
recently overhauled their estates in Westminster,
knocking two flats into one and three into two, a
kind of surgical treatment made possible where the
walls are of loadbearing brick which will assuredly be
impossible in the tower blocks recently built of loadbearing reinforced concrete. Yet from the Peabody
tenements of the 1870s to Herbert Morrison's LCC
flats of the 1930s, and then to the tower blocks of
Birmingham and Glasgow in the 1960s, one can see
only a slippery line of descent from one optimistic
'solution' of the housing problem to the next, each
one increasingly inhumane and inflexible, and each
one more rapidly made obsolete. The Peabodies were
slums in seventy years and Morrison's flats in less
than forty, so that, with increasing speed of improvement in the standard of living, our brave tower blocks
are likely to have an acceptable life of barely twenty
— only a third the way through the repayment of the
instalments on the loans by which they are built.

The fundamental fault of tenements and flats is, to
repeat, the hypocrisy of double standards that they
express: those who design them would never be seen
dead living in them. The architect-spinster who pro-
pounded a doctrinaire defence of tower blocks in
response to an article of mine in the *Sunday Times*
was tracked to earth by another reader, via the *RIBA
Directory*, to her cosy home in a Kensington mews

cottage. What I find profoundly impressive in the
Garden City pioneers of the generation 1890—1914 is
that, inspired as they were by the bourgeois arcadia
of Bedford Park, they resolutely refused to accept
double standards, but insisted on sharing the same
middle-class, or classless, kind of home with those for
whom they built, such variations as there were being
of size rather than basic character. Jonathan Carr
himself had his own substantial Norman Shaw villa,
Tower House, situated in the heart of Bedford Park
— ironically since replaced by flats. In the industrial
cities such togetherness could be inspired by philanthropic tact: in the 1840s, for instance, the pro-
digious Lady Charlotte Guest, while making sure that
her iron magnate husband Sir Josiah Guest built a
great Gothic mansion for her at Canford Manor in
Dorset, nonetheless deliberately lived in the modest
eighteenth century manager's house when she visited
their Dowlais ironworks, then the world's biggest, at
Merthyr Tydfil.

The most spectacular planned industrial village of
the generation after Owen was Saltaire in Yorkshire,
built in 1850—63 as a single enterprise when Sir Titus
Salt moved his mills out of the congested centre of
Bradford. The design by the Bradford architects
Lockwood & Mawson has great dignity: the terrace
houses, with their continuous rhythm of round-
headed arches over doors and windows, underneath
broad eaves on brackets, are a cross between the rue
de Rivoli and an ideal Quattrocento city of Tuscany,
of the kind depicted in the background of paintings
by della Francesca or Veneziano; while at the same
time they have the down-to-earth practicality of the
nearby hill villages such as Baildon or the Bronte's
Haworth. But in other respects Saltaire is less than
ideal, or almost 'too ideal', in that Salt left nothing to
chance: the institute and cottage hospital are grimly
paternalistic and the whole street layout is a uniform
grid, down to the smallest details, such things as
clothes lines being banned. Across the railway line the
village faces a monumental antithesis of God and
Mammon, in the form of the giant-columned Congre-

C

gational-Chapel-cum-Salt-family-mausoleum on one side of Victoria Road and the vast alpaca and mohair mill on the other. Sir Titus himself lived in a Gothic mansion by a London architect on a nearby hilltop. Meanwhile, at Halifax, Colonel Akroyd was building his no less paternalistic 'almshouse' villages at Copley and Akroydon, designed by Scott and his pupil Crossland.

The dangers to which such cossetting could lead, with the industrialist fattening up his workers like prize pigs, were dramatically illustrated by the fate of the American model town near Chicago, named Pullman after its founder and his railcar factory. It was laid out in 1884 by an excellent Chicago architect Solon S. Beman, with neat little brick houses in the American equivalent of an Arts and Crafts vernacular. George Pullman provided just everything for his workers, from clubs and playing fields to a system of fifth-column spying for discouraging industrial militancy. Nemesis came as early as 1893 in a total and prolonged strike which crippled the firm, and which pointed, at a time when some English philanthropists were becoming fascinated by the pioneer settlements of America, an awful lesson in the tensions created in an industrial community consisting only of 'tied cottages'.

The nearest thing to Pullman in Great Britain was W. H. Lever's Port Sunlight on Merseyside, where the soap factory was begun in 1888 and the houses a year later, designed by a variety of Cheshire and Lancashire architects in an elaborately picturesque confection of local styles, particularly half-timber. The cottages were tied directly to employment at the factory; and in spite of Lever's high standards of accommodation, his generous landscaping and tree-planting, and his remarkable feat of making a soap factory of all things lie down peaceably with the workers' cottages, facing them across a tree-lined avenue, there is an undeniably almshousey atmosphere about Port Sunlight, which leaves it permanently fixed in the social scale of the time when it was created. 'No man of an independent turn of mind can breathe for long the atmosphere of Port Sunlight. That might be news to your Lordship, but we have tried it,' wrote a trade unionist in 1919 to Lever, by then Lord Leverhulme. 'The profit-sharing system not only enslaves and degrades the workers,' he added. 'It tends to make them servile and sycophant.'

The Quaker George Cadbury was more subtle when he and his brothers moved their chocolate factory out from the centre of Birmingham; not only was the Bournville Village Trust established as a separate organisation from the chocolate firm, but an effort was made to attract residents from a wide spectrum socially, including middle-class commuters into Birmingham itself. This was made possible by the socially advantageous siting of Bournville to the south-west of the city, immediately beyond the posh suburbs of Edgbaston and Selly Oak. Thus Bournville succeeded in being, more than any other planned community in Britain since, a mixed society; it is almost impossible to distinguish the homes of chocolate workers from the homes of commuters, all adapted by the local architect Alexander Harvey from the more modest Norman Shaw types of cottage. Cadbury laid particular emphasis on the therapeutic value of growing vegetables, so the gardens are spacious. But there is a certain archness about parts of Bournville too, particularly the village green with its opulent Quaker Meeting House.

Altogether more relaxed as well as more sophisticated than Bournville is its younger sister among Quaker chocolate villages, New Earswick, built on the outskirts of York by Joseph Rowntree, beginning in 1902. Its earliest cottages, softly roughcast but with the bright scarlet pantiles of the local vernacular, have long front gardens, some of them approached by little bridges over a brook; but there is also the makings of a comprehensive footpath system, separate from the roads, and gravitating not towards a solemn chapel but towards the sprightly secular Folk Hall.

Rowntree's architect-planners were a pair of Yorkshiremen practising at Buxton, Parker & Unwin. A tough and down-to-earth tradition of working-class cottage building had in fact been evolving for years in the colliery villages of the North Midlands and South Yorkshire. Raymond Unwin (1863–1940) started his career as an apprentice engineer at the Staveley Coal and Iron Company, and did not set up in architectural practice with Barry Parker until 1896, when he was 33. The previous year he had designed a church for the model mining village of Barrow Hill (Mr Barrow being Staveley's Chairman) but little is at present known of the extent of his opportunities for designing cottages 'on the side' while he was still working in industry. Unwin undoubtedly owed to his late start in architecture his acute practical sense of the complexity of everyday family life, and also his political stress on cooperative management as the means of bringing the good life to the many. By contrast his brother-in-law and half-cousin Barry Parker (1867–1947) was a typical product of the Arts and Crafts Movement in the wake of Morris, and was at his happiest when designing open-plan living rooms in intense Art Nouveau colours, purple, orange and green.

Not that Unwin himself was unsophisticated. Though born near Sheffield, he was brought up in Oxford, where his failed-businessman father had become a private tutor, and he must have been just as impressed by the precinctual seclusion of the colleges as Philip Webb, the son of an Oxford doctor, had been. But his mind broke out from that seclusion, when as an undergraduate he attended lectures by three remarkable men: Canon Samuel Barnett, the East End London vicar who as part of his assault on the slums was then founding Toynbee Hall in Whitechapel with the help of Oxford graduates as a pioneering centre of citizens' advice and welfare work; John Ruskin, who as Slade Professor had gone far beyond the normal bounds of art criticism to attack the stifling of creativity in an industrial society (he had just established his ideal farm community of St George's Guild at Totley, near Sheffield, and was writing about its aims in his series of tracts called *Fors Clavigera*); and Edward Carpenter, the scientist and philosopher, who shortly afterwards himself withdrew to a small agricultural settlement he had founded at Millthorpe, also near Sheffield. Unwin visited Carpenter, first in vacations and then from his nearby colliery, and he was no doubt as impressed as William Morris himself was by the attempt at Mill-thorpe to find a genuine 'simple life'. Morris observed that Carpenter grew his own produce and sold it at the local markets, and concluded: 'It seems to me that a very real way to enjoy life is to accept all its necessary ordinary details and turn them into events by taking interest in them: whereas modern civilisation huddles them out of the way, has them done in a venal and slovenly manner till they become real drudgery which people can't help trying to avoid.'

It was this passionate desire to sanctify the ordinary, which Morris himself rarely achieved, that meant so much to Raymond Unwin, and his partnership with Parker was perfectly complementary in that Parker was able to inject poetry into an ordinariness which in Unwin's hands might have become merely dull and anonymous. But there was actual poetry in Unwin's vision too, in his case of a semi-political kind, deriving from the American Walt Whitman, whom Carpenter knew well; Carpenter himself wrote a long Whitmanesque poem called *Towards Democracy*, full of exhortations to England to awake, which had a profound effect on Unwin. It is difficult for us now to understand the extraordinarily liberating effect which Whitman's windy rhetoric about democracy had upon young men at that time, who were moving out of the traditional hierarchies of the towns and devoting themselves to semi-pantheistic garden-worship in the suburbs. Whitman was similarly the inspiration for another Northern architectural pioneer, Charles Holden, who came from Bolton, where Whitman's closest English friend, J. W. Wallace, was the centre of an intellectual circle which also included W. H. Lever's principal architect in the second phase of Port Sunlight, Jonathan Simpson; Holden and Unwin almost certainly knew each other through the Northern Art Workers' Guild, where they had friends in common such as the brilliant suburban villa architect Edgar Wood. It is not clear when Unwin himself first visited America, which later gave him his favourite platforms; but certainly not only American rhetoric but actual American achievements in community building had from the start a powerful influence on the Garden City Movement.

Ebenezer Howard himself, the humble shorthand writer who, rather than Cadbury or Rowntree or Unwin, was the movement's undisputed leader, had worked from 1872 to 1876 in Chicago, then familiarly known as the Garden City. As Walter Creese has suggested, Howard must have been aware of F. L. Olmsted's newly built garden suburb of Riverside; Olmsted in his turn had been inspired by his visits to England in the fifties, where he was 'ready to admit that in democratic America there was nothing to be thought of as comparable with [the] People's Garden' of Paxton's Birkenhead Park. Howard was not an articulate man, so we know little in detail of the influences upon him; he mentions the proposals of Edward Gibbon Wakefield for the organised migratory movement of population, by Herbert Spencer for copartnership forms of land tenure and by James Silk Buckingham for building a new city. Certainly the immediate spark was Edward Bellamy's utopian novel about Boston, *Looking Backwards* (1888) — the same book which stimulated William Morris to write *News from Nowhere* (1890). Howard must also have had in mind Morris's exhortation in *The Earthly Paradise*:

> Forget the spreading of the hideous town;
> Think rather of the pack-horse on the down,
> And dream of London, small, and white, and clean,
> The clear Thames bordered by its gardens green.

But the success of Howard's slim volume, when in 1898 it was published under the title *Tomorrow: A Peaceful Path to Real Reform* (retitled in 1902 *Garden Cities of Tomorrow*), had much less to do with Morris and Bellamy than with the simple diagrammatic quality of Utilitarian utopias fifty years before — Buckingham's New Victoria for example, published in 1848 and rather similar to Saltaire (which may indeed have owed something to it). Howard's central proposal was that London's population should be systematically decanted to new groups of 'social cities' of 250,000 people set self-sufficiently with their own commerce and industry in the midst of the countryside; each social city would consist of a central core of 58,000 people connected up to a ring of six independent and widely spaced garden cities, each of 32,000. This brilliant concept, very similar to the most recent plans of the 1960s for larger New Towns (such as Peterborough) was illustrated by poky little diagrams of no visual value whatever. But this in a way was Howard's genius: having had a social and communal idea of fundamental value, he did not try to design it all himself in the way that Lever had done. He restricted himself to these simple explanatory diagrams of the basic principles; and then, having rapidly gained financial and political backing, he held a limited competition in 1903 for the design of the First Garden City at Letchworth, in which a partnership of two of Shaw's best pupils, Lethaby and Ricardo, was deservedly defeated by the little-known firm from Buxton, Parker and Unwin.

Two years later Parker & Unwin were again chosen to plan a major new community, this time by Mrs Henrietta Barnett, wife of the founder of Toynbee Hall. She had inherited a considerable fortune (her father being the Mr Rowland who made macassar oil for men's hair) and, when her husband left the slums for a canon's stall at Westminster Abbey, she decided to devote her genius for organising and fund-raising to the task of salvaging the landscape northwards from Hampstead Heath, which was threatened with rampant suburbia by the proposed extension of the Northern Line of the underground railway. First she bought what is now the Hampstead Heath Extension by public subscription and handed it over to the London County Council; then she persuaded Eton

College to sell the other 243 acres of their estate to a non-profitmaking Hampstead Garden Suburb Trust, modelled on the one which Howard and his followers had established for Letchworth.

Of the two settlements, Letchworth is the more interesting as a strategic plan, in that it has from the start been a virtually self-sufficient community, with an interesting mixture socially; Hampstead Garden Suburb, on the other hand, is of incomparable quality as a detailed environment, in that under Unwin's masterful control it attracted a wide variety of investment (private owners, private builders, copartnership societies, charitable bodies, the Trust itself, and the nonprofitmaking Garden Suburb Development Company) at a time when Letchworth was floundering in the absence of adequate capital or of an adequate mains electricity supply. Letchworth has some excellent groups of houses, particularly by Parker himself, who lived there, but it lacks an adequate centre and its landscape is so lushly overgrown that at times it overwhelms the architecture instead of partnering it. Hampstead Garden Suburb's setback by contrast was not aesthetic, but social, in that it became the victim of its own prosperity: after 1918 the low-cost copartnership housing was virtually given up, and even those houses which had been inhabited by artisans were gradually absorbed into a uniform upper-middle-class complacency.

The founder of the Garden Suburb, Mrs Barnett, had certainly travelled in America in the nineties, and she specifically states that it was there that she was first impressed by the possibilities of communal open space in front of the houses, eliminating the customary walls and fences. Unwin and his fellow architects, particularly those who came from a nonconformist background, had become increasingly interested in the New England settlements of the American pioneers, who had after all been escaping in their day from the restrictiveness of the political and religious Establishment. Not that such communal settlements were without precedent in England itself: Fulneck, for example, the Moravian village in Yorkshire begun in 1724, was the birthplace of Benjamin Latrobe, architect of the Capitol; and there was William Penn's Quaker retreat at Jordans in Buckinghamshire. At Hampstead the communal front gardens of America were restricted to certain special culs-de-sac where they were appropriate — Linnell Close for example, a group of hip-roofed brick villas of a self-consciously neo-Colonial primness.

The more conventional groups of houses, designed by a galaxy of different architects, Unwin arranged in varied terraces and clusters around narrow culs-de-sac, the twelve-foot width of driveway being sanctioned (in defiance of the byelaws) by a special Act of Parliament; they are connected up laterally by footpaths, giving access to allotments and tennis courts in the generous backland behind the gardens. Unwin was violently critical of the 'monotony' of suburbs of the Willesden-Tooting-Catford kind; and by restricting densities to 12 houses (about 40—45 people) to the acre, and exquisitely relating each line of cottages to the contours and to old trees and hedgerows, he achieved a special sense of place in every road, instead of the uniform grid pattern of the spec builder. Yet however dedicated Unwin was to improving the suburban cottage, he did not try to improve it out of existence; in spite of the seductive illustrations of medieval towns, especially in Germany, in his bible *Town Planning in Practice* (1909), he kept his own cottages closely in tune with the vernacular of high-class spec building in the tradition of Bedford Park and of high-class philanthropy such as Bournville. It was, in the Smithsons' words, 'English popular architecture so expressive of our climate'.

Already in *The Builder* of 1910 one of the culs-de-sac at Hampstead was being described as 'intended for superior artisans' — the point being that, as in the New Towns fifty years later, the jobs available and the enterprise needed for the move meant that the working-class men attracted were predominantly skilled. Unwin, with his industrial experience, knew instinctively how to pitch his cottages to the aspirations of 'superior artisans'; and, in spite of subsequent gibes from architects about the imposition of middle-class standards upon working-class people in the cottages which, under his influence as Chief Architect to the Ministry of Health, became the norm of the post-1918 council housing estate, the evidence suggests that Unwin knew what he was doing. The real middle-class imposition comes from those obsessed with physical health who sweep old cottages away in favour of hygienic tenements, thus making a revolutionary break in social patterns which often consorts strangely with the unrevolutionary temperaments of the officials who think such buildings suitable for other people to live in. Unwin by contrast recognised that social health depends upon a stable evolution which resists exploitation by passing technological fashions, and accordingly he based his work on traditional vernacular models, whether from the country village street or from its suburban brother, the artisan terrace.

My own stress on the overriding importance of the small English family house depends on a similar belief that, even though evolution may in some respects have speeded up, it is still evolution, not revolution. For nearly fifty years now architects have been brainwashed by a barrage of propaganda from the apostles of the Modern Movement, particularly Le Corbusier, to the effect that we live in a time of rapid and fundamental change, for which only radically new solutions can be appropriate. 'They may not like it now, but they will get used to it' or 'Why should we allow them to have what they have always been used to when they obviously are not capable of knowing the range of other possibilities available?' — these are the arguments adduced by the older 'modern' critics such as J. M. Richards in favour of tower blocks and open plan living rooms for council tenants. The separate rooms of the small cottage are supposed by such pioneers to be irremediably bourgeois and cosy — as though cosiness were a crime. Yet it is precisely those romantics, who are still excited by the nostalgic Popular Front vision of the slim towers of workers' flats heroically punching at the sky, who are in fact ramming middle-class attitudes down working-class throats. Of course it is fun to live in a high block of flats in Mayfair in the week when you also own a country cottage you can escape to at the weekend; of course it is exhilarating to swim in a fish bowl of plate glass, when you can afford to pay for the extra central heating and to distance yourself far enough from the neighbours' prying eyes; and of course it is elegant and spacious to have a single open-plan living-and-dining area when your family keeps its hands uniformly clean. Yet to take just one example of the realities of working-class life, it was found in the Park Hill flats at Sheffield, where each family was provided with a single large living-dining room and a tiny kitchenette, that residents were prepared to undergo amazing physical hardships in order to eat their high tea within that kitchenette; the practical point being that, if the father of the family is employed in heavy engineering and comes home in dirty boots and overalls, he wants to be able to sit down to a meal immediately on hard washable surfaces, instead of being forced to strip off and have a bath in order to avoid soiling the living room carpets.

Old patterns of life die hard, and that is why the suburban tradition of family houses with gardens, from Henry II to Raymond Unwin, must still be the heart of our environmental designing. It is curious now to remember the spate of articles by Gaitskellite sociologists, immediately after Labour lost for the third time running in 1959, who put over as though it were some axiomatic truth the plausible hunch that it had all happened because the working classes were becoming middle class. Yet most of the detailed evidence (Goldthorpe's studies at Luton, for instance) is to the contrary: even if a man is making £50 or £60 a week, far more than the average schoolteacher, he will still regard himself as working class and continue to have a traditional pattern of life, the difference being that all the pent-up demand for equipment and gear which was stifled in days of poverty is now able to billow out in the form of cars, fridges, washing machines — and soon dishwashers, tape-recorders and television cassettes. The way of life is still basically the same — it is just *more* of the same. Even amongst those who have had higher education, changes of life-style are much less evident in the science laboratories, with their nine-to-five routine, than among the sociologists themselves.

In fact the position is, in my view, exactly the reverse: the middle classes are increasingly becoming working class. Ever since the vernacular revivalism of Nash and Devey and Norman Shaw, the middle classes have increasingly desired to possess the roots of the simple life contained in the cottage; and the disappearance of servants has, despite temporary inconvenience, actually liberated their masters so that they can enjoy a simpler, less hierarchical life. Any house agent can confirm the ever-increasing tendency of middle-class people to become disillusioned with high-rise or picture window or open plan, and to turn back to the old artisan terrace house in search of something which more closely relates in simple practical terms to the gradual evolution of the family.

Yet it is extraordinary how little is taught to architectural students and students of planning about the actual detailed make-up of the vernacular cottage, not only in terms of its functional performance in the narrow sense of turning switches or pulling plugs, but in the deeper sense of a range of visual symbols which stirs feelings no less real for not being easily expressible. So we must next turn the microscope on the ordinary threshold.

The formal but personal exhibitionism of the front garden, its avenue in miniature flattering the visitor to the threshold, is displayed here in a stone cottage at Stock Plain, near Sheffield. (Edwin Smith)

3

The Space that Lies Between

There is nothing like treading the boards of old-tyme democratic politics for middle-class persons like myself (or for that matter, for architects and planners) to find out about the ordinary doorstep — to see what the milkman and the postman saw. It was a total education in environmental values for me suddenly to be forced through the embarrassment barrier as an undergraduate by instructions to canvass every family in a suburban village, not choosing houses according to the architectural values of the Buildings of England volumes, but, in Ruskin's words about the painter's proper attitude to Nature, 'selecting nothing and rejecting nothing'.

In those far-off days of the Early Affluent Society, one soon noticed on the council estates that the doorbell which went 'ding-dong' instead of just 'ding' denoted a Tory voter, an overmighty subject with pretensions to gracious living. Yet it was the unpredictable variety of each threshold which was so much more fascinating: never again would one fall into the trap of discussing the English suburban cottage in terms of 'soulless monotony'. Simply because it was rooted in the ground, it enjoyed a limitless flexibility of contact outwards into the community, via pathway, garden, yard and pavement, overlaid by a minutely hand-stitched coverlet of gnomes, chrysanths, trellises and crazy paving. Conversely, one began to have the first spasms of doubt about the then architecturally fashionable solution of the collective tower block of flats, of the species inspired by Corbusier's *Unité*, in that it had self-evidently achieved that proud unity only by denying diversity and by severing the family from its traditional human contacts at ground-level. The patchwork quilt of individual identity seemed to have been traded in abruptly for a uniform blanket of machine-mown lawn. 'Public space' and 'private space' had been crudely and fiercely defined by the slamming of doors in the lift hall. Yet the quality of life in built-up areas depends more than anything else on what does or does not happen in the space that lies between, in the semi-public or the semi-private, or in a mixture of the two at different seasons and different times.

In 1967, as an assistant editor of the *Architectural Review*, I was asked by my editor, the redoubtable J. M. Richards, to put together a special issue of the magazine which would illustrate 'the best of current housing design', together with a text explaining 'what we think should be done'. He made quite clear that what was wanted by him and by the other editors was a typical AR tract on the great god Urbanity, and his cosmetic soul-sister Townscape. My idea of importing into the argument some sociological evidence indicative of what ordinary people actually wanted was scornfully dismissed by the proprietor, de Cronin Hastings, alias Ivor de Wolfe, with the words 'But *we know* what should be done.'

I became convinced on the contrary that we did not know, and that most of what passed in the mid-sixties for 'good housing design' at high densities was in fact a fundamental violation of the lives of those families who had to live in it — and council tenants clearly had little choice. I can remember a discussion with one of the contributors to the issue, Roy Worskett of the Ministry of Housing, when we suddenly came to the resounding conclusion that almost all the most renowned high-density housing schemes were dangerous rubbish, precisely because they were conceived of merely as 'housing' and not as part of the fabric of a total living community. The no-man's-land of communal lift halls and open landscaping was no substitute for the individual back yard in a diverse neighbourhood with pubs and shops.

My wife and I had ourselves set up family two years before in an ordinary two-storey artisan terrace house in the South-East London suburb of Lee, in a road with a (to me) attractively mixed social and racial character; and it was increasingly borne in upon me by commonsense and by personal observation that this kind of house did in fact satisfy not just myself and my own family but an extraordinarily wide range of ages and income groups. These quite anonymous little houses, built by Victorian speculative builders were in fact marvels of sophisticated

design, based not so much on self-conscious artistic decision-making as on the gradual evolution over the centuries of the ordinary family, which is itself, anthropologically, something very sophisticated.
Local architects in recent years had showed their own instinctive awareness of this by living in that kind of house themselves, or at least in the updated version of it which Eric Lyons had designed for Span; but it became obvious that they had totally failed to relate what was good for their own families to what was good enough for other people's. Estates of high council flats, even where the architects were as eminent as Lasdun or Stirling or Spence, suddenly seemed to me by contrast to be extraordinarily unsophisticated, in their crude elimination or neglect of the everyday activities of family life.

Once the members of a family are hoisted off the ground, be it the fourth floor, or the twenty-fourth, certain vital links that are normally taken for granted disappear abruptly from their relationships with their neighbours, and indeed with the very earth itself. They find that the traditional threshold, which has its two or three steps up to the front door overlooked across the street by as many as twenty different neighbours standing on their own scrubbed doorsteps or sitting in their net-curtained bay windows, has been replaced by a door into a lift hall, which is an anonymous and almost windowless space with only three or four other entrances, none of them overlooked by anyone. They find that the traditional back yard, with its effortless ability to absorb on equal terms the baby's pram, the toddler's toys, the housewife's washing lines and the dog's kennel, everyone of them closely overlooked from the kitchen window, has disappeared completely, a single door to a lift hall offering no kind of substitute for an escape route at the back. And they find that, apart from the pathetic G-string gesture of the windowbox, the traditional self-protective clothing of the garden has gone too — the front garden with its semi-public display of roses, rocks and gnomes, and the back garden, with its semi-private sandpits, shrubs and sheds. In their place the blocks of flats are surrounded by mindless expanses of open lawn, which are the responsibility and pride of no one, fenced off and peppered with little notices saying 'No Ball Games'. Dorothy Parker might have amended herself to say: 'If all the useless grass verges in municipal housing estates were laid end to end, I would not be in the least surprised.' Certainly, as the recent 'built form studies' by Sir Leslie Martin's team at Cambridge have proved, they could be combined to form either a full-sized football pitch for the community or individual gardens for each family, even at densities of over a hundred people to the acre.

Not only do the flatted estates impose a bureaucratic anonymity which violates the individuality of family life — no pets, no washing lines, no trellises, no colour wash, and all the doors painted uniformly olive-green — but they have gone on to deny fundamentally the changes and chances of a rapidly improving standard of living, which is at last making it financially possible for most people to breathe the freedom of doing their own thing. It was a shock for me as a well-brought-up propagandist for modern architecture to realise that it was in fact in the much-abused 'monotonous sprawl' of the LCC cottage estates of the twenties, at places like Becontree and St Helier, that this freedom had over the years been able to blossom more generously than anywhere else in council housing — blossoming literally in the private gardens and psychologically in the well-rooted growth of family life, a growth expressed architecturally in the sixties by the burgeoning of packaged bathrooms and toolsheds.

Take the front door itself for a start. The most important thing to be arbitrarily eliminated in a block of flats is the individual threshold — and I was relieved to find that my own intuitive emphasis on thresholds in the *Architectural Review's* special housing issue of 1967 was backed up scientifically a year later by the social surveys of Shankland, Cox & Associates' Childwall Valley Study, in which the architects analysed a large Liverpool Corporation estate of the late fifties as a prelude to designing an estate of their own for the council on an adjoining site. As the Childwall Study demonstrated, we may take completely for granted those two or three steps up to the door of an ordinary terrace house, but they have in fact an extraordinarily varied and sophisticated role in linking the semi-public with the semi-private.

In the first place the threshold overlooks the public highway. In her book *The Death and Life of Great American Cities*, Jane Jacobs emphasised the crucial importance of the watching eyes of residents in maintaining law and order, and this is one of those obvious observations which nonetheless need to be drummed home repeatedly into the heads of architects and planners. 'Law and order' does not necessarily imply real crime: there is within any built-up area an extremely wide variety of small nuisances — noise and smell and obstruction — which do not in any way justify calling in the police but which nevertheless need to be kept constantly under control by the vigilance of residents. Put at its simplest, such watchfulness means little more than the old parliamentary expression 'I spy strangers', in that residents whose houses face each other across a street in the normal way are able to notice anything or anyone out of the ordinary and just check within themselves, hardly with a conscious thought, whether there might be anything slightly wrong. It is not so much the dramatic incidents of burglarly or brawling that recur, but the humdrum problems associated with such trends as increasing road traffic, with heavy lorries parked in unsuitable places and revved up at unsuitable hours. The only time my wife and I have ever called in the police was when we thought a house opposite was being burgled at five in the morning, although in fact the teenage son was being innocently picked up by his workmate in the large black van with no external markings which woke us up. Then there is the problem of young children who run out into the road without a care when temporarily out of sight of their mother; in an ordinary street they will still be in sight of the neighbours on their thresholds.

Road safety training in schools is that much more urgent for children living in flats, just because they have not been brought up with the regular habits of the pavement.

Jane Jacobs's stress on these negative opportunities of the street, on its role in communal self-defence, was the direct result of her bitter experience of urban renewal projects in New York, with their frightening rash of unobserved muggings. In the more modest sense of aimless vandalism, there are ominous signs of similar dangers in the graffiti-covered walls, urinated staircases and smashed armour-glass louvres of British high-rise housing — such barrack wastes as Lansdowne Green in Lambeth, Ladywood in Birmingham or Hutchesontown-Gorbals in Glasgow. But the main advantages which residents find in the street are much more positive than mere security and much less esoteric than the kind of clattery hothouse Naples-in-the-suburbs for which Jane Jacobs and her Hampstead acolytes have such a romantic affection. Whatever the delights of such rare cockney kasbahs as Portobello Road or Shepherd's Market, the virtues of the vast majority of English streets lie not in trinket stalls or bright lights, but in the much quieter human relationships which are the humdrum necessities of family life in the suburbs.

The first such necessity is what can only be called *neighbourliness*; and underlying it is the never-ending human quest for *identity*, for measuring oneself against one's fellow men. I come out on my front doorstep of a Saturday morning, enjoying the knowledge that my wee plot is 'mine all mine', quite as possessively, I assure you, as any of Capability Brown's clients coming out into their giant porticoes. My diminutive porchlet, striped brick and plaster under a gable, is in the Ruskinian version of round-arched Northern Italian Gothic used in 1872 at Shaftesbury Park, Battersea, though in this case the pattern dates from about 1890; before my feet the two grand scrubbed steps lead down to the ornately cusped cast-iron of the coalhole cover; and thence the broad tiled avenue, blue and red and all of ten feet long, leads out through my front garden, past my striplet of lawn, past flowery borders and luxuriant creepers, to my low wall of blue brick and wooden gate which separate me from the public pavement. From my raised-up vantage point I can gaze imperiously straight across the road to a dozen or more houses of exactly the same vintage, and by pivoting obliquely to the right, two or three on the same side of the road (there is a street corner to my left). At almost any time of the day there is likely to be someone similarly flaunting herself or himself on their doorstep who will recognise me — and I will recognise them. It is easy to dismiss, as something perfunctory, that all-important casual nod of greeting to one's neighbours. It may be all over in a couple of seconds without anything of apparent value said, more often nothing whatever said at all; but it is, I believe, one of the absolute necessities of human life that we should so recognise our neighbours and be recognised by them. Within the apparently endless built-up area of a great city, simply to nod to one another means in effect admitting that you are you, someone particular whom I know, and I am I, someone particular whom you know, and admitting that between us we belong to the same spatial relationship of people and place in the local community of the 'urban village'. It does not necessarily matter whether we are friendly or not: as G. P. Wibberley, London University's Professor of Countryside Planning, has put it: 'The great thing about the village is that, even if you are not loved, at least you can be hated — you will not be ignored.' Now to most of us suburbians such neighbourly noddings of the head must seem a ridiculously obvious or banal fact of life, certainly not worth publishing; but the whole trouble about high-rise estates of flats is that the obvious and the banal tend not to happen. The tenant emerges from his tower-block flat, not onto a threshold with a view of his neighbours, or even for that matter of any other passersby, but into a confined walled-in lift hall, with the doors of three, or at best four, other flats, totally devoid of any steps on which to stand and enjoy the

84

view — because there are no steps and there is no view.

The question of numbers is actually very important in establishing the closest ties of neighbourliness — this is where quality of life does paradoxically depend on quantity. In my street, with sixteen or seventeen different families within view immediately I emerge onto my threshold, there are sure to be at least three or four with whom I shall have something in common. To be precise in my case, there are our next-door neighbours to the left who have only recently arrived but are old friends, sharing identical interests with my wife and myself (teaching and planning respectively); then there is the retired spinster immediately opposite, who likes to sit out on her doorstep and amuse the children, as well as reminiscing to me about the Hulton Press in its great days when she worked for it; and then there are her Irish neighbours, a husband who stokes the boilers in one of London's last surviving workhouses and takes photographs of professional quality in his spare time, and his breathlessly, garrulously kind wife, full of odd scraps of knowledge, who baby-sits for us and often has our children over to tea with hers. There are at least half a dozen other friendly families whom we see less frequently: our next-door neighbour on the right for instance, a bus driver who has done decorating work for us in his spare time and whose teenage daughters used also to do some baby-sitting; then there is the family across the road whom I know through the Labour Party, and another who has a son of the same age as ours, and then a rather hearty lady who enjoys chatting up our children (as well as needlessly shouting at the Nigerian ones round the corner). With all these people and others further up the road or round the corner, we can have chance contacts and conversations at almost any time; and I hope they feel themselves equally recognised by us in return.

The situation on the fifteenth floor of a tower block can be disastrously different. Like most of the architects and planners who design them, I have no

The slow, inefficient, vandal-prone progress of the low-cost lift breeds a sullen apathy in those who wait for it. Pearl Jephcott's Homes in High Flats reports average waiting times of over ten minutes for the lifts shown here at Red Road, Glasgow. No wonder mothers keep their children cooped up on high or else lose control of them. (Marilyn Stafford)

personal experience of life up there; so once again we have to rely on commonsense and personal observation on the doorstep, fortified by assistance from the sociologists. One of them, Ed Cooney of the Institute of Community Studies, carried out as long ago as 1961 a survey of privacy in postwar housing at Bethnal Green. Having noted that privacy is so vital to English people that no word describing its opposite — presumably it would be 'community' — is in fact in colloquial use, Cooney tested the extent to which privacy had been achieved in different types of block without dragging in its evil shadow, loneliness. He found that on the floors where there were only four or five flats, the sheer lack of numbers in the neighbours tended to make newcomers extremely wary of making contacts at all. If it has been easy enough for my wife and me in a terrace house to find at least three firm friends among sixteen families, what happens to people on the fifteenth floor who find that the total available choice is only three? With such a small number there is no guarantee that every one of them might not be indifferent or hostile; so is it sensible for the newcomer to greet them at all? Yet a great deal of rubbish was talked by architects and planners about possible communal benefits from building tower blocks; when the *Architectural Review* published in 1960 its glamorous photographs of Denys Lasdun's so-called 'cluster block' at Bethnal Green, it committed itself to the ineffable absurdity of describing the outcome as 'a vertical street'. Whether anyone at the *Architectural Review* has ever tried walking up a vertical street I shudder to think — or ever seen anyone doing so, except in Outer Space or on the Wall of Death. The cluster block was supposed to encourage neighbourliness by the way in which it grouped together round a common lift shaft what were in effect four separate tower blocks, with only two flats per floor. Theoretically, therefore, there were eight families to each floor rather than four or five; but, such was the curious funnelling and spiralling effect on gusts of wind caused by Lasdun's layout, with the access galleries and bridges to the lift shaft left absolutely open to the elements, that the social effect in practice, as Cooney discovered, was that families on the same floor but in different blocks of the cluster rarely got to know each other at all. Each pair of flats became an isolated cul-de-sac; and thus, far from cementing together communal living, Mr Lasdun had actually achieved a dwelling with greater privacy and isolation than any previously known in London.

In the normal street by contrast, with its multitude of diverse neighbours, there are complicated gradations between close personal friendships at one extreme and occasional acquaintance at the other, with the opportunity for each family to achieve the range of relationships it desires. But there is also the wider context of the neighbourhood, the 'urban village', represented by the passers-by on the pavement. The pavement is in fact another of those features of everyday life in suburbs which is taken by all of us for granted, at least until it disappears disconcertingly into the rimless landscape of lawns in a new housing scheme. It brings the outside world very close to the house, but by confining it within rigid parallel lines only four or five feet apart, between the garden and the gutter, it succeeds in disciplining what might otherwise become intrusion. Passers-by know instinctively that they are not to stray beyond these parallel lines, and children and dogs are naturally brought up to walk within them. It is a matter of choice for the individual householder whether he wishes to be more or less exposed to the pavement: he can have a low wall or a thick hedge or a high fence, or he can have none of these things but rely on net curtains instead; or again he may simply enjoy seeing and being seen clearly. On the open landscaping of so many high density housing estates there is no such choice. One of the most frequent of all complaints in such estates is about the noise and confusion caused by the games of the older children — that is, the nine, ten, eleven and twelve-year-olds. This is partly because of our chronic failure to provide facilities for play midway between the toddlers' sandpit and the teenagers' dance hall, but it also has very much to do with the absence of the customary guidelines for the public path. Where there is no clear pavement but only a broad stretch of greensward, the subtle gradations of semi-public and semi-private are uniformly ironed out (or, literally, mown down) in favour of a smooth grass surface, which may look good to visiting delegations of burgomasters and commissars but means very little practically to local residents, except that children and dogs can rush across it, right up to their windows, without let or hindrance.

What makes the lack of fences worse is the fact that passers-by are increasingly motorised; it may be just about possible to keep ten-year-old boys off the living-room windows of ground-floor flats, by planting dense shrubs and spiky cobbles, but it is very much harder to keep out the noise and pollution and visual disruption of heavy lorries, for example, with their disconcerting habit of revving up at 5.30 in the morning. There has been an inexcusable delay by Governments in making sure that the road haulage industry pays the true cost of making its activities socially acceptable. A Ministry of Transport working party recently recommended the setting up of lorry parks by local authorities, but it is surely the industry who ultimately should pay for these by appropriate tolls. Action against lorries in London, which has been obstructed by the reluctance of the police themselves to enforce laws on obstruction, is at last under way after the success of an experimental GLC lorry parking scheme in Tower Hamlets, which came into force in November 1971. But in most places anarchy persists, with drivers taking their lorries home with them for the night; and this is all the more insidious on flatted council estates with 'open landscaping', in that the other tenants there, feeling themselves to have so little personal claim on the open space outside their blocks, will tend to accept with weary resignation what in roads with individual houses would be greeted by active protest and petitions to the Town Hall.

In spite of its modest size, the family car is, by sheer weight of numbers, becoming even more menacing to family life when parked amidst council flats than the juggernaut lorry. In estate after estate the dream of 'freeing space on the ground' by breaking up the street and building high — that mirage of Cartesian logic in *La Cité Radieuse* with which Le Corbusier captivated a whole generation of housing architects — has turned instead into a nightmare of low-level sprawl of Noddy-houses on wheels. The car is in effect a piece of mobile architecture, a sitting room on the move, sometimes a bedroom when stationary. Those who designed the shimmering Corbusian skyline of Roehampton, and who incidentally forgot to bring up a bus service to it for the first five years, nonetheless assumed there would be a car ownership level of under twenty per cent; accordingly vehicular constipation on the 'estate roads' has since become acute. Yet the sudden swing of the Housing Ministry in the mid-sixties — not so much a swing as a panic — towards car parking standards in new estates of as much as one hundred per cent garaging (that is to say, one per family) plus fifty per cent hardstandings for visitors, has made the situation even worse than before in some high-rise estates: the obvious 'solution' has been to build multi-storey or underground car parks between the blocks, but these have proved extremely difficult to police — once again, because they are outside the network of semi-public, semi-private supervision (supervision in the most literal sense) which exists in the traditional street. The result has been a doubling of evils: the new car parks are left almost empty, while tenants park their cars instead along the choked estate roads, so that ambulances and fire engines cannot get through. Once the density drops below a hundred people to the acre, just as houses-on-the-ground for everyone become possible, so do individual garages. There has been much discussion on the relative merits of grouped garages as against those which are 'integral' with the house, with the big car-door built into it on what might be called the fire-station principle of rapid commuting (sometimes on seeing a row of new 'town houses' with their gaping garages I have a fantasy that the model parents' bedroom in the future will have not only a tea-making machine, but also a greasy pole straight down to the driving seat for late sleepers). It seems certain anyway that most people will continue to want, as far as possible, to have their cars parked outside their own homes, or at least be able to bring them out in the open air very close by, so that the necessary car-washing and repair work can be done in pleasant conditions and interspersed with conversations with neighbours and with children.

In new estates it is vital to keep the access roads as short as possible. The layout studies group of the former Ministry of Housing quickly established in their comparative appraisals of housing schemes that there were enormous variations between estates of the same density in terms of the percentage of open space which had been covered by tarmac; and the more wasteful schemes included not just the philistine road-hog type emanating from borough engineers, with vast turning circles for space-age dust-carts, but also some of the more architecturally dogmatic Radburn layouts, separating pedestrians from traffic in long parallel rows of highway and greenway. At the highest densities the best buy is invariably a courtyard type of layout, with the garages located round the periphery in short access streets, where most of them can still be integral with the houses (as in the Merton Architect's Department's brilliantly concise Pollards Hill estate of houses-on-the-ground at 110 people to the acre). Refuse disposal is ideally done in paper sacks, which once a week are wheeled on electric trolleys to peripheral collecting points.

It is much more important to concentrate in such ways on minimising the hard surfaces at the front of the house, thus maximising the soft gardens at the back, than it is to indulge in elaborate theoretical diagrams of traffic segregation. People cannot be forced to segregate their lives, least of all children; and in fact the conflict between children playing in streets and cars parked in them is by no means a foregone conclusion when thoroughly examined. So much depends on the particular configuration of a street and of its relationship to other streets in the neighbourhood. Our own road in Lee is L-shaped, and thus the only regular intruders are the driving schools, who find the right-angle bend instructive for their pupils; its very abruptness in fact gives the road the all-important residential quality of a low 'design speed'. Speed of traffic has far more effect on the residential environment than complicated systems of vehicular-pedestrian segregation — a point proved by a visit to the handsome Roundshaw estate, designed by Clifford Culpin & Partners on the site of Croydon Airport, where all the intricacy of the terraces and decks over the access roads is insufficient to prevent pedestrians from strolling unconcernedly down to the verges of the main spine road of the estate along which speeds of 50 m.p.h. are easy. There are two much smaller estates close to my home which show what different design speeds can do for otherwise conventional access roads. One is a modish 'mixed development' of tower blocks and terraces in plum-coloured brick where the houses-with-gardens for the larger families are arranged around wholly traffic-free courtyards; yet these courtyards are flanked by a new road which runs absolutely straight for three hundred yards, thus allowing cars to rev up to impressive speeds immediately next to where the greatest numbers of children live. The other estate by contrast consists merely of four-storey maisonettes in conventional pitched-roofed slabs, set at right-angles to a railway embankment and architecturally rather dreary; but the environment is transformed, especially for the children, by the way in which the single estate road is made to snake in and out and around each block, in a series of right-angled S-bends, so that it is physically impossible for any driver to manage more than 15 m.p.h.

Given such slow speeds of approach, there is in fact a naturally close identity between the kind of hard surfaces required for parking cars and the kind required for the ball games of older children. For example, in the otherwise excellent estate of two-storey houses (72 to the acre) at Woodway Lane,

Coventry, designed by Fred Lloyd Roche when he was at the Midlands Housing Consortium, Ministry sociologists have coldly noted that the carefully segregated Radburn layout has not worked as the architect intended. The 'front door', which opens onto a landscaped 'greenway', reserved wholly for pedestrians, is rarely used by most families, and by some not at all. This is partly because children have to be kept away from such open areas, which afford no barriers between their games and other people's windows, and partly because the door gives access directly into the living room, with consequent problems of dirty feet on fitted carpets; but it is mainly because mothers, fathers and children all want to play together as a family at the 'back door'. This opens by contrast into a small hard-surfaced yard, which is overlooked from the kitchen window and enclosed by a fence, thus being wholly suitable for prams and toddlers; while beyond that is the garage court, again adequately enclosed, in which cars can be washed and footballs kicked, without generally causing damage to the house or infringing its privacy. In fact, given the enormous amount of space on the threshold which is nowadays occupied by 'visitors' handstandings' as well as garage forecourts, it is surely commonsense to use such hard surfaces for play as well as parking, and to fence them off solely for play until the level of car ownership increases. There is admittedly a danger of drivers backing their cars out on top of invisible children; so the ideal arrangement seems to be to sink garages very slightly below ground, with the children's playspace a half-level up, sitting on the garage roofs. But to be convenient enough to be used, and used without danger, such garage-playgrounds need to be quite small and immediately next to the houses of the families involved — and there must be no aesthetic prejudice against the necessary netting to fence off ball-games.

A more profound reason than mere convenience why the family car tends to be parked prominently next to the family home lies in its value as self-advertisement. There has in recent years been far too much snide talk about 'status-symbols', indulged in by middle-class people who have enjoyed such symbols themselves for years and now heartily resent the fact that the great mass of other people are busy acquiring them too. People never talked about 'keeping up with the Joneses' in the days when the Joneses were all middle-class and therefore respectable. It is sad that such *de-haut-en-bas* sneers about other people's aspirations should have become a reflex reaction, not only in the idle chatter on the cocktail circuit and at the golf club bar, but also in the straight-laced puritan morality which has castrated modern architecture, particularly in the local authority departments concerned with 'housing'. That we should actually wish our home and our car to be clearly identifiable from our neighbours' homes and cars is not some kind of vice in us, or even a harmless weakness at which others can smile; it is in fact an essential part of the survival kit of personality that keeps us sane in what would otherwise be the drab anonymity of the urban filing cabinet. The whole point of suburban culture, its glory in fact, is that, detached or semi-detached, we are able to find in it our personal identity. In what planners are pleased to call a conurbation each one of us has a desperate need to identify himself: we are deservedly proud of the things that are peculiarly ours and no one else's; and, among other things, we feel a special need in a densely built-up area to pick out our own distinctive family home. I particularly remember a cartoon in *Punch* which showed a little boy and his mother walking dwarfed between absolutely uniform high blocks of flats, with the mother turning round and saying: 'Wave goodbye to Granny.' The fact that a natural and desirable yearning for recognition and for identity should have been prostituted by the advertising agencies, as a means of stimulating the acquisition by each family of expensive consumer goods — colour television being the latest — is not in itself an adverse comment upon it; in fact it confirms its crucial psychological importance, as the admen know all too well what things really get under our skin.

But if the car, of whatever shape or colour, washed or unwashed, is an important part of the public face which identifies a family, it is nonetheless only part of the extension of a whole facade of 'home', which is centred upon the front garden and the front doorstep. I have for long been fascinated by front gardens, and yet they are just another facet of domestic life in the suburbs which is taken for granted — by the professional expert, that is, not by the ordinary householder. It is extraordinary to see the imaginative ingenuity with which the owners of a row of absolutely identical terrace houses can conjure up out of their front gardens a series of totally different environments — some with hard paving, some with cottage flowers, others with elaborate fantasies of gnome or windmill. As Peter Wale remarked in a very perceptive article in the *Sunday Times Magazine* about the Kentish suburb of West Wickham, the essence of such variegated super-villages lies in the intricate iconography of their personal landscapes, as intricate in their way as the Japanese garden. Householders go to any trouble to obtain for their front gardens the two or three dozen paving stones or bricks or ceramic tiles of their choice. In our neighbourhood a large private estate has just been completed, in a sub-Span style of cross-walled terrace house, using a rustic scarlet brick with a mottled tone and a crinkly texture; and many a weekend car boot must have been stuffed with contraband, for in the surrounding half-mile of suburban terraces there are now at least ten front gardens which are gloriously bejewelled with bright walling — an epic of dispersion comparable as a subject for archaeological research with Roman pottery up Indian rivers or Coca-Cola bottles in the ramparts of Da Nang.

There is nothing to be ashamed of in family image-building of this kind, a cross between jackdaw and peacock. There is, however, everything to be ashamed of in the attitude of an architect-planner who forbids such creative pleasures to his clients but enjoys them in his own home. It worries me in the citations of the RIBA Architecture Awards — the annual opportunity for juries of eminent architects to scratch each other's backs — that the word of praise which recurs more often than any other is 'consistent'. From Pugin to the Smithsons, our architecture has been subjected to a hundred and thirty-five years of puritanical assault against 'shams' and 'facadism' and in favour of what the High Church Victorians called 'honesty' and our own generation calls 'consistency'. Having chosen his dominant material (brick, timber, concrete) the honest or consistent architect is supposed to feel himself honour-bound to stick to it regardless of the profound psychological differences in a home between 'the front' and 'the back' and even 'inside' and 'outside'. In a uniform terrace of 'town houses', exposed red brick will sometimes be used inside as well as out, and the white-painted softwood of the kitchen worktops will be reflected also in the continuous white framing of the garden fences. As far as possible there will be smooth lawns at the front and smooth lawns at the back. How offensive to such 'consistency' the individual front garden must seem, and how insane the desire of most of us to have it different. And yet in every other century the facade has been a most important part of even modest building, as it is the part which holds out a hand to the visitor and prepares him for the personality that lies behind it.

There are, of course, a few people who do not wish to keep up a neat front garden and, so long as their undergrowth is free from vermin, they are perfectly entitled not to; but one hears altogether too much about these 'delinquents' from architects who use such occasional deviations from the norm as an excuse to sweep away front gardens altogether. There are certainly special difficulties of responsibility where houses are multi-occupied; but this is merely the drawback of the block of flats under another guise. Far from the pressure of modern city life leading to a general neglect of the gardens of simple family houses, the opposite is surely true: the lesser black-backed bureaucrat shows an almost desperate desire at the weekend to shed his formal plumage and don a protective skin of dungaree, shaking off the dust of the city pavements into his own private habitat of living plants, so that on the Monday morning he has to be summoned reluctantly, like Cincinnatus, from his cabbage patch.

Of course there will always be a minority who want to live in flats instead and merely have a window box (the 1963 Ministry survey of families living at high density found 29 per cent of tenants happy to remain on high in their multi-storey blocks, and correspondingly 71 per cent who wanted to move down to ground level). Yet even a tiny strip of earth on an upper cill can in itself be a highly intricate patchwork, as Gertrude Jekyll was able to demonstrate back in the nineties to a young millhand who wrote to her from Rochdale for advice on what to plant. But at least in the context of an economical structure of loadbearing brick it can be found possible to do what Southwark Council did at the remarkable Bonamy Estate off the Old Kent Road, 136-to-the-acre but only four storeys high: each family maisonette at upper level was provided with a living-room-sized roof-terrace with, built into the front of it, a massive precast concrete trench-shaped window box — what the Americans called a 'planter'. I reported in the *Architectural Review* for November 1967: 'There can surely be no other housing scheme in Britain [at this density] in which much of one courtyard (finished less than nine months ago) now has its skyline composed entirely of flowers' — an effect enhanced by the way the brick architecture had consciously been kept quiet as a vernacular background to whatever the tenants decided they wanted to plant.

Similar ideas have governed the same borough's much-delayed North Peckham scheme, of five storeys this time, with an ambitious sequence of pedestrian streets and piazzas and playgrounds at second-floor level, as well as terrace-balconies. As an estate it is too big and too dense, but if such numbers of people have to be accommodated on so little land, it is a surprisingly intimate and friendly way of doing so. Unfortunately the Southwark department soon shed most

D

of its anarchic youngsters and, under the vigorous but insensitive direction of local Labour politicians intent on the quantity of the housing programme regardless, set to producing instead (in the Aylesbury and Heygate estates) what are surely the most inhuman highrise prefabs ever built in this country — including what Laing's handout proudly proclaims to be 'the longest system-built block in Europe'.

The Bonamy tradition of private places on the roof has been carried on elsewhere in South London by Tony Kirk's team at the London Housing Consortium South Group; but their Stockwell Park courtyards at Brixton are so monastically introverted as to seem oppressive. The fact is that such juggling with courtyards and roof terraces would not be necessary if only the density could be brought down from 136 to under 100, so that all family dwellings could be at ground level; and, once that is made possible, there can be little doubt that in a free vote there would be a massive majority in favour not only of back yards or back gardens but also of front gardens, or at least planted thresholds, however tiny in acreage. It does not need much skill in horticulture to enliven a walled and paved surface with the odd creeper or shrub-in-a-pot.

But whatever the image, flowers or no flowers, exhibitionist or subfusc, the need for privacy, or semi-privacy, remains paramount: the need of the nuclear family to keep the casual passer-by at arm's length. I am sure that the main reason for the proliferation of notice boards discouraging public access to Span estates — notices which I remember Ian Nairn protesting rather too much about in a television programme about Span — is precisely that the architect, Eric Lyons, however humane he has been in other ways, has in front of his houses systematically eliminated all the more natural systems of protection by fences or hedges. There is something slightly absurd about a great expanse of grass, 'freely landscaped' as the handouts put it, which then has immediately to compromise its freedom by being peppered with little notices. In the high-density council estates this is

PLEASE DO NOT WALK OR PLAY ON THE GRASS

This area has been laid out as an amenity to
be enjoyed by all the tenants on the estate.
Will you please help to preserve its appearance
by preventing .... or to the area

...... Manager

The wastes of open landscape at Lee Bank, Birmingham, can be kept nice only by fire-denying notices. Yet the ground is wide enough for hundreds of useable private gardens. (Marilyn Stafford) often far from amusing; for example, amidst the wilderness of off-the-peg tower blocks from Messrs Wimpey which Birmingham Corporation has seen fit to erect all over the Lee Bank redevelopment area, the broad green acres of intervening landscape have been sown with menacing notices:

> PLEASE DO NOT WALK OR PLAY ON THE GRASS. This area has been laid out as an amenity to be enjoyed [sic] by all the tenants on the estate. Will you please help to preserve its appearance by preventing damage in the area.
> J.J. Atkinson, Housing Manager.

It is a funny kind of keeping up appearances which excludes walking and playing, as though they were equivalent to spitting and shitting; yet this kind of municipal fascism, with its embattled 'laager mentality' against teenage vandals, has rapidly become the high density norm. The Greater London Council is only the largest of a multitude of authorities who have specialised in laying out open spaces where the children of an estate can freely play, except that large notices saying NO BALL GAMES are then erected in order to tell them that they cannot. In the competition-winning Leith Fort estate at Edinburgh, for example, the notices saying

> CHILDREN ARE NOT ALLOWED TO PLAY ON BALCONIES
> By Order City Architect

are actually stuck on the walls of what were originally designed by the architects as 'play decks'. Caretakers on such estates can either become petty tyrants or else acquire a Nelsonian eye towards such games.

Worse still are the actual thresholds of flats: in place of the secure and dependable progression from pavement to gate to pathway to doorstep, there are the uncertain and signless wastes of communal lift halls and access balconies. It may indeed be possible to prevent innocent play on the greensward 'by order', but it is virtually impossible outside a police state to prevent malicious vandalism and urination on staircases or in lifts. Such 'communal areas' are in the most literal sense unsupervised by families, in that no one overlooks them, and they are therefore solely the responsibility of the caretaker, who may live several blocks away. Some authorities are now replacing even these caretakers with a system of so-called 'flying squads' (what the tenants' leaders have called 'men on the run'). Le Corbusier's rant about 'creating space on the ground' has led all too many architects, from Roehampton onwards, to adopt his idea of raising the blocks themselves on stilts (or pilotis). Whatever the relevance of this extra space as a shady loggia out of the Mediterranean sun, in a Northern climate it is bound to be a dank and depressing undercroft and, furthermore, racked by gusts of wind, which are funnelled furiously between the tall towers and slabs, eddying in circles between them and then sucked through beneath the stilts. Sir Basil Spence's twenty-storey slab of maisonettes across the centre of the Gorbals is a particularly deplorable example of this, the dirt and litter blowing about between raking diagonal struts, megalomaniac in scale and coarse in texture. If funnelled gusts can destroy the cooling towers of a power station, as they did at Ferrybridge in 1967, it is not surprising that they are uncomfortable to the ailing body of an elderly lady. British architects have in recent years shown a criminal disregard for what is dignified by the technical name of 'microclimate'; it simply means 'making the best of the weather' in the ways that the builders of vernacular cottages in the country villages handed down as commonsense from father to son.

The sheer unpleasantness of the communal areas of flats makes it likely that those who resort to them will be up to no good, and will not be disturbed; the crypts and vaults of high-rise flats are increasingly abandoned in the evening to the tender mercies of Hell's Angels. The resulting damage and filth are invariably blamed upon the tenants, with the obvious implication that the working classes are incapable of looking after themselves or behaving properly. Few middle-class people, however, have to live in blocks of flats, and when they do there is often a permanent caretaker's flat built into the basement, on the French principle of the *concierge*. There is no evidence that unsupervised places for which no one is responsible are any better looked after in middle-class areas — bus shelters or public telephones, for instance. Yet the bitter irony of it all is that historically, as we have seen in the previous chapter, the tenement block was provided with all those open landings and balconies precisely in order that the tenants could be easily supervised and sluiced out — in the same Utilitarian tradition of paternalism as Bentham's panopticon prison. The comparison then was with the stews and rookeries, compared with which the communal staircase, regularly scrubbed, was indeed a great improvement; but nowadays the comparison is with the individual suburban house-on-the-ground, semi-detached or terraced, where the owner or tenant can exercise complete self-control without being supervised at all — except by the all-important doorstep-to-doorstep observation of neighbours across the street.

At the very least, the one, two or three steps of the ordinary threshold do offer the sanction that strangers can be thrown down them — and this is not as fanciful a notion as it may seem, in this age of the door-to-door salesman. I am just such a salesman myself when canvassing politically, and I know full well that the relationship between me and the person I am talking with is to my disadvantage as a persuader if, at an ordinary house-on-the-ground, I am literally on a lower level. If I say 'I am one of the three Labour candidates for this Ward' from a position down below in the pathway, it is that much easier for the housewife to give her time-honoured reply 'Not today, thank you' and shut the door abruptly before I can retaliate one step higher with 'What about tomorrow then?'

In a block of council flats, by contrast, where the only separation between the private home and the public access to it by way of balcony or lift hall is the thin plank of the front door, one finds oneself putting one's foot through the opening almost without intending it. I have a shrewd suspicion that door-to-door salesmen, let alone the Mormons and Jehovah's Witnesses, have a far better chance of overcoming the objections of the housewife when they catch her, so to speak, without a threshold. The same applies, if less aggressively, to the day-to-day encounters on the doorstep with the milkman and the postman, or, for that matter, with neighbours who come to call (and are sometimes too garrulous to go). The raised level of the threshold makes the householder just that little bit more dominant, and this is sensed instinctively by the caller, so that the householder can bring the conversation rapidly to an end at any time without appearing to cause offence. The tenant of the flat has no such advantage. I have noticed, when canvassing in tower blocks, how old people in particular respond to the insecurity of the unobserved lift hall by barricading themselves behind an elaborate sequence of padlocks and chains, and will invariably begin the conversation through the letter-box — hardly an attractive opening to a human relationship. The great virtue of the traditional front door is that it enables private business to be carried on in public. The householder wants to keep strangers out of his inner sanctum but to talk with them without being overheard by neighbours; on the other hand, it is essential to be overlooked by the neighbours, to overcome the instinctive fear of muggings on the quiet.

But behind all the functional complexities lies that one simple emotional need for identity, for self-assertion, for a threshold which stands out as one's own. Such self-expression can be anything from the straightforward scrubbing and painting of the stone steps that is so characteristc of even the grimiest lanes of Lancashire's cotton towns, to the much more elaborate variety of decoration and equipment made possible by affluence. It is a sign of the times that tenants of the pretty little £8-a-week council houses just round the corner from us have added coach lamps to their front doors. The car itself is often parked in front gardens, which can sometimes have distressing results for the environment of the older suburban terraces. One house in my road actually has a couple of sailing dinghies parked in front, these dinghy owners incidentally not being among the middle-class immigrants. Certainly it is much easier to add an individual car port or garage to a detached or semi-detached house at the lower densities preferred by Unwin; it is fascinating to observe the ingenuity of the many eminent architects at Hampstead Garden Suburb, who from as early as 1911 (Bunney & Makins at 16 Meadway) found themselves forced to add garages to houses which had already been built to their designs just before the car became fashionable.

On council estates the problem is not merely that there is little provision for parking anything in the way of personal possessions in front of one's home, but even the front doors are painted uniformly lime green or primrose yellow or pale blue, according to the dictates of some architectural assistant at the town hall, armed with the British Standard Colour Code catalogue. The servility of the landlord-tenant relationship is stressed by the uniform, rather in the way that 'red doors' indicate a particular brand of 'tied house' in the pub trade. And the lack of a threshold exposes the home to a bureaucratic equivalent of full-frontal nudity (rent collectors, encyclopaedia salesmen, Mormons) from which the self-respecting tenant automatically retreats behind a veil of net curtains.

Not that the net curtain is itself anything to be sneered at — as it so often seems to be by the trendy and as it certainly is by most architects. It is in fact a most sophisticated device for marking off the semi-public from the semi-private, and probably dates back to the early Middle Ages, when it would have been some sort of rough-woven sacking. There is an instinctive delight in being able to look out from one's home and see the goings-on in the street, in the confidence that those in the street do not realise one is there and could not peer back even if they did. It puts the net curtain in the same category as what American interior designers call the 'modesty panel' in an office desk — the panel which means that you can see your secretary's legs, whereas she (lucky girl) cannot see yours. The sensitive architect can combine this one-way vision with just enough see-through to be tantalising. The great Lutyens, for example, in his last major country house, Middleton Park near Bicester (1938), was faced with the task of accommodating an earl who had married a film star; so in the domed state bathroom of pink onyx and white marble, he gave the shower alcove a gilded door of purdah glass, which meant that Lady Jersey could see all of Lord Jersey approaching, whilst he could delight only in the outline of her filmy silhouette. (Until recently the house was the National Provincial Bank managers' training college, and the shower bath was the high point of each manager's stay there.)

The net curtain is itself a sophisticated kind of purdah — a touch of Eastern promise in suburbia. After lighting-up time the more exhibitionist householder does not immediately close his main curtains, but for an hour or so gives his neighbours the pleasure of looking in through the net upon the silhouettes of a television supper or the preliminaries to a dinner party. This kind of exposure, mind you, can be overdone; when Colonel Seifert's Royal Garden Hotel first opened in Kensington High Street, I remember how fascinating it was to observe from the coffee bar across the road the couples in their bedrooms embracing and sinking slowly from sight. The see-through dress is the see-not-too-much-and-suggest-a-great-deal-more dress; and far from being just a recent whim of the rag trade, it has in fact a long architectural ancestry in the half-indoor, half outdoor spaces chronicled in the previous chapter, which reached their first climax in the orientally influenced work of Nash: verandahs, balconies, loggias, terraces, pergolas, gazeboes and above all, bay windows. Readers of Bamber Gascoigne's book on the Mughal emperors can trace the source of much English suburban romanticism in the state apartments of the Red Forts at Agra and Delhi: bungalow pavilions with net-curtain walls of white marble and delicately projecting bay windows, perched above the agricultural landscape on a man-made cliff face of pink limestone. It was in fact on the engravings of Mughal buildings by the brothers Daniell that S. P. Cockerell based Sezincote and John Nash the lacy stucco of the Brighton Pavilion.

It is hard to exaggerate the importance of the bay window in achieving an easy and natural relationship not only between the house and the landscape, but between the family and the community — a relationship which, by means of the shimmering net curtain, has true romance. There is much that an architect could learn about designing good suburbs from the works of those romantic novelists such as Barbara Cartland, who so skilfully blend veiled exoticism with stark respectability. The trendy minority merely replaces the net and the lace with less subtle alternatives such as Venetian and Pinoleum blinds. The point is that the projecting bay window enables each family to participate fully in the life of the street, while keeping it at arm's length. The twitching of the net curtain, far from being merely interfering or neurotic, is in fact a precondition of the best in the mutual helpfulness of community life.

For example, we have across the road from us a lady, who is in some people's view a confounded busybody, as she does not hesitate to tell us facts about ourselves; yet it is precisely because she is an inveterate curtain-twitcher that it was she who realised a couple of years ago that the elderly spinster next door to us was dying. Our neighbour had for some months retreated into herself and defied friendship, and her doorway was out of sight round the right-angle bend, so we did not know that she had quietly taken to her bed; whereas the 'busybody' could see from across the street that she had not been out on her doorstep for some days and that the milk bottles were beginning to accumulate. The upshot was that an ambulance swiftly collected her, and when she died a few days later, she was not in utter loneliness but at the home of her nephew. Would she, I asked myself, have been discovered at all had she been in a block of flats,where her doorstep would not have been overlooked at all by anyone's bay window? Obviously it is the sensational cases of dead bodies in flats some weeks or even months after death (three in Portsmouth in the last two years) that hit the news pages of the papers; yet this kind of thing is only the tip of an iceberg of non-communication in estates without doorsteps. The Roman Catholic priest at Roehampton, Father Simes, has told me emphatically that what his flock lack most of all in the social life of their high flats is quite simply *gossip*: the common -or-garden chat about events in the neighbourhood over the common-or-garden fence of the neighbour. Far from idle tongues being merely the servants of the Devil, they have latent within them the possibility of serving the caring community simply by giving it the ordinary doorstep news service.

But the positive attraction of the curtained bay is, to repeat, its romance, combining freely with veran- dah, balcony and bedroom oriel, in a flexible series of half-outdoor, half-indoor areas for comfortable relax- ation in our temperate climate. Nash's Brighton Pavil- ion, with its negligée of Indian trellises given firmness and uplift by Holland's earlier bows, and his Blaise Hamlet cottages, with their intricate rookery-nookery of tile and timber, seem far more attuned to the reali- ties of our affluent society at the present day, albeit they are over 150 years old, than the thin-blooded and flat-chested facades of most council flats. High- rise estates, as we have seen, are strapped by their official architects into the architectural equivalent of the Liberty bodice ('Oh Liberty, how many crimes...') with all the familiar indignities of school uniform in terms of approved materials and colours, and lists of rules stating 'Thou shalt not': in the case of the block of flats, not only 'Thou shalt not hang out washing' and 'Thou shalt not play ball games', but also 'Thou shalt not keep pets'. The flexible facades of houses-on-the-ground, with their curtained bay windows — many different patterns of curtain, incidentally — are replaced by the absolutely uniform concrete panel of the industrialised building system, in which any sign of individuality is made to seem an anomaly or an offence.

The crucial point is that the visual diktat is only the outward and visible sign of a social and managerial diktat, represented by that uniformed caretaker who keeps the children off the grass. It will be a matter of disbelief to future generations that Labour councillors in particular, who can hardly be unaware of the fund of initiative amongst ordinary people, should have had over the years an attitude to their rebellious tenantry as high-handed as a nineteenth century Irish aristocrat. There can be absolutely no justification for forcing tenants all to have the same colour of front door. The architect may plead that a mixture of colours will spoil the purity of his design, but no design is truly functional, let alone humane, which cannot accommodate within it such minor freedoms. For the sake of the total environment of the community, the overall design must act firmly as a frame, stressing if possible in its materials the special character of the neighbourhood and its geography; but it must not be more than a frame, in terms of what has to be insisted on. The obsessive uniformities of detailing imposed upon leasehold tenants by the paternalistic Great Estates of the past — Grosvenor, Bedford, Calthorpe, Moray — may aesthetically be worth preserving in complete historical authenticity by means of Article Four directions and Section Eight directions and other refined tortures of planning control, but surely in the context of present-day society such dictatorship, riding roughshod over the consumer, is an easy way out for the architect, which avoids the very real aesthetic difficulty of designing for a densely packed democracy of individuals.

To allow full scope for the householder's personal self-expression without resigning the community to a degeneration into environmental chaos, the architect has to tackle the much more difficult task of separating out the various time-scales involved in his houses: the permanent structural frame (usually repetitive brick crosswalls for terraced houses) which is likely to last at least two hundred years; the non-structural finishes (what used to be called ornament, but 'honesty' does not allow us to call it that any longer) which are likely to be altered considerably within fifty; the partition walls inside the dwelling, which are likely to be re-arranged within twenty; and the decorations of the internal surfaces, which often will not survive more than five. Clearly the place for the architect to insist dogmatically on his own aesthetic ideals is in the permanent structure, where he is fully entitled to dramatise boldly the appropriate materials for the place; yet, as we have seen, he far too often insists on being dogmatically 'consistent' at the other extreme as well, finishing the inside walls in exposed brickwork or even rough-shuttered concrete. But however bold the structure, the operative word, externally as well as internally, must be 'appropriateness'. It is significant that Alvar Aalto himself, while relating romantically the brick, copper and timber of his exteriors to the surrounding pinewoods, respects the commonsense demands of the Finnish climate by making his interiors a total contrast, a mechanically sophisticated cocoon finished in elegant synthetic materials, none too permanent. In less sensible hands, the hairy, pock-marked concrete of the sixties has proved just as resistant as the smooth white plaster of the thirties to the need for the individual family to express its own personality.

This has, I am sure, been one of the underlying reasons for the popularity of Eric Lyons's Span estates, and the widespread imitation of them: that, living and working in a Thames-side suburb as he does, he has instinctively understood the hierarchy of change which the suburban family demands. Externally Lyons has played off against the permanent structure of his solid brick crosswalls a light (and, in a generation or two, expendable) infill of tile-hanging or weatherboarding and window-boxes; while internally he has provided simple plaster finishes with a minimum of built-in furniture (except in the kitchen) — he has even publicly defended the basic right of the occupier to move his own wardrobes about. Among the public housing authorities, by contrast, even the most enlightened have tended to opt externally for an absolute impermeability of even concrete surfaces. The St Mary's estate at Oldham, for example, designed by the Ministry of Housing Development Group as a working textbook of how to put into practice the official Parker Morris housing standards, has a gratuitously clinical alternation on its elevations of continuous glass-and-metal window bands and continuous concrete spandrel bands, with no attempt whatever to identify the individual house, even though none of it is more than five storeys high; while inside each house the absolutely identical wall-to-wall expanse of window confers upon every family an institutional sameness of surroundings for which no amount of meticulously researched, but permanently built-in, storage space can compensate.

Sentiments about flexibility for the tenant, so that he can control his own environment, may suggest to architect-readers that I am a disciple of the Dutch guru, Professor N. J. Habraken, author of *Supports*, and that I am advocating the kind of moveable-wall solution now being developed for the Greater London Council by Nabeel Hamdi and Nic Wilkinson, under the code-name PSSHAK. All I can say is: I am not, interesting as the ideas of these architects are. (In fact I confess defensively that I first discussed the separation of different time-scales of structure and infill, in a radio talk in 1968, before I had ever heard of Habraken.) The fallacy of PSSHAK, it seems to me, is that it diagnoses wrongly the time-scale of change within the dwelling. As I have suggested, the likely life of the internal walls of a dwelling is about twenty years, by which time a major re-jigging of the mechanical services and consequent room uses is likely to be necessary (compare the GLC's present revamping of its neo-Georgian flats of the late thirties, and then allow for a gradual speed-up of the cycle). Any major changes in demand by families in less than twenty years are much more likely to be met by selling one house and buying another, as many couples do when their children begin to walk;

or in terms of council housing by applying for a transfer. Even assuming that a sufficiently well-insulated movable wall can be developed by PSSHAK within the Government's housing cost yardsticks, it seems to me highly unlikely that most ordinary families will want to introduce a profound sense of insecurity into their homes by shifting the walls around at will. The GLC and the borough councils are likely to do far more for the convenience of their clients if they simply ensure that there is a sufficient variety of dwellings in size and character available in any particular neighbourhood, so as to enable families to move around freely while staying within the comforting boundaries of their home 'village'.

In any case the response to demand which tenants really want is much more social and human than narrowly architectural; for the principal reason besides aesthetic dictatorship for the dead uniformity of external decoration on council estates is administrative. The decoration is normally carried out by the council as landlord and not by the tenants themselves, and thus a single repetitive colour is simply more economical to apply ('economies of scale'). An extreme example of this was the recent redecoration by the Greater London Council of the Flower House Estate on the Lewisham-Beckenham road; the flats there, though with Georgian-shaped windows and hipped roofs, had painted wall surfaces of plaster which were all-white-gone-grimy in the approved dogma of 'early modern'. Without consulting the tenants at all, the GLC proceeded to repaint alternate blocks of flats in battleship grey and ripe apricot. It is high-handedness of this kind that frustrates the natural pride of tenants in their own homes; by the merest whim of some graduate tastemonger in County Hall, the individuality of hundreds of families is submerged in camouflage like a wartime aerodrome — and submerged much more aggressively in apricot and grey than ever it was previously in dirty white. With regard to inside decorations, there has usually been a false antithesis based on political prejudice: in order to save the public purse some

111

cash, Conservative councils have insisted that tenants should do all their own works, regardless of hardship; Labour councils meanwhile, in order to cater for the needy, have insisted paternalistically that the council should do it all, thus mounting a positive disincentive to the more able-bodied tenants from taking any trouble themselves or expressing any of their own pride in the home. What in fact is needed is a flexible system similar to that recently instituted at Sheffield, by which each tenant who wants to do his own decoration is free to do it, and is given a grant, in the form of two or three rent-free weeks each year, in order to cover the cost of doing it. It should then be possible to give him a completely open hand in choosing the colours of paintwork, so long as he restricts it to those surfaces which were intended to be painted. Meanwhile the council would continue to decorate for the elderly and the disabled, and also for other tenants who are not keen on do-it-yourself; they, needless to say, would not get the rent-free weeks.

Even now tenants are occasionally able to take at least their threshold into their own hands. Close to my home, for example, there is a flat on the end of an access balcony, where the tenant has been able to put a gate across the balcony without incurring official wrath; thus the cul-de-sac of the balcony end has become a private forecourt to the flat — virtually an extra room. In the Vanbrugh Park estate at Greenwich, Chamberlin, Powell & Bon designed their terrace houses to be entered through front gardens, which are screened from the garage courts by a rather monumental pergola of brick piers and concrete crossbars, with one opening per house. This opening was intended by the architects to be filled with a standard low privet hedge and a chain hanging between wooden posts — all very neat and municipal. But the tenants, almost immediately they moved in, began to fill it, according to individual taste, with an extraordinary medley of trellises and climbing plants of different patterns and colours. The effect may not have been quite what the architects expected — in fact they were horrified when first they saw it — but it has turned out to be extraordinarily successful visually as well as socially, the individuality of the screening and planting being firmly contained (again on the principle of separating time-scales) within the uniformity of the pergola.

Such self-expression identifies not only the individual family but the society of an individual estate. It also symbolises an all-too-rare relationship of trust and cooperation between the council tenant and the council landlord, and there is no reason why it should not be extended to a far wider self-determination in the layout of an estate's communal 'public' spaces too. Why should the tenants not decide on their own landscape, or at least be responsible, jointly with elected councillors, for instructing the officials who design it? When the tenants of the earlier part of the appalling high-rise redevelopment along Battersea Park Road — the subject of Carlos Pasini's marvellous television film *Where the Houses Stood* — asked permission from Wandsworth Council a couple of years ago to fill their two large grass spaces with either allotments or a football pitch or both, they were summarily refused. All must remain green and purposeless. Of course serried rows of beans and random chickenwire fences might not look exactly nice — that no doubt was the immediate reaction of the Architect's Department — but until architects can design council estates to accommodate such things without their looking unpleasant, then they have only themselves to blame if tenants subsequently demand to be allowed to mess things up. A landscape which looks beautiful only when it is unused is like a Victorian nude. It is not surprising that the higher density estates which have no courts or pitches for the older children, let alone positive encouragement by play leadership or youth clubs, are increasingly subject to vandalism.

At the same time it is interesting to notice how this varies from place to place: at another Battersea estate, Winstanley, although there is superficially the usual mixture of high-rise towers and low-rise slabs, a Ministry of Housing survey found a relatively high level of consumer satisfaction and a relatively low level of vandalism; and it is just possible that this might be because the architect, Andrew Artur of George Trew & Dunn, insisted firmly on planting, not just a token shrub or two, but dense groves of semi-mature trees, so that the whole estate is unusually leafy and relaxed in atmosphere.

Vandalism, which is so much encouraged by 'open landscaping', can only really be checked on existing estates of that type by a new approach to management. The deplorable remoteness of most housing officials in the GLC and the new London Boroughs has certainly given warning of the dangers inherent in local reform elsewhere in the country. At the moment housing management consists largely in employing that uniformed caretaker to keep children off the grass, notionally obstruct ball games and tentatively deal with mechanical faults as best he can when they occur. Any tenant with more profound complaints is supposed to confide them to his friendly neighbourhood rent collector, who in his turn is supposed to pass them on up the hierarchy, step by step, so that 'prompt' action is taken. In fact, as everyone knows, there are interminable and inexplicable delays before 'they' come and do something about it. As often as not, the rent collector fails to pass on the message at all or simply misunderstands it. This is largely not his fault: the prevalence of attacks on rent collectors, particularly in the unsupervised spaces of open landscape or high-rise lift halls, has led to a drastic drop in quality among recruits; not surprisingly there are few candidates for a job which involves furtively looking over one's shoulder for possible robbers, and fewer still who can bring to it any kind of enthusiasm for social work. The sooner that all rents are paid by Giro or by cheque into a computerised accounts system — which merely means tenants going to the Post Office, without having to open a bank account — the sooner it will then be possible for the housing authority to employ, instead of rent collectors, properly qualified housing assistants who can concentrate on the families really in need of support and who can also look more widely at the needs of the community. If such officials can be employed not from the central town hall but from a district office serving the neighbourhood, so much the better — particularly if it is the headquarters of a multi-disciplinary neighbourhood team dedicated to community development, as described in Chapter Six.

But even radical changes in the face of officialdom are of small importance compared with the promotion of self-help by the tenants and residents themselves — self-help which has been pioneered in London in the most unfavourable circumstances by the squatters' associations who take over empty houses to make homes for the down-and-out. The idea that on the ordinary council estate the tenants are not helpless but can do things for themselves to improve their own surroundings, is rapidly gaining ground. The tenants' associations that have been springing up all over the country in response to the recent substantial increases in council rents have found themselves increasingly concerned not merely with reacting to financial matters in the narrow sense but with that much wider range of human needs which trade union leaders call (wrongly) 'fringe benefits'. The more lively tenants' leaders have in fact found themselves raising repeatedly problems of the environment — of traffic conditions, of playgrounds, of vandalism, of landscaping, of maintenance — even if that horrid word 'environment' is not one that has come as readily to their lips as it would to the committee of a middle-class civic society. Tenants' leaders have suddenly been breaking through the barrier of many generations of inferiority complex in their relationship with officials and councillors.

It is in fact essential, both for people's self-respect, and for the enhanced standards of upkeep such self-respect will self-impose, that local authorities should be able to hand over as far as possible the management of their estates to the tenants themselves, together with the necessary sum of money which would in any case be spent on maintenance. If it is possible in the private estates of Wates and Span for residents, as part of their covenanted terms of purchase, to

115

exact a levy upon themselves in order to employ the outside services of gardeners and groundsmen, then it should equally be possible on the council estates for a clear proportion of rent to be set aside each week to cover the tenants' own maintenance of their estate. If residents themselves were made financially and administratively responsible for their own communal environment, then at the very least the incidence of vandalism should decrease, and at best there should be a real chance of creating a lively and attractive environment which almost anyone would be proud of as his own. Irresponsible behaviour is encouraged in a situation where no one has responsibility; it is only natural that adults should stand aside when they see twelve-year-old boys smashing up their estate if the 'communal spaces' are no real concern of the community. Here again the resistance to such reforms in the Town Hall has extraordinarily slight foundations, namely the traditional desire of the housing department not to reveal exactly in what proportions tenants' rents are spent between such minor items as maintenance of the estate on the one hand and such major items as the servicing of the extortionate interest charges on the housing deficit on the other. On all estates in fact, management committees should be formed, consisting largely of elected tenants' representatives, but with local councillors also who would have a veto on certain matters (the Local Government Act understandably lays down that on decisions affecting the expenditure of public money there should be a two-thirds majority of councillors voting). Where estates are small, a district committee could combine the management of several (this has now been done in Camden and other London boroughs). The next stage would be to involve private tenants and landlords in the locality as well, in a joint residents' association, so as to avoid treating the council tenant as a separate species of animal. Such joint management committees could in fact form the basis of neighbourhood councils of the kind recently elected at Golborne Ward in Notting Hill (see Chapter Six again).

Such reforms in our attitudes to the semi-public should not be too difficult to bring into being, even on high-rise estates where the ready-made instrument of democracy, in the street and its doorsteps, has almost disappeared. Much more difficult, as we shall see, are reforms in attitudes to the semi-private, in that family houses which have not got back gardens are castrated irreparably.

A modern pattern for compact but private family houses was set in 1955, in true Picturesque tradition, in an aristocratic model village: Rushbrooke in Suffolk, designed by Llewelyn-Davies & Weeks for Lord Rothschild. (de Burgh Galwey, Architectural Review)

4

The Space Round the Back

If the front of the house is semi-public, the back is semi-private. While it is fascinating and entirely justifiable for us, as members of the public, to enjoy the variety of self-advertisement in the planting and paving of other people's front gardens, it is slightly unhealthy for us to peer, as voyeurs, into their back gardens. Perhaps it is for that reason that municipal authorities who, in the nineteenth century tradition of health and hygiene, are always keen on throwing every germ open to destruction, should be so bent on getting rid of such 'backland'. The word 'garden' is admittedly to some extent a misnomer, as it automatically implies gardening, and of course the administrators and planners are quick to jump up and point out that not everyone does so — that in fact most back gardens are a 'mess'. But all that means is that the officials do not happen to like a particular kind of human liveliness — their own back gardens in the posher suburbs are probably a different sort of mess.

It is indeed extraordinary how various the activities are which go on in the private open space of family houses. As a local solicitor John Dolding wrote recently in a passionate letter of complaint to Lewisham's Planning Officer, about the council's pre-1971 policy of systematically eliminating private gardens from the redeveloped slums, 'A garden in Deptford, however small, is somewhere the toddlers can have freedom and safety, can later ride their tricycles, keep rabbits, guinea pigs, tortoises, build their private dens, make a noise without annoying mother, and invite their friends. Father can garden, respray his motor-cycle, build a shed to do his woodwork in, keep pigeons. Mother can sunbathe, clean her carpets, sling the rubbish into it (without bothering anyone else), natter over the fence and foster friendship and neighbourliness.'

The fact is that though you and I may have some idea of what our immediate neighbours on either side do out at the back, at least some of the time, what the next lot of families beyond them do behind their fences is unknown territory. The administrator, who likes to have us all neatly filed and tabbed, finds himself amongst back gardens like a medieval explorer going off the edge of his map — 'There be dragons,' he thinks (or courting couples) — and with the natural instinct of fear, he becomes violent. 'Nonconforming uses,' he cries, as he pens those censorious paragraphs in the Borough Development Plan which insists that all such uses should be utterly expelled from any area which is 'zoned residential'. For the sake of public relations, this all tends to be dressed up as a progressive campaign against the abuses of 'backyard industry'; and certainly there used to be many cases, and there still are some, where such industries do pose severe problems of noise from panel beating and metal scrap, and of atmospheric pollution from soapworks and tanneries. But nowadays, with more and more such industries becoming electric-powered and clean, the Victorian crusade against the factory round the corner tends often to seem misplaced. Noisome factories and squalid car lots are one thing, small precision workshops are quite another.

It is one of the most important features of the social life of our suburbs that back alleyways and back gardens should give sanctuary to the specialised craftsman, who has very often operated there for generations. Close to where I live, in ordinary lower middle-class suburbs, we have knife-grinders, mica-splitters, Turkish Delight makers, security printers of postage stamps, and a Japanese food warehouse. Such small factories and backyard workshops provide useful employment for the local community, much of it skilled, and they help to stabilise it a little in the midst of ever-more-frenetic commuting. Some of them also help to employ the elderly and the disabled. Now that the crusade against the excesses of Victorian laissez-faire has succeeded in disentangling most of the worst factories from the surrounding houses, a much more flexible approach needs to be adopted by planners.

The crusade of hygienic zoning did not have its first great victories until the building of the postwar New Towns, where factories were restricted to the ghetto of a single 'industrial area', ironically enough just at the time when cleanliness became the rule for the kind of mobile, science-based industries which tend to move to new towns. At Stevenage the consequences were absurd, particularly before the by-pass was built: every morning almost the entire working population surged across the A1 from the residential neighbourhoods on one side of the road to the industrial area on the other, and every evening they surged back again, with indescribable traffic chaos at the junctions at each peak period. It is interesting to notice by contrast that, in the plan for Milton Keynes, industry is once again going to be spread more naturally and more evenly across the whole urban area, thus saving time and saving road space. In fact in the inner areas of our cities, from which so much industry has recently been decentralised, there is now a positive necessity to provide convenient premises for small firms where new products can be fostered in the early years of their existence. The owner of a small precision engineering business, for instance, who at one time claimed to possess the only centrally heated, air-conditioned railway arch in South-East London, told me that after he had outgrown it, he had had great difficulty in finding a suitable slightly larger site in the same area.

There is in any case a widespread tendency nowadays for people to have their own domestic workshops. This is all part of the so-called 'leisure revolution' brought about by the shorter working week — though a more accurate name for it for many people would be the 'second jobs revolution'. The ability of trade unionists to survive recent long strikes has not been merely handed to them by social security benefits, but has often been reinforced by their own spare-time earning capacity as motor mechanics, carpet layers, furniture repairers, electricians.

In people's own homes the do-it-yourself market is still in its healthy infancy, and at the same time affluence has been making it possible for most of us to acquire more and more equipment and gear, so that storage space outside the main volume of the house has become increasingly essential. Even if the family car stands out visibly in the open with no roof over it — and, for security reasons, many drivers prefer that — some kind of smaller shed is bound to be needed for all the implements that go with it and its upkeep, and with the upkeep of house and garden. Accordingly, in the back gardens of the suburbs, as we have already noted, there is an incredible proliferation of sheds presenting a Hansel and Gretel skyline of ready-made or home-made pixy houses — instant Noddyland. Seen from the railway, they can look like exhibits lifted straight from the catalogue of Bernard Rudofsky's prestigious exhibition of tribal architecture, 'Architecture without Architects', the illusion of an aboriginal village being particularly strong in the cliff-hanging pigeon lofts outside Newcastle. Yet the rigid puritanism of their professional education has brainwashed planning officers into viewing back-garden sheds with absolute abhorrence: 'shacks' is the word that is spat out regardless.

Allotments are particularly unpopular for their unkempt appearance, although emotional wartime memories of 'dig for victory' are enshrined in mandatory Acts of Parliament protecting many of them; yet 'dig for pleasure', in what we are now supposed to call 'leisure gardens', somehow fails to secure the same claim on official tolerance in peacetime. (Since I wrote all this, Sir Colin Buchanan has as usual said what needs saying better than anyone, at a recent Housing Centre Conference: 'Often, when I am travelling by train, I look out at the rows of fairly poor houses that back on to the railway lines... but I see bits tacked on, I see flowers in the gardens, little patches of mown grass, greenhouses, pigeon lofts, and of course sheds, and I feel that those houses, miserable though they may be in so many respects, nevertheless provide in difficult circumstances a creative outlet for the occupants in a way that a flat in a tower block, where you can't drive a nail into the wall without permission, does not and never can. If I had to pin it to one single piece of advice, I think I would say, "Don't forget the sheds." A man must have a shed... I do not like neglected allotments, but I like the individuality expressed in the shacks and sheds when there is no undue regimentation by an over-zealous local authority pursuing some totally false aesthetic ambition.') Where something nasty in the woodsheds does seriously impinge on the visual environment, the local authority can surely absorb it gently into the landscape by planting trees and shrubs around it and, in the case of allotments, growing well-trimmed hedges, just as Sir Raymond Unwin did so successfully at Hampstead Garden Suburb sixty years ago.

Let no one in any case imagine that sheds are some primitive throwback; they are on the contrary the harbingers of our future freedoms. Allotments may indeed be less popular than they were, but that is because they were wholly detached from the dwelling, and thus tended to be used by men merely as a means of escape from their wives. In the more cosy uxoriousness and more equal partnership of the nuclear family, at a time when the home has become so much more comfortable simply to sit in, the husband has naturally preferred to cultivate his own backyard as a direct extension of it — and not just for flowers or veg. The electrically heated greenhouse steaming with rare cacti, the mechanical workshop plugged in with power tools, the semi-commercial craft studio kitted up with kiln and lathe — these can all be found with increasing frequency in the back yards of Victorian artisan cottages, and not merely those that have been taken over by the middle classes.

The greenhouses and workshops of the working classes remain in fact resolutely immune from the aspirations of *House and Garden* or *Design Magazine*: the furniture made there, for example, is unrepentantly repro and the flower patterns are close relatives of the British Legion floral clock. The competitive instinct of the gardener is aimed not at some tasteful bourgeois ambience of gracious living but at the gross excitement of the tour-de-force: the mighty green marrow, the lascivious-looking leek, the individual prize dahlia or chrysanth, the profusely tinted rose — in every case, the magic of fertility. This is the sort of thrill which has packed in working-class crowds at international exhibitions ever since the Great Exhibition of 1851, whose architect, Sir Joseph Paxton, was himself a self-made gardener of working-class origin. The ceremonial unveiling for instance of his giant Victoria Regia water lily (1836), grown in the back garden of a duke and in a pavilion which was a prototype of the Crystal Palace, combined aristocratic grandeur and proletarian grossness (both blatantly sensual) of the kind which still deeply offends the respectable bourgeois but would be immediately appreciated by a champion leek-grower in County Durham.

Competitiveness in the back garden (and the similar competitiveness of brass band contests and the bowling green, described by Brian Jackson in *Working Class Community*), is specially characteristic of those people who tend to be wrongly characterised by most sociologists as 'lower middle-class' but could be much more accurately entitled 'working-class with aspirations'. It is the skilled mechanic, the small shopkeeper and the junior clerk and their wives (C1 and C2 in the admen's scales) who are the backbone of the suburban bazaar and jumble sale; it is they for example who, as recent researchers have shown, give birth to the majority of the top beauty queens — those impersonal male fantasies which seem more like a sexual equivalent of the prize dahlia or pumpkin (or the Victoria Regia lily) than an exhibition of the real thing.

Obsessive private fantasies are no doubt in part a mental compensation for dull drudgery at work and excessive matiness from workmates. A man tied to a production line in shifts can work out his frustrated longings for lone achievement by employing himself decisively during his so-called leisure time in the 'secret garden' at the back of the house. Both in intent and in practice such gardening is poles apart from the cultivation (in both senses) of the professional upper middle classes (the admen's ABs). A manager or civil servant tends to enjoy during the working week considerable job satisfaction but also a certain loneliness of decision-making; so at evenings and weekends he can aim, conversely, at a relaxed and gregarious atmosphere, his garden becoming a landscape to be walked through or sat in at leisure in the company of friends and neighbours. You can see this difference of attitude very clearly in a couple of nursery garden catalogues my wife happens to have at the moment: Bees of Chester are an artisans' nursery, their illustrations indicating no regard whatever for landscaping but concentrating instead on splendid individual specimen blooms in close-up, intended no doubt for forced growth in backyards, followed by prize-winning in the local hall. Wallace & Barr of Marden, by contrast, are pure bourgeois: a super Lutyens/Jekyll-style stockbroker's arcadia on the cover and tastefully tinted flowers in picturesque clusters inside — what Gertrude Jekyll herself called 'drifts' of colour — with the variegated herbaceous border as the climax.

The trouble is that architect-planners, because of their own social background, have naturally tended to accept the middle-class assumption, that the purpose of gardening is to create a landscape to be wandered through; and accordingly, given the tiny size of patio-garden possible at the standard (and excessive) density in inner city areas of 136 people to the acre, they have thought it better to abolish such private space altogether in favour of creating a single stockbroker-size garden-landscape for everybody to share in common. Stephen Mullin has perceptively recalled how 'Roehampton was praised for political reasons: once upon a time only the rich had parks, now the poor could have them as well. What this argument ignored was that the whole point of the rich man's park — like the three that made up the Roehampton site — was that it was *private* to his family, whereas the parkland of a housing estate is entirely public and not specially belonging to anyone at all.' In any case, Mullin added, the argument quickly took a twist into a cruder real-politik: 'It was actually claimed by some architects that the provision of all this open space would help to engender in the tenants a greater sense of respect for public property. But in fact, as we know, exactly the opposite has happened, because the tenants did not feel it was in any way theirs and they saw no reason why they should bother with it, when they were not allowed to walk on the grass, look at the grass or even smell the grass.'

Privacy in fact is of paramount importance to most families, the five-foot wall or fence around the garden plot making an incalculable gain in their happiness. That this can be done even at densities of over 100 to the acre will be demonstrated from recent examples in the next chapter. All that needs stating at this stage, loud and clear, is that *privacy is nothing to be ashamed of*. There is an unfortunate tendency for middle-class administrators, particularly those who have had their finer sensibilities blunted in the enforced togetherness of the boarding school, to imply that a sense of privacy is purely the product of guilt and shame. (How well I remember our Amazonian house matron, Miss Taylor, striding through a communal bathroom of thirteen-year-old boys, who were all desperately trying to put towels round their torsoes, and contemptuously snorting 'It's all right, boys, I've seen 'em all before.') There is a very profound sense in which the simple pitched-roofed cottage-home of the English village is able to symbolise in its bricks and timbers the most intimate fondlings and feelings and movings-together-into-one of the family partnership: not for nothing, as we have already noted, was the 'cruck' or 'fork' of curved oak trunks which made up the basic pitched roof of the early medieval timber cottage called after the same private parts of the human body which we still call the 'crotch' or the 'fork'. Prudery is one thing, but a sense of exclusive delicacy quite another; and I believe that the ordinary Edwardian semi-detached, even allowing for variations in cultural assumptions between classes and between races, is nonetheless an exceptionally sophisticated type of home which allows for an extremely subtle gradation of degrees of delicacy and of exclusiveness, controllable to a large extent by the family's own use of such flexible barriers or half-barriers as fences, hedges or lace curtains. The voyeurism and gossip which such exclusiveness stimulates in those left outside it are again far too easily despised; such stimulating interest in each other is the lifeblood of neighbourliness, leading, as we have seen, to admirably positive responses of community care in emergencies.

The variety of human relationships can sometimes be specially enhanced where there is a network of back alleys behind the gardens. These alleys have for long been on the clearance list of both police and planners as the sparking tinder of vice — which no doubt they can be, just as they can also (it depends on how you look at it) be the scenes of the most heavenly transports of lovemaking between the rightfully betrothed. A formal kiss in the public street on the exposed front doorstep of her home is fine enough, but then so is putting your hand up her skirt in the alley round the back — different experiences, each in its proper place.

Do new town planners ever think about the possibility of lovers' lanes, of the kind which the Victorians so richly provided for in their suburbs? Or do they put the blinkers on, like the author of the official guidebook to the Northamptonshire boot-and-shoe town of Raunds, who says that 'no probable meaning has yet been discovered' for the name of a little narrow lane there called Titty Ho? With the right to be fertile should go the right to be furtive too. The open communal spaces beloved of architects are a grim reminder of Andrew Marvell's lines: 'The grave's a fine and private place, But none I think do there embrace.' In a sense the trend to 'permissiveness' has made the provision of really attractive semi-private places more important than before, as the new freedom does not (whatever the older generation may think) mean blatancy, but greater intimacy; and certainly in the average high-rise estate any goings-on on those open lawns are horribly inhibited by the lack of seclusion. What do courting couples do on such estates?

'Permissiveness' is in fact only the psychological

aspect of increasing freedom of activity of many kinds for families (apart of course from the pensioners, the disabled and the unemployed). Here again it is important not to misjudge the situation through middle-class spectacles. Nothing has been more remarkable in the sixties and seventies than the perpetuation, indeed the blossoming, of distinctively working-class attitudes and activities among the 'new rich' of £50-a-week workers. When a man passes £2000 per annum he does not suddenly turn into a different animal, as though taking the pledge: he does not exchange the working men's club for the golf club, the local pub for the kebab house, the pools coupon for the deposit account, or Coronation Street for the late night arts programme. What in fact he does, to the despair of the trendy, is to buy more and more and more of the same, particularly more hardware, and thus he satisfies at last a pent-up demand for material goods which was frustrated for so long in times of unemployment and austerity. Fridges and washing machines and dish-washers in the kitchen, TV sets and record players and cocktail bars in the lounge, cars and boats and sports goods in the garage, greenhouses and pigeon-houses and dog kennels in the back garden and windmills, gnomes and ornamental pools at the front — all this is enough to drive the sensitive bourgeois intellectual into a Ruskinian wilderness of crying 'Woe, woe, woe' unto materialism. Yet, as Raymond Williams has argued, it is not that our culture has necessarily got better or worse with greater affluence, it has simple become *more*.

However unpalatable it may be to the intellectual neo-peasant, the fact is that, even in a highly developed country such as Great Britain, for most people the materialist dream has barely begun. It tends to be assumed far too casually by those pundits who have themselves never lacked bourgeois comforts, that we already have had something fully-grown called 'the Affluent Society', since way back in Mr Macmillan's 'never-had-it-so-good' days. Yet the long series of strikes by lower-paid workers — the dustmen, the postmen, the miners, the railwaymen — has

begun to bring home to people what has actually
happened: that the affluent society so far has
meant most significantly the widening of the dif-
ferentials between the £50-a-week family and the
£15-a-week family. In that context it is no use
preaching environmental remedies for Eco-Doom
which involve a return to a simple life unless those
enduring a hard life are allowed to escape from it.
Blueprint for Survival is in its essence the most practical argument for Socialism produced for a generation; but in its detailed application it needs to rid
itself of a kind of middle-class sneer against working-
class affluence, because assuredly those doing the
sneering will be the sort of people who have themselves enjoyed such comforts virtually since birth:
cars, cameras, central heating, and so on. 'My God —
the working classes — they're doing it like rabbits' is a
dubious reaction when it comes from middle-class
people who have themselves been doing it too for
years as of right. One could say cynically that the
middle classes were never really worried about the
effect of cars on our environment until the working
classes started getting them, and the mythology was
born of the council house with the Jaguar parked
outside it. It is this kind of hypocrisy which Anthony
Crosland has exposed in his critical remarks about
'middle-class amenity interests'; and those who believe (as I do) that Crosland's Keynesian philosophy
of strength through economic growth is ultimately a
policy of global suicide must think all the more carefully about how any alternative policy of restraint
can be justified to a low-paid miner for whom 'prosperity' is still a primary aim, however well his wages
compare with those of the Indian peasant.

The answer to these conflicts over consumption
lies, I think, in a much more careful analysis of what
it is materially that gives families satisfaction, not in
terms of a mere piling-up of hardware, but in terms of
meaningful personal activities. I suspect that the loneliness of the longest-stalked leek grower depends less
on the extravagant purchase of gear than on the
generous provision of space — the space *outside* the

house rather than inside. Granted it was the pro-liferation of hardware itself that led the Parker Morris Committee in 1961 to recommend that higher space standards inside council houses should be made man-datory by Whitehall, particularly for storage space; but the fundamental failure of the committee was its inability to follow through with an equally perceptive understanding of how the equipment that was stored was likely to be used: that the back garden is no longer something detached from the house, but is in effect an 'outside room'. It thus seems anomalous that, when Parker Morris recommended meticulously, room by room, the precise square footage that was to be the minimum for private space inside the house, he and his committee should then have failed completely to specify anything of the kind for private space out-side; yet if they had, surely the disasters of high-rise in the sixties would never have happened. But some-how the argument that 'most people aren't interested in gardening', meaning that most people are not sophisticated herbaceous-border-type gardeners, has been used as an excuse for ignoring the basic neces-sity that people should be able to define the boun-daries of their human privacy — their territoriality, to use the anthropologist's term. It is rather as though the fact that most English wives are plain cooks had been used as an excuse for not insisting on the pro-vision of kitchens.

Undoubtedly space on the ground is the most im-portant consumable commodity in short supply — and we shall discuss in the next chapter just how scarce it may be. As a suburban builder of 'town houses', Neil Wates confirms that the first priority of purchasers, and their first major criticism after sett-ling down, is invariably 'more space'. High-minded intellectuals and self-appointed amenity guardians may loosely deplore the prospect of 'Los Angeles', even though they themselves may have enjoyed for some years the benefits both of car ownership and of such space-consuming recreations as yachting and mountaineering; but meanwhile the rest of the popu-lation is beginning gleefully to prepare for it. There is,

129

E

as we shall see, a fundamental difference in any case between English suburban densities of 40–80 people to the acre, and the genuine Los Angeles of only 10–20; so 'Los Angeles' is a term of abuse in England, not an accurate prophecy. Furthermore the problems of congestion created in London when only 10 per cent commute by car have already led to a growing realisation of the importance of public transport, given the fact that, even when every household does possess a car (a state which planners are given to describing inaccurately as '100 per cent car ownership') the majority of individual members of that family are likely at any time *not* to have access to it. The miniature scale of Britain's geography means that far fewer families than in France or Scandinavia have opted for 'second homes' in the country; and in spite of the evident demand for country cottages, caravans and glorified beach huts (and the so-called 'mobile homes' which are solidly plumbed into the same meadow year in, year out) most families have not become anything like as mobile as some planners, particularly in transportation, would like us to think. The Nationwide Building Society's recent survey on *Why do people move?* showed that 23 per cent had gone to get a more spacious house, compared with 22.4 per cent who had been shifted by a change of job. Even for those who do have second homes, it will be in the 'first home' that the majority of the family's equipment will be stored, from vehicles to machine tools to camping gear to artist's materials, so that at the very least the small back garden shed will tend to become a big back garden shed.

It is not surprising that the planners of the new city of Milton Keynes, Lord Llewelyn-Davies and Walter Bor, who have had considerable experience in preparing planning schemes for American cities, have placed a renewed emphasis on lower densities, meaning space between houses, or at the back of them. The density of 45–50 people to the acre in the first generation new towns, which was dramatically increased to over 75 to the acre to create the more 'urban' atmosphere of Cumbernauld, has now at

Milton Keynes been equally rapidly reduced back again to an average of 45 — to justifiable sneers of *'Plus ça change'* from the Town and Country Planning Association, the garden city pioneers, who had always advocated the lower densities. Yet it was only eight years ago that the TCPA's president, Sir Frederick Osborn, was virtually howled down, and certainly jeered at, by a crowded audience of architects when he rose to question the otherwise uncritically received paper at the RIBA on Cumbernauld, given by Sir Hugh Wilson. As ex-manager of Letchworth and Welwyn, Osborn was then regarded by the profession merely as an Edwardian crank, so it is satisfying that he has survived to be proved right in his persistent and unpopular advocacy of the humane garden.

That new average of 45-to-the-acre at Milton Keynes actually conceals considerable variations from clusters of town houses at 60 or more down to palatial villas at barely ten; and the plan for the new city is also notable for including large areas for water sports and two top quality golf courses. Admittedly these advantages are partly the product of old-world English pragmatism, as large lakes have to be created in any case in order to control the flooding of the Ouse valley and it just so happens that golf is the favourite sport of the Chairman of the Development Corporation, Lord Campbell. But there was also the immediate problem of how to attract higher executives to set up home within the boundaries of the new city, so as to avoid the one-class uniformity of earlier new towns, which had suffered from the cultural and social impoverishment of losing their executives to the surrounding villages. Campbell and his planners had made up their minds to be spacious, after a series of initial planning seminars with experts such as Professor Melvin Webber of California, at which they had attempted to predict what the pattern of society might conceivably be only thirty years hence. This was made the starting point for establishing a planning framework which could perpetually adjust to any possible changes in society, as individual wealth increased. Earlier new towns by contrast based their layout rigidly on the particular pattern of society which then happened to exist: accordingly, the better parts of Harlow and Stevenage, labouring as they do under the strain of having provided garages for only 20 per cent of householders, already possess an extraordinary atmosphere of the period piece (*At Last the 1948 Show*), encapsulating in ideal terms a permanent outdoor and life-size museum of British society at a particular historical moment — in just the same way as Welwyn encapsulates the Twenties, Hampstead Garden Suburb the Edwardian brand of Liberalism, and Saltaire the heyday of the railway age.

But the Milton Keynes prospect of rapid change must not be misinterpreted as total revolution, in the way that the prewar 'modern' visions were revolutionary. On the contrary, the more fluid, mobile and spacious family life becomes in the next thirty years, the more essential in an evolutionary sense will be the traditional fixed points of home — the family's base camp. Increasing spaciousness will be felt not merely in the need for storing hardware and for 'painting the landscape with living things' but also in the expansion of the interior of the home out into the back garden in order to accommodate a more active social life. Already there are more than twenty different brands of 'home extension' on the market, and although at the moment these tend themselves to be unsatisfactorily closed and finite as structures and difficult for our children to extend any further — a flat-roofed one of timber and glass, for instance, is called the Doric — they do at least form some kind of response to the growing need in the suburbs, particularly among the home-bound wives with young children, for the more extensive reception of visitors and friends. The sales brochures invariably illustrate the home extension in use for that increasingly important suburban occasion, the coffee morning.

This increase in home entertaining is only part of a much wider network of suburban societies and associations; even the one-class (skilled working class) pattern of earlier new towns did not prevent them from spawning an incredible variety of clubs and committees, which the more spacious surroundings of Arcadia made possible (and which the immigration of large numbers of strangers made vitally necessary). Indeed, as with Professor Gans's Levittowners, the apparent uniformity, even monotony, on the surface bore no relation to the fact that most inhabitants enjoyed a much richer and more diverse social life than any they had known before. By 1961 Harlow Development Corporation's liaison officer could report that within the new town there were already 443 separate associations. Committees are certainly a growth industry in the suburbs and new towns, even though at the moment it may seem always to be the same stage-army-of-the-good who sit upon them — but then, as Brian Jackson points out, that is characteristic of the unobtrusive working-class style of administration by 'linkmen' (as against the more overt middle-class brand of 'leadership'). The whole vexed question of 'public participation' is discussed in Chapter Six; a sidelight upon it is the impact it may have upon the scale of the reception rooms in people's homes. In the rapidly expanding Pre-school Playgroup Association branches, for example, the committee member who has the advantage over her fellows is the one who has a large living room suitable for meetings, and at present this usually means in a Victorian villa.

But, to repeat, the fixed points will remain, in particular that crucial fixed point which lies somewhere between the front door and the back door, at the centre of the main living room. The trouble is that it becomes increasingly unclear exactly where or what this is. Through man's existence on earth, right up to the present generation, the hunter has come home to the hearth, and it is significant that as late as the Edwardian period or the twenties the fireside was still the all-important focus of the whole house. In fact, as part of their creation of a super-authentic natural cottage life for the commuter, the English architects of that period, such as Shaw and Lutyens, considerably elaborated the hearth, sometimes into the almost separate room of the inglenook. Yet suddenly and absolutely, the Modern Movement switched to the all-electric; it was perhaps the most shocking feature of all about the revolutionary white-walled architects of the thirties that they called the bluff of the cottage and triggered off the elimination of the hearth from hundreds of thousands of homes, as families gave up solid fuel for heating in favour of gas or electricity.

There has of course been an obvious logic in this, and few people who enjoy central heating today would wish to drag themselves back to the fetching and carrying and stoking of the open fire. Except, that is, for the living room: I think it is extremely likely that one of the significant symbols of prosperity and well-being in the next stage of the affluent society is going to be the re-introduction of a single central open fire into the house. This will be largely visual, a symbol of emotional warmth, rather than thermal: for it is all too clear that the television set has proved a less than inspiring centrepiece for the family living room and there are in any case signs that, as with cigarette smoking, some of the younger generation may be less glued to it than their elders. There may well be an increasing tendency for one corner of the living room to display a keyboard or dashboard, replete with a multitude of switches for quick changes of atmosphere in lighting, heating and entertainment, and this symbol of technological prowess will no doubt be tarted up with the same kind of pseudo-streamlining that flatters the motorist. But this elaboration of artificial controls will make it psychologically all the more important for the family to enjoy the natural and apparently uncontrolled flickering of the naked flame on the handsawn logs (or at least on the smokeless fuel). And those who cannot afford the real thing will at least be able to buy a visual memento of it: the colour magazines have already begun to illustrate ranges of fireplace designs, with overmantels in old Adam, which can be clipped on to walls, like the smile of the Cheshire Cat, regardless of whether there is any chimney behind them or not. Pasini's film on high-rise flats in Battersea showed an example of great pathos in the tenants' association secretary's tenth-floor flat, which he had bedecked not only with a dummy fireplace — physically detached from the wall so as not to anger the council by leaving the marks of fixing — but also with a sensationally elaborate ceiling of coffered tiles. The glow within the chimneypiece frame, if it is not actually a cocktail cabinet or a stereo speaker, is most likely to be the perennial coals — the 'switch on the logs in the fire' of Betjeman's poem. It is likely however that the really switched-on will increasingly react instead in favour of the authentically rustic fireside, which the wealthy are already rediscovering in their second homes in the countryside. In such places the traditional hearth, no longer being necessary for simple functional reasons inside the house, can equally well be bodily transferred to the outside: the open-air barbecue oven, which is the focus of Sir Basil Spence's cottage on Beaulieu River, was a portent for England at its date (1961), although already a commonplace in the States.

The great advantage of the temperate climate of the British Isles is precisely that it does make possible an unusually elaborate sequence of private spaces at the back of the house, suitable for different kinds of conviviality at different seasons, even without the artificial aids of the mechanical engineers. *The Architecture of the Well-Tempered Environment*, which forms the title of Reyner Banham's book on the air-conditioned dream, has so far been developed mainly for those parts of the technologically developed world which suffer from extremes of temperature and humidity, and therefore have to employ mechanical aids to alleviate them. It is widely believed by the British, however, that whereas other countries have climates, we only have 'weather', which is sent from God, or at least from the Air Ministry roof; and whereas climates call for artificial controls, 'weather' simply has to be tolerated and talked about endlessly. It is typical that our leading school of architecture, the Architectural Association, should have a separate department of Tropical Architecture — and no doubt it would have one of Arctic Architecture too, if enough people lived up there — yet meanwhile it almost totally neglects to teach students about the architectural handling of British weather. As we have already noted, it has been one of the most distressing features of the recent mania for high-rise flats that ignorance of the smaller variations of the weather has often led to the creation of extremes of climate, provoking in particular the intolerable gales which are wrung from the eddying wind when it is buffeted about between tower blocks. Many householders suffer from the high wind speeds at the upper levels, where it can be impossible to open the windows for large parts of the year, particularly when the sheets of plate glass, inhuman in scale, are of the side-hung pivoting type, so neat in its appearance on the elevation, but productive of a howling gust from the slightest crack of opening.

Such climatic brutalities are compounded by the inadequate insulating properties of many of the synthetic infill panels used for the outside walls of high-rise flats. Alex Hardy and Peter Sullivan of the Newcastle University School of Architecture have emphasised in their research the importance of heat storage in materials. For traditional Northumberland cottages, Hardy points out, the sites were chosen with instinctive care to provide windbreaks and suntraps, so that the thick masonry could continue to radiate its stored warmth long after the sun had gone down. This means that a sensibly designed patio or terrace, with surfaces of heat-reflective paving but with no mechanical aids whatever, can give the Northumberland cottager a climate as good as Kent, adding as much as ten degrees to the local temperature and prolonging conditions for sitting outdoors by at least an hour on summer evenings. Most architects today pay no attention at all to this traditional country-builders' knowledge of fair-weather design, handed down by word of mouth by generations of men who never knew the jargon term 'micro-climate'.

136 What is worse, most modern forms of cheap con-

struction are so palpably inadequate for heat storage that they materially add to the heating bills of the unfortunate occupier; and not surprisingly, the all-electric council flats propagated by the professional find little acceptance amongst tenants, whose soaring bills for central heating do not even qualify for rebates in the way that their rents do. Those who are able to switch off their heating systems often do so, and then rig up paraffin heaters instead, the unhealthy humidity of which causes concrete walls to 'sweat' with condensation and breed fungi. Paraffin is in any case notoriously unsafe. I shall always remember vividly my first canvassing as a council candidate in the winter of '67 in a brand-new half-finished row of GLC maisonettes, one of which was already a blackened shell, burnt out a month before by an overturned paraffin heater, killing two children. This is the kind of bitter end product of a situation in which the Treasury's rigid budgeting of capital on an annual basis forces Ministries in turn to force local authorities in turn to force their architects to hold down capital costs to the minimum, while very little regard is paid to 'cost-in-use'. Maintenance work after all comes easily enough in a regular dribble from the revenue account — except of course that the bills for heat and light come out of the wages of the wretched tenant. Amidst the technological euphoria of Banham's book, the reader is suddenly brought down to earth by a school at Wallasey, which heats itself purely from stored sunlight, at no cost to the public purse whatever. It is significant that the architect, Edwin Morgan, was not an eminent London consultant but merely the chief assistant to Wallasey's borough engineer; as an architectural equivalent to *The Man in the White Suit* in the old Ealing film, he might well have succeeded in bankrupting some of the country's heating engineers and suppliers, so it is perhaps just as well for them that he died soon afterwards, with the secrets of his design virtually unknown.

It is in the sensitive zone between the indoors of the private house and the outdoors of the private garden that it would be rewarding to make a detailed study of the micro-climatic qualities of such sophisticated Edwardian architects as Lutyens or Parker & Unwin, with their elaborate sequences of sheltered space, from bay window and inglenook out to loggia and verandah and out again to garden terrace and pergola. The superlative garden at Sissinghurst Castle in Kent, begun by Vita Sackville-West and Harold Nicolson as late as 1931, is in the same Edwardian tradition; contained as it is amidst the labyrinthine fragments of a long-demolished Tudor house, it demonstrates on a summer evening an extraordinary range of possibilities in the manipulation of the natural environment without any aid from technology. Within an almost rectilinear grid dictated by Nicolson's classical mind, his wife created a dozen or more separate 'outdoor rooms', each of which is planted to provide a slightly different atmosphere, in heat and light as well as colour and smell (and smells, incidentally, are likely to become increasingly important to us in our leisure time, when we lead our working lives in an even more deodorized lack of atmosphere). What is so impressive at Sissinghurst, or for that matter in the environment of a well-preserved Lutyens house-and-garden such as The Deanery at Sonning or Grey Walls at Gullane, is the intricacy with which the designer has played upon the response of the human senses at a human scale, whilst at the same time underlaying it all with the clarity of a classical discipline. Such intricacy — or, as Robert Venturi would have it, 'complexity and contradiction' — is going to be increasingly possible for affluent people to afford in the purlieus of their own homes; but it should also be possible to achieve it equally in the more humble backyards of planned housing, as Lutyens himself demonstrated brilliantly in such little-known estate villages as Milton Abbot in Devon and Upper Slaughter in the Cotswolds.

All these related aspects of privacy, intricacy, cultivation and micro-climate are in the end, to repeat, a matter of *identity* — of each family's possession of its own special territory. It is difficult for planners to recognise that, however accurately a house may be described as a slum by official criteria of unfitness, the pulse of family affection is likely to be beating just as strongly within its walls as in any 'desirable residence of character' in the Green Belt — probably more strongly in fact, because the residents, not being particularly mobile, are likely to have lived there for that much longer, building up a network of sisters, cousins and aunts of the 'extended family' kind analysed by Young & Willmott in Bethnal Green. When people are uprooted, if only because redundancy forces them to look for jobs elsewhere, they have a desperate need to put down new roots as quickly as possible, to bind up the wounds of separation and to reassure themselves that they still belong. Eric Lyons made a full-blooded response to this nuclear loneliness with the cosy embrace of his landscaping on the Span estates, cannibalising the Victorian gardens of demolished mansions in order to provide a kind of instant maturity of lushness for the newly arrived young couples. I was myself brought up in the grounds of the Royal Military Academy, Sandhurst, where my father had a permanent civilian job; the vast majority of other families there were serving out a two-or-three-year Army posting, and accordingly had to engage in hectic socialising to collect a new circle of friends within their first few weeks from arrival. Perhaps the most extreme examples of such temporary root-planting can be found in the bedsitters of students, usually occupied only for one academic year at a time (less than thirty weeks, excluding vacations). It is no good providing an intricate and attractive variety of rooms, as Peter Chamberlin did for New Hall at Cambridge, if the internal walls are then faced uniformly in white brick, so that even Sellotape has to be banned by the authorities for leaving dirty marks; the existence of a special Chamberlin-designed metal picture-rail is no substitute for the student's freedom to create her own environment in those first few weeks of the autumn term. Acres of pinboard are the first requirement for an instant change of scenery.

Universities, particularly the new foundations, are a good barometer of the architectural profession's sensitivity to its clients, as they have had similar basic requirements and all-too-similar out-of-town sites, yet have turned out quite differently. Can it be coincidence that those with the most student troubles happen to be those with the least humane architecture: Essex with its plum-coloured towers, Warwick with its white-tiled rectangles, Kent with the ruthless sub-palazzo symmetry of its first two colleges? It tends to be forgotten that the famous sit-in at Warwick, which in its turn led to the discovery of documents indicating undue pressure from business interests, started merely as a protest against the inadequacy of the residential and communal buildings — the cries of 'airport lounge' against the characterless common rooms of Rootes Hall being particularly appropriate in view of the similar accommodation designed by the same architects, Yorke Rosenberg Mardall, for the airports at Gatwick, Stansted, Luton and Newcastle.

The most successful socially of the new universities are those where the architects have on the contrary responded to an intricate human scale, York and Lancaster, both of them much criticised by other middle-aged architects for being 'pretty' and 'picturesque', as though these qualities were sins. Lancaster, by Peter Shepheard and Gabriel Epstein, is of brick and possibly a little too dense in layout for subsequent growth, in spite of its linear (open-ended) plan; whereas York, by a team under Sir Stirrat Johnson-Marshall and Andrew Derbyshire, has exploited the latest in adaptable technology, being entirely prefabricated in a version of the steel-framed CLASP system. For a fast-growing university, with unpredictable consequences from research, this means that the walls can be non-loadbearing and easily removable, and the buildings laid out almost at random around an elaborate interlocking of lakes created by the landscape architect and historian of the Picturesque, Frank Clark. Andrew Derbyshire freely admits that this bewildering diversity amidst the uniformity of the prefabricated panels has led even the vice-chancellor, Lord James, to tell visitors proudly 'This is the English lecture room' when actually opening the door to a broom cupboard; but Derbyshire suggests that it is precisely this sense of discovering hidden corners for themselves, corners which outsiders would find confusing, which gives the inhabitants of a Cotswold village, equally uniform in material, the feeling that they alone as residents know it and possess it. There is the analogy of the way in which lovers only gradually discover the hidden secrets of each other's bodies, secrets which they alone then share. This discovery of possession is indeed crucial to our happiness.

The family life of individual cottages at Walworth has been ruthlessly obliterated by the clinical repetitiveness of the London Borough of Southwark's Aylesbury estate — 'Europe's longest system-built block' is the contractors' proud claim. (Peter Baistow, Architects' Journal)

5

Less Density More Light

Only when he can show signs of understanding the intimacies of the threshold and the backyard, and the need to defend there the rights of the individual family, can the architect-planner hope to justify to his clients his customary enthusiasm for turning the telescope the other way round and 'talking about Jerusalem'.

Although the community must in the end try to be more than just the sum of its separate households, it has to start by being just that — for no amount of subsequent community planning in terms of clubs and clinics and nurseries can assuage in hindsight a failure to provide in the first place for the basic home comforts of mothers and fathers and children. The priorities have become blurred, I suspect, partly because those professionals who have enjoyed the privileges of higher education have had a tendency to be brainwashed by an ideal of community, particularly at Oxford and Cambridge, which specifically excludes the desires and demands of the nuclear family. Towers of learning, of ivory or of purple brick, are, to put it mildly, not the best places in which to appreciate domestic privacy, particularly for those who have already been brought up away from their families in the enforced community of the boarding school.

For the young upper-class revolutionaries at the Architectural Association in the thirties, the architectural contemporaries of Auden and Spender, the word 'community', or rather its jargon equivalent 'comprehensive development', naturally came to mean a regimented collective of workers' flats, of the kind derived from the Berlin *siedlungen* of Gropius and the Tauts or from the visionary projects in Le Corbusier's *Cité Radieuse.* A special favourite of the pundits was the Cité de la Muette at Drancy, near Paris, designed by Beaudouin and Lods, in which Roehampton-type towers of flats could first be photographed as an erected fact — even though the reality of this particular Cité was far from *radieuse* in that it lay empty, unconnected to public services, until it was requisitioned as barracks during the war.

Another response to hazy ideas of working-class solidarity was the vast multi-storey slab derived from the Marxist flats of Vienna — the curving walls and window banks of Quarry Hill in the centre of Leeds, for example. Just as the physical expression of 'community' in an Oxford college (or a public school) is an institutionalised set-up of dining hall, common rooms and communal bath blocks, so at Quarry Hill the much-praised efforts at community building turned out in reality to be little more than a comprehensive health centre and a laundry stranded in the middle of the main courtyard.

The point is that talkers about Jerusalem delude both themselves and their clients if they imagine that the promised land depends for its quality of life on a mere hand-out of 'communal facilities'. It is likely to depend far more, as we have seen, on the availability of private open space attached to each home, which can be used in an infinite variety of ways as each family sees fit. Yet time and again, when comprehensive redevelopers condemn an area for having a 'deficiency of open space', all that they mean is that it has a deficiency of *public* open space in terms of communal parks and playgrounds. The provision of this open space, to reach even such rule-of-thumb standards as the Greater London Development Plan's 2½ acres per thousand people, has then depended for its achievement on the ruthless sacrifice of almost all private open space.

The rebuilding of historic inner-city neighbourhoods is parcelled out into comprehensive development areas, each of them with its sub-list of 'community provision' (shops, clinics, park, old people's homes and so on) each one neatly separated out from the next, making what is in effect a large-scale built diagram of the administrative and financial separatism which exists between different council departments grant-aided by different Ministries. Such disintegration of the community can go to ludicrous lengths: some old people's homes, with warden-assisted flatlets attached, have needed the coordination of the pantomime horse, with the front legs grant-aided by the Department of Environment as 'housing' and the back legs by the Department of Social Services as 'welfare' — one department threatening to pay up its share in a different year from the other department.

But even a low-density suburb of houses-with-gardens, such as the Arbury estate on the north side of Cambridge, has suffered drastically from visual and social disintegration at its centre: instead of a varied and lively High Street of continuous frontages, it has been presented with a totally unrelated gaggle of separate structures dotted about amongst unusable grass verges: church, pub, library, shopping parade, secondary school, doctors' surgery. Eric Lyons's village street at New Ash Green, by contrast, depends for its liveliness of atmosphere as much on the subtle juxtaposition of shops and offices, workshops and community hall as it does on his intricacy of brick and tile. Similarly in the far eastern semis of Birmingham, behind the official Anglican noticeboard of 'the Church of St Philip and St James' at Hodge Hill, there co-exists under a single roof a sports centre, a youth club, a couple of playgroups, a young mums' club, a café, an old people's day centre and a parish church, all interchangeably enjoying the same sequence of spaces, with altar platform and kitchen as the only fixed points. Hodge Hill is notable also as a product of voluntary enthusiasm in an area of so-called monotonous sprawl.

It is in the high-rise estates that the disintegration of 'communal facilities' is particularly painful, the grass-and-tarmac verges around the towers being interrupted at random by the isolated pavilion blocks of school or clinic, plus, as they say on the plan, an occasional 'OP's home' or 'POS' (public open space). A stranded Victorian pub, its raggedly exposed side-gables of stock bricks or Flettons crying out feebly at their forcible severance from the next-door homes, provides a last refuge of nostalgia in brown paint and engraved glass, thanks merely to its not having been profitable enough to the brewers to merit rebuilding. Such survivals, however, give almost as much of pain as of comfort in their familiarity, mutely witnessing that to build a new estate an established community has been invariably broken up, before the newcomers in the flats moved in. The larger the development area, the more ruthless the scattering of the previous inhabitants, followed by an abrupt new intake from similar dispersions elsewhere. Even in high density areas where some 'overspill' is unavoidable if light and air are to be let in, it should surely be feasible to make it possible for most of the families who want to stay in their own areas to do so (although contrary to romantic social-worker myth, by no means all of them will necessarily want to stay). Redevelopment should in fact be implemented in phases and not all at once, with one group of streets being rebuilt to take in the families rehoused from the next group and so on, in a gradual crop rotation within the same limited field. What has tended to happen instead is that over the past decade schemes have grown ominously larger and denser, and single building contracts for vast unified flatted estates have become the inner-city norm — partly for reasons of bureaucratic convenience, very much (as we shall see) for reasons of technological expediency, and above all for reasons of architectural megalomania.

If the first major heresy of Jerusalemites is to imagine that 'community' equals 'communal facilities', the second is to imagine that 'visual uniformity' equals 'social cohesion'. There is an unspoken assumption shared by many architects that an outward appearance which is repetitively 'consistent' (that favourite word again) is some kind of sacramental indication of an inner harmony amongst its inhabitants. Pugin's fallacy about 'Christian architecture for Christian people' is in effect brought up-to-date as 'hygienic architecture for hygienic people'. Of course the Georgian terraces and the garden-suburb semis were also architecturally consistent, but there the flexible brick structure, easy to add to or to alter, was set in a humane counterpoint to a patchwork landscape of private gardens laid out by individual owners. It is the inhumane sameness, and lack of escape from sameness, that makes the large-scale battery-hatch slab of flats so repellent. Every family, arriving as strangers, finds it difficult to set any personal mark upon the concrete walls or the mown lawns to identify its special home. The architect's mania for consistency has both stimulated and concealed the real cause of the increasing size and sameness of new estates: the increasing adoption until recently of industrialised building methods, otherwise known as prefabricated building or system building. What we experienced in the late sixties was a monstrously energetic wagging of the architectural dog by its technological tail, in that, once it had been decided technically to build with factory-made components, it became essential economically to keep open for them the longest possible production runs. In the fifties, when most houses and flats were still built with loadbearing brick external walls, an estate for two or three hundred families was considered large and an estate of over a thousand dwellings was exceptional. Alton East and West at Roehampton for instance (making a total of 3079 homes) and Park Hill and Hyde Park at Sheffield (995 and 1322) were justified only by special pleading about their exceptional hillside sites, which were said to demand unified treatment.

By the early sixties there was mounting criticism on all sides, especially in the wake of the Rachman scandals about profiteering landlords, about the slow progress of slum clearance, but the real reason for this was not grasped: that the Government, and through it the nation as a whole, was not spending nearly enough on housing. Even as late as 1971, when annual expenditure on defence and education had long since passed the £2,000 million mark, the total subsidies to public authority housing consisted of £157 million from national taxes and just over £60 million from local rates — plus of course £302 million doled out to mainly middle-class house purchasers in terms of tax relief on mortgage interest. The pressures on cost-conscious local authorities were exacerbated for the best of reasons, when they gradually adopted the higher standards of space and equipment within the home suggested in the Parker Morris Report of 1961 and eventually made mandatory by the Government in 1967 (with certain important exceptions). At the same time, with full employment and growing pressure from public opinion to control the numbers of Commonwealth immigrants entering the country (the Act to limit them was passed in 1962) there were difficulties in attracting a sufficiently large labour force, skilled or unskilled, for traditional methods of building. Shortage of staff led to costly delays on site. So when the prophets of industrialised building promised methods which were cheaper, quicker and far less labour-intensive, they were taken to be a possible panacea, even though it soon turned out that many of them were slower and more expensive.

It was not realised that there would be such difficulties in coordinating the supply of building components to the widely variable sites and conditions of a 'low technology' industry — difficulties which had, heaven knows, occurred often enough even in the 'high technology' industry of the motor car. In the case of the Greater London Council's ambitious new town for 90,000 people at Thamesmead, just across the river from Ford's at Dagenham, even the first 1,500 houses ran into acute trouble, in that delays in production not only wasted men's time but also led to serious industrial trouble because of the non-payment of expected overtime and bonuses. It was also forgotten amidst all the talk about management, that the majority of time wasted on housing schemes is not wasted on the building site at all, but in the compulsory purchase of land, the rehousing of the expelled inhabitants, the architects' design work and the obtaining of Government loan sanction; and in any case, even after the possibly quicker erection of the basic structures, there still remain many of the 'finishing trades' such as painting and landscaping — let alone the preparation of the site in the first place (in the case of Thamesmead, the draining of the marshes into a huge lake). If speed proved a chimera, so did economy, with the Thamesmead flats already coming out at over £11,000 each two years ago.

But the greatest illusion of all, — and the only one which in the end would matter to the consumer, to the slum-cleared tenant — was that prefabrication, with its modular components slotted together, would by definition be on the side of greater freedom and flexibility for the home. It all depended what was being prefabricated: a false analogy was made with the 'light and dry' steel-framed systems which had been pioneered by the Hertfordshire County Council and later by the CLASP consortium in the Midlands, for the building of one- and two-storey schools, with simple and repetitive room spaces and relatively modest demands for load-bearing and sound insulation. When the Tory Government woke up in 1963 to the urgent electoral demand to deliver more houses, it so happened that the kingpin of CLASP, Sir Donald Gibson, had just become the Director-General of Research and Development at Mr Geoffrey Rippon's renamed Ministry of Public Building and Works: that Ministry then confidently spawned the National Building Agency to advise local authorities on which building systems, of nearly three hundred suddenly sprung upon the market, would be the most suitable to use for family homes. It soon became apparent that light infill walls were quite insufficient to keep one neighbour's record-player or loud laughter off another neighbour's desire for peace; only at York University, in a modified version of CLASP, were residential standards of quietness approached at a reasonable cost in a 'dry and light' system.

The Government's advisers turned instead to a totally different type of prefabrication, 'wet and heavy', for local authority housing schemes. On the Continent, especially in France, where high slab blocks of flats had become traditional, the reinforced concrete frame had gradually been extended to make up a totally reinforced concrete building, composed throughout of loadbearing panels, each of them a whole storey in height. These wall panels, stuffed with reinforcing rods, made the structure totally rigid; the easy adaptability of the prewar semi, in terms of throwing two rooms into one, could be made possible only in fantasy with a laser beam. In any case the lifting tackle of tower cranes required to heave each panel into place was so costly to the contractor that it could be made economic only through the 'long erection runs' of the high-rise tower or, better still, the high-rise slab. In rare cases, where sites were exceptionally open, it was still possible to build ordinary houses-on-the-ground in heavy panels, but only, as at Skelmersdale, on the condition that there was an authoritarian straightening out of the buildings into long monotonous terraces, so that the cranes could run alongside on their special railway tracks without interruption. Even if the lack of speed and lack of economy of much concrete-panel construction came as a surprise to its fans, its crippling environmental limitations were already perfectly obvious in 1963–64 when Sir Keith Joseph seized upon it as the one possible means of reviving the laggard annual scoreboard of dwellings completed. The limitations were no less obvious a year later when Richard Crossman and Bob Mellish used the same means to hitch the housing programme to Mr Wilson's 'white heat of the technological revolution' — a white heat, incidentally, which in the concrete-walled flat has tended in the winter to congeal into a grey dampness of fungus-blotched walls, unless the tenant turns technologist himself and controls the ventilation according to instructions not normally supplied. The gas explosion which in 1968 ripped out one corner of the East London tower block of Ronan Point, killing five, was an almost inevitable nemesis for years of technological conceit; it emerged at the public inquiry that a 60 to 70 m.p.h. gust of wind could have brought the deck of cards down just as easily.

'More slums are likely to be built in the next five years than in the past twenty' was my own gloomy prediction in the *Architectural Review* for November 1967; and it was easy to be proved right by such galloping examples of architectural inflation as the 31-storey towers sticking up bleakly on Glasgow's eastern outskirts at Red Road Balornock, or the

400-yard slab block of ten to twelve storeys called Wendover on Southwark's Aylesbury estate at Walworth. Both schemes have been proudly advertised in the technical press by their contractors for setting new records in system building, the Red Road towers as Europe's *highest* and the Aylesbury slab as Europe's *longest* — yet another pair of Gold Medals for the British lads. Such competitive commercial propaganda, exploiting as it did the sincere desire of Labour councillors to get rid of their slums as quickly as possible, exhibited the characteristic hysteria of high risks: every 'heavy system' contractor had rapidly come to realise that rich pickings would be his only so long as he could keep up a sufficient production rate to cover his massive expenditure on factory plant, and to make a profit he had therefore to maintain a minimum annual output of at least a thousand dwelling units — at least one monster estate every year. Most of the big contractors had shopped hurriedly abroad for their systems, which they imported on licence: the Balency system from France by Cubitt's for Thamesmead, the Larsen-Neilsen from Denmark by Taylor-Woodrow for many brutal GLC estates as well as Ronan Point, the Camus system from France by the Liverpool firm of Unit, and the Jespersen system from Denmark by Laing's (who, with assistance from the Ministry, turned it into 12M-Jespersen at the chillingly clinical St. Mary's Estate at Oldham). All-British systems were developed by concrete beam specialists such as Bison and Reema, as well as by Wates (with their more flexible method of on-site battery casting) and by Wimpey (with their No-Fines technique of patent shuttering). Between these contractors and their less hardy rivals, and between the various suppliers of packaged mechanical services, there ensued some bitter infighting to collar the most lucrative clients: councillors and officials found themselves wined and dined and taken on trips to Paris, and it is not surprising that a few of them were led astray, as subsequent corruption inquiries have indicated.

150   The road to this reinforced concrete hell was

naturally paved with good political intentions, expressed in this case in the annual Dutch auction of housebuilding statistics: 200,000, then 300,000, then 400,000. It is often forgotten that more than half of each of these figures (much more than half when the Tories were in power) referred to private enterprise houses-for-sale, mostly in the outer suburbs; the total number of council houses built in any one year never rose above 203,900 (out of the 1967 total for all houses of 404,400). Yet ever since the early thirties (Arthur Greenwood's Housing Act of 1931) successive Ministers of Health and Housing had blithely assured the country at regular intervals that clearance of slum houses was only a ten-year job to complete. As the *New Left Review* cynically but justifiably observed, at any particular time 'the number of officially recognised slums tends to correspond, more or less exactly to the number of unfit houses (usually about 3 per cent of the nation's total housing stock) which the Government thinks it can pull down within a given period (usually five years) plus a slightly larger number which it hopes to clear later (usually about 3.5 per cent).' Yet all the time, incredible as it may seem, no Government actually *knew* how many slum houses there were: the official national statistics were nothing less than a fraud, consisting as they did only of the demonstrably phoney figure of 847,112 houses 'represented' as slums by the local authorities in 1955. Each authority made out its own list of 'unfit' houses according to its own peculiar standards of unfitness, and they did it in such an arbitrary and subjective way that the ludicrous situation arose of more slums being 'represented' as existing in Tunbridge Wells than in Llanelly, in Hoylake UDC than in Cardiff, in Aylesbury than in the Rhondda.

Many Labour councils had apparently hidden their faces in despair of ever being able to do anything about the hideous decay they were presumably elected to remedy, so they preferred not to quantify it; while paradoxically there were some Tory commuter-belt councils who were unexpectedly zealous in identifying every possible pocket of unfit houses remaining in their locality, even if this involved de-molishing delightful old cottages which could be better rehabilitated. Take the city council of Cambridge; as early as 1932, under the Greenwood Act, their city surveyor plotted the destruction of the exquisite medieval alleyways of Botolph Lane, St Mary's Lane and Round Church Street; the first two are still happily with us, but in Round Church Street the weatherboarded cottages and raised sidewalk of Tan Yard, with Prziborsky's famous hairdressing saloon, finally bit the dust in 1962 to make way for the entrance to a multi-storey car park, even though the 'slums' were by then inhabited mainly by aesthetically minded dons who had no need whatever to be rehoused.

Meanwhile in the inner areas of the major cities, the areas of real housing stress, the programmes of new building were not even sufficient to cater for the increase of population and the increasing rate of household formation (a jargon phrase which means in effect that young couples are marrying earlier, but can't stand living with their in-laws). Many of the council houses had to go to families displaced by other public projects (schools, roads, parks, clinics) even though the 'housing need' of such families might be negligible. One of the penthouses on top of the Brandon estate towers in Kennington, for instance, was let to the Hon. Thomas Pakenham (Lord Long-ford's heir) — other residence, Tullynally Castle in Eire — and the architectural historian of country houses, Mark Girouard, just because their previous flat in Paddington had had to be compulsorily acquired for another LCC housing scheme. When I used to visit their panoramic eyrie for meetings of a Victorian Society sub-committee, I could not help wryly recalling the advertisement in *The Times* for Wimpey's the builders, in which a similar pair of tower blocks in Coventry and Harlow were captioned 'The Stately Homes of England'.

At last the Labour Government decided to break through the official miasma of false optimism by instituting a National Sample Survey of House Condition, carried out by a nationally recruited team of public health inspectors to a common set of standards: they reported in July 1967 that, although some 700,000 houses had been slum-cleared since the 1955 estimate of 847,112, the total number still unfit amounted to a staggering 1,800,000 — between 11 and 12 per cent of the entire housing stock — of which about 1,100,000 were likely to be treated as part of slum clearance areas. On the then current rate of 70,000 cleared each year, it would clearly take at least twenty years to remedy matters — and by then of course higher living standards would have led in any case to a redefinition of the term 'slum'. The regeneration of our homes, as politicians and planners seem rarely to appreciate, is a continuous and never-ending process, not a simple statistical 'housing problem' requiring a once-for-all 'solution'.

In this connection the much more alarming output of the survey was that another 2,500,000 dwellings (15 per cent of the total national stock) were partially defective and therefore, unless something were done about them, they also would degenerate into slums. In historical terms this meant that, even after the worst pre-byelaw or 'early byelaw' streets of the 1850s and 1860s had been redeveloped, there was still a mass of standard byelaw houses of the 1880s and 1890s, basically decent as family homes, which urgently needed to be brought up-to-date in plumbing and damp-proofing if they were to avoid decay and demolition. It was to save these that the Labour Government acted wisely in introducing, through the 1969 Housing Act, a set of major new powers for local authorities to designate General Improvement Areas, based on the ideas for environmental as well as structural rehabilitation contained in the Ministry's pioneering study of the Deeplish neighbourhood in Rochdale; not just plumbing and painting of individual houses, but tree-planting, diversion of traffic and provision of parking and playgrounds for a whole area. Economists such as Lionel Needleman of the LSE have calculated that, given the steep rise in building costs as well as the greater flexibility of older houses in meeting changes in living standards, it would be worth spending as much as half the cost of a new house in order to give an old one an extra 'life' of thirty years. The real test of a Government's housing programme is not in fact the number of new houses it builds but the quality and condition of the total national housing stock, old as well as new.

The tragedy of the sixties was that this new 'total' approach to housing came too late to avoid the consequences of the stepped-up programmes mounted by both brands of Government in the previous six years. By 1966 as many as 25.7 per cent of the council 'dwellings' put out to tender by local authorities were in multi-storey blocks (five storeys and over) compared with 14.2 per cent in 1960 and 8.7 in 1957; by the second quarter of 1972 the figure had dropped full circle back to 8.3 per cent. Similarly industrialised building rose to a peak of completions from 30.8 per cent in 1967 to 41.3 per cent in 1970, and then dropped to 25.5 per cent only two years later.

Vast flatted estates of 136 people to the acre marched across territory previously occupied by family cottages. The GLC's Ledbury Estate on the Old Kent Road, for instance, with its grey cliffs of Taylor Woodrow Larsen-Nielsen units, has its ten-storey point blocks set arbitrarily at a diagonal to any of the existing street lines. In 1967, before it even went up, I remember the group leader in charge, Derek Bottomley, lamenting to me at his drawing-board in County Hall that he had ever had to design the estate, as the area covered by it had consisted very largely of pleasant, improvable houses-with-gardens. Similarly the builder Neil Wates told me how much he personally loathed the environment created by local authorities using his own firm's highly profitable system of prefabrication.

That has indeed been the predicament of sensitive souls in the industry: they have always been able to blame someone else, and in the last resort the fifteen councillors on the housing committee of any particular local authority. It is they, so the argument runs, who pay the piper, and it is they — particularly the

Socialist and the working-class — who persist in demanding as their tune that there should be the maximum number of 'units' stacked up on each available acre of territory. Certainly the politicians have been quite as susceptible as any architects to the lure of megalomania implicit in the tower block: there is after all no more impressive way of indicating to a poorly housed electorate that political salvation is on the way than by pointing to the skyline and saying 'Look at our housing programme.' When I first stood for Lewisham Council in 1968, opinion amongst the ruling Labour group had in the past few months begun to move strongly against the building of any more tower blocks, yet when our election manifesto was published, lo and behold, there on the front page was emblazoned the aggressive skyline of the trio of point blocks at Lewisham Park.

Architects and councillors are never happier than when, instead of abusing each other for the neo-slums they are building, they can join unanimously together to abuse a third party, the Government, as an excuse or even as a justification for the multi-storey flats that have in such great numbers been built. The five-part argument runs like this: (i) the country is over-populated and has too little land so we have to build densely and up; (ii) we must protect the Green Belt around our cities, and preserve a firm division between town and countryside, but if we went on building cottage estates of the prewar post-Unwin type, such as Becontree, London would stretch from Birmingham to Southampton, so we must build densely and up; (iii) we have in any case got far too little land within our own municipal boundaries, and we have many thousands of slum-dwellers to rehouse, so we have to build densely and up; (iv) the Development Plan for our city has zoned these inner areas as being suitable for high density living, so we must do what the Plan says and build densely and up; (v) we have recruited some bright young architects who have shown us (1952 version) that at this high density we do not have to build gloomy five-storey blocks but can build beautiful twenty-storey towers-in-the-park instead, or (1972 version) that at this high density we do not have to build gloomy twenty-storey towers but can build nice intimate five-storey courtyards instead. These five arguments have been the core of the case for multi-storey flats put forward over the past generation by every major British city, architects, planners and councillors alike, and obviously they have to be taken, and rebutted, seriously.

First, there is the growth of population — the most imponderable and unprovable, and therefore most easily hysterical, of hypotheses. Certainly the numbers of Indians and Brazilians and Indonesians cannot go on rising indefinitely at their present rate, without perpetual crises of famine. But the fundamental problem is not the abnormal concentration of people but the unequal distribution of resources — not the quantities of statistics but the quality of life. There is nowhere in the world more densely inhabited than the bits of six countries impaled upon the axis between Birmingham and Bonn; yet even within that statistically crowded area, there are the rural beauties of the Weald of Kent, the forest of the Ardennes or the vineyards of the Moselle. The unpredictable and alarming increase in the British birthrate around 1960, led as it was by the Queen herself, seems to have exhausted itself, and the latest figures from the Registrar-General at the time of writing (June 1972) indicate on the contrary what is almost the ecological ideal of Zero Population Growth, partly no doubt as a result of the Abortion Act and free family planning.

But the crucial problem in any case is not population *per se*: even if we have nearly achieved ZPG, we still have to learn how to live within our means — not just living within the limits of our own resources as a nation, but progressively de-escalating our demands upon the resources of other countries. And it is the mineral and mechanical resources which are scarce, much more than land — even though 'shortage of land' has been turned into an alibi for every kind of abuse from gazumping to homelessness. Clear and precise studies have been done at Wye College by Professor G.P. Wibberley and Dr Robin Best which

156

show that, even at the present land take for development of 60,000 acres a year, there will be quite sufficient left for agriculture in thirty years' time — assuming (and here's the rub, environmentally) that the present pace of mechanisation and intensified yield continues. But if agriculture cannot confine itself within smaller boundaries to its own satisfaction, priority should be given to the reclamation of the many thousands of acres of non-agricultural land which are derelict or waste — not merely the worked-out craters of mineral extractions but also the un-drained marshland of the estuaries (barring bird sanctuaries) and even the extra land which can be summoned forth from the sea on the Dutch pattern (as the engineer Bernard Clark vainly proposed for Foulness). Assuming that we can hold our population level and that we can use and reclaim our existing land acreage more wisely, the real question for the apocalyptically or eschatologically minded is: what kind of life-style will we and our fellow-citizens be demanding a generation hence?

My own belief (and like all such predictions, it can in the end be no better than a belief) is that the slightly larger land take needed for family-houses-with-gardens could be more than compensated for by the more relaxed and undemanding life-style that could go with it. A man who at least grows his own flowers, if not his own vegetables and chickens as well, is likely, in the tradition of William Cobbett or Eric Gill, to be slightly more contented with his own self-sufficiency without lashing out on consumer goodies of a heavily mechanical type; conversely, a man who is shut up in a cut-price penthouse on the fifteenth floor, sans earth, sans grass, sans birds (except of the penthouse type), is by definition extremely likely to seek satisfaction for his impotence by laying in great stocks of purchased goods. Perhaps we should be prepared to allow a little extra land for homes in view of the relief to resources of adopting a more pastoral mode of life — an argument preached for years in the wilderness by Frank Lloyd Wright.

This brings us to the second key argument, about

the kind of countryside we want anyway, and whether a slightly more spacious way of life in the inner city would automatically mean bungalows from Battersea to Bournemouth. Is it possible in a permissive society to maintain the primal chastity of the Green Belt — what Neville Chamberlain, in his innocence, proposed originally to call the Green Girdle? To answer, this, we have to be absolutely clear what the planners mean by all those figures of people to the acre which are so gaily bandied about — to be precise, we have to distinguish between 'net density' and 'gross density'. All the figures with which I have already thickly sown this text — 136 to the acre, 100 to the acre, 50 to the acre and so on — are all 'net' figures of the number of people on the housing estate in the narrow sense, within the boundaries of the immediately surrounding roads. These net figures are the meaningful ones in terms of personal comfort and architectural design; in terms of the physical contact between families, 100 to the acre is indeed exactly twice as dense as 50 to the acre, and it certainly feels like it to those condemned to suffer it. In terms of land take, of space actually occupied by buildings, of farmland actually obliterated, one might logically suppose that exactly the corollary would apply: that 100 to the acre flats would occupy only half the amount of land that 50 to the acre houses would occupy. But in reality this is not so at all, because the only meaningful figure of physical land take (as against personal contact) is the one which goes beyond mere homes and gardens and includes shopping centres, schools, offices, factories, road and rail, and everything else for which the local community uses its territory — that total figure of people to the acre being 'gross' density. Take Milton Keynes: the average net density of the houses will be about 40 people to the acre; whereas the gross density, arising from 200,000 people on over 22,000 acres, will be only ten to the acre.

Robin Best has skilfully demonstrated that these figures of gross density give the lie conclusively to all the basic arguments in favour of building densely and up 'so as to economise on land'; because whatever the density — 20, 120, 220 or even 320 — the football field and cricket pitch remain the same size, the railway lines continue along the standard guage, the supermarket shelf still stocks the standard packets. So a rise in net density from 45 to 50 (as in the first generation New Towns) to 75 (as at Cumbernauld), although it undoubtedly makes a marked difference to the confines of family life, achieves remarkably little in terms of saving land, as the schools and churches and factories are still taking up the same amount of space; and in fact at the higher densities there may well be actually a *bigger* land take for roads and car parking space, because of the intensity of traffic. No one can visit Cumbernauld without being conscious of the drastic swathes of land cut through by the dual carriageways which canalise the traffic towards the single major shopping centre; whereas Lord Llewelyn-Davies's team, after a disillusioning defeat by the engineers in favour of a similar 'coarse mesh' of spaghetti at Washington New Town, succeeded at Milton Keynes in establishing from the outset the economic benefits, both in land and in structure, of a 'fine mesh' of medium-sized roads with ground-level traffic-light-operated junctions.

Really substantial gross savings of land can only be achieved in schemes at about five times the net density of Cumbernauld, at New York or Chicago (or Gorbals slum) levels of 300 or more. The Peabody tenements, given the large size of many Victorian families, were usually over the 500 mark when they started. There is still an argument for building to such densities, and it is at this moment being demonstrated on the ground for ordinary council tenants by, of all people, Eric Lyons, in his rather ominously entitled World's End scheme at Chelsea. It was given Government permission, in true guinea-pig style, as an experiment, Lyons's argument being that the economy in land would mean that extra money could be spent on providing excellent 'communal facilities', including a gymnasium and a nursery for the kids, and clumps of trees growing out of the earth-filled 'newel posts' of the multi-storey car parks. In fact the amount of extra money available for luxuries has been very little, because of the high structural cost of the twenty-storey tower blocks.

Similar arguments were put forward in the early fifties by Kadleigh, Horsbrugh and Whitfield in their two visionary schemes for High Paddington (over the railway tracks) and for the Barbican. As now executed at 200 to the acre by Chamberlin, Powell & Bon, the Barbican does genuinely have the luxuries of city lights, in the unique provision of the Royal Shakespeare Company's theatre and the London Symphony Orchestra's concert hall. But all is not socially what it seems: originally the estate was intended to include a good deal of low-rental accommodation, but because of soaring costs, it now provides only posh pieds-à-terre for the kind of people who are lucky enough also to have thatched cottages, and even large country houses, ready for their getaway (with children) at weekends — just the kind of Chelsea residents who will not be housed by that council in World's End.

The rural escape routes of the rich really give the lie to the sedulously peddled myth of the popularity of extreme high density: when Theo Crosby, for example, revealed to the press in 1964 his Government-commissioned Taylor Woodrow scheme for rebuilding Fulham, he actually had the face to instance the happiness of those who live at 250 to the acre in Mayfair and Knightsbridge mansion flats as a justification for housing working-class people at a similar density; he added that his courtyards would be just the same size as a Georgian precinct such as Manchester Square (a square which is, incidentally, given over nowadays to offices). Such are the dangers of a purely visual approach to community building, uninformed by any understanding of the differences in family life between the affluent and mobile and the impoverished and immobile. The implicit deceit of such arguments is in any case that, to tot up the real cost to the community of high density schemes in land take, one should add to the net site not only the extra road widths and flyovers for the honeypot attraction of traffic to the city centre, but also the extra acreage of countryside consumed by 'second homes'. In the end the theoretical arguments for extreme densities are being defeated in practice by the choice of the consumer, who is now fleeing from the flats of Inner London even faster than from Venice. The population of the Inner London boroughs, which had gone down by only 148,000 (4.4 per cent) between 1951 and 1961, went down by a further 475,000 (almost exactly 15 per cent) in the following decade.

The opposite extreme argument, for a very low density, was put forward with persuasive charm from 1934 onwards by Frank Lloyd Wright, in his various schemes for what he called Broadacre City. Although this had a rather hierarchical division into areas of minimum houses, medium houses and larger houses, its basic tenet was neither urban nor suburban but the American pioneer smallholder's dream of half-an-acre of land for every family — very similar to the Homes for Heroes put up in 1919 for returning English soldiers by the Agricultural Resettlement Board under Sir Laurence Weaver. This kind of net density, not 70 to the acre but more like seven, assuredly *would* make London stretch to the sea in all directions; but it is not of course what English architects mean by 'low density' when they criticise 'monotonous suburban sprawl'. Such giant prewar cottage estates of the LCC as Becontree and Downham in fact conform closely to Unwin's ideal of 12 houses (35—40 people) to the acre; and private enterprise estates of the same period are also often at about 35 to the acre.

Once again the crucial question is not so much net housing density, but gross: what gives the Outer London suburbs their remarkably low gross density (Bromley for example has three times the land area of Lewisham, which is one of the least dense of the Inner London boroughs) is partly the amount of public open space that has been preserved as fields

F

and woods, and also as private sports grounds, but also partly the amount of largely unused land which has been left standing semi-derelict in the curious patches that tend to be left over between rival laissez-faire speculations. There are also substantial areas where Victorian stockbroker villas stand in an acre or two of land each; and there is no reason why the grounds of these should not be developed too, so long as fine trees are preserved, along with those houses ranking as historic buildings, which can be converted into flats. There has already been a good deal of building in the outer boroughs, but this has been overwhelmingly in the form of private estates for owner-occupiers, which do little to relieve the over-crowded areas of Inner London. There has been a similar imbalance between Solihull and Birmingham, between Altrincham and Manchester, between the Wirral and Liverpool — with the Conservative con-trolled 'executive dormitories' defending their green acres and allowing only low density development, often at as little as 30 to the acre. What this has meant is that the Inner London boroughs and the cities of Manchester, Liverpool and Birmingham have accordingly been thrown back upon the meagre re-sources of land within their own boundaries; and this has correspondingly led in most inner areas to the adoption of excessively high densities of between 120 and 200 to the acre — high enough for all the dis-advantages of family life in flats, yet without any of the compensating luxuries which are alleged to be possible at the really high densities of over 250.

I am not suggesting, in view of the wish of so many families to remain in their traditional neighbour-hoods, that the densities of the inner suburbs can be allowed to drop to the 35—40 of the LCC cottage estates or the 45—50 of the first generation New Towns. The sensible average density to adopt, it seems to me, is around 80, which makes it possible, Cumbernauld-style, to provide virtually every family with a house-on-the-ground, but which can be varied slightly up or slightly down (say between 50 and 100), so as to respond on the one hand to the particular demands of the landscape or historic buildings, and on the other to the situation at the centres of towns and villages (popular for small flats amongst some of the middle-aged whose children have left home). Eighty to the acre is certainly not sprawl — it means neat little terraces of town houses with small gardens, sufficient to house all Londoners decently. But even given the declining population, it will not be possible to bring down the densities of the inner areas from 136 to 80, without encroaching on the Green Belt, unless there is help from the outer boroughs in allowing unused land within their borders to be purchased — in the case of London by the GLC and in the case of the other big cities by the new metropolitan authorities set up for the first time in 1973. Otherwise the inner boroughs will be forced to tear their remaining pleasant landscape to pieces in order to achieve a ruthlessly uniform 80 everywhere.

The most striking imbalance between inner and outer suburbs at the moment is not so much in density — though that, as we have seen, is striking enough — but much more in terms of the kinds of society and community that are growing up there. For a start, the Inner Boroughs are containing an ever higher proportion of council housing — almost 50 per cent now in Lewisham, 85 per cent soon in Tower Hamlets — while the Outer Boroughs become more and more uniformly covered by the lusher pastures of the owner-occupied home. But what is even more striking is the differential rate of obsolescence between the dense areas of council flats and — leaving on one side the homes of the owner-occupied — the lower density areas of prewar council cottages. Not only are the dense five-storey blocks of neo-Georgian flats built in the thirties already having to be revamped at vast expense (a programme started by the GLC before it handed over most of these estates to the boroughs in April 1971) but it is extremely dubious how worthwhile as a public investment such work is; for by mid-1972 it was costing £6,000 per flat (well over half the price of a new one) to provide

dwellings which, albeit with a new bath and sink unit

and central heating, would still continue to exist in an environment of grimy tarmac courtyards totally unsatisfactory for family life. It is ironic that the 50 per cent Government grants for environmental works available in General Improvement Areas, intended primarily to be the means of resuscitating areas of privately owned homes, are increasingly being applied by councils instead to areas of prewar flats.

Many of the postwar estates are by now almost equally slummy, with a rapid turnover of dissatisfied and sometimes violent tenants — Noble Street in Newcastle-upon-Tyne, for example, built in 1956, and many of Liverpool's Everton flats of around 1960. Meanwhile the prewar cottage estates, even before being supplied with new baths and sinks and heating — in the case of the GLC's St. Helier estate, by means of a packaged home extension swung in over the roof by crane — are surviving wonderfully well as attractive family houses, particularly now that the trees and shrubs are in full maturity. The estates may still be excessively one-class and thereby somewhat impoverished culturally and commercially (few good shops) but they are notably stable and satisfied communities with a considerable response to the GLC's current offer of individual freeholds — the plethora of new porches, picture windows and crazy-paved stone facings put up by the new owners being in themselves the emblems of personal pride and vitality.

Yet absurdly it is these increasingly attractive, even at times idyllic, model villages of the twenties that are being held up as butts for scorn by architects. Take Mr Geoffrey Spyer, for example, whose book *Architect and Community* (1971) is a neat encapsulation of all the fallacies and fantasies I have been attacking in this book. His comment on the LCC cottage estates is: 'While the new suburbs provided better standards of light, air and open space than the more densely built-up central areas, the improvements in living conditions were largely marginal [sic] ... Architecturally they were dreary. The enormous scale of the developments, their monotonous regularity and their

164

meanness created a subhuman environment which was only relieved over the years by the few trees and bits of green which managed to survive the monstrous sprawl.' It would be hard to invent a more total travesty of what the visitor today actually sees, in terms of blossoming gardens and mature woodland. Welwyn Garden City is similar, and even better are some of the provincial estates put up in 1916—20 before the Geddes Axe enforced economies: Curtis Green's at Chepstow and Winchester, C.H. James's at Lincoln and Adshead & Ramsey's at Moulsecoomb outside Brighton. Perhaps the LCC's best of the twenties was Dover House Road, which is now on the bus route to Roehampton and is said to have had Russian visitors drooling over it, rather than the famous flats up the road (to the embarrassment of their hosts).

The disastrous social consequence of the imbalance in quality between cottage and flat is that the denser inner-city areas are being rapidly deserted by the younger, more lively and more skilled sections of the population. The actual number leaving Inner London in the five years 1966—1971 — the latter half of that 15 per cent figure already quoted — was an explosive enough announcement at the Greater London Development Plan Inquiry, in that it turned out to be nearly twice as many as the GLC had expected and predicted. But much more important is the fact that the inner areas such as Stepney and Shoreditch, Bermondsey and Deptford, are increasingly being deserted by their traditional artisan leadership and are being left to degenerate into a lumpen proletariat of hotel porters, kitchen staff, cleaners, the disabled and the unemployed. This raises serious problems for public participation in planning (see Chapter Six). The number of single-parent families in such areas has increased alarmingly; yet as far as I know there has been no major study by sociologists of matrimonial breakdown as a symptom or cause of housing stress.

Where have the young and skilled gone, in their escape from Cobbett's 'Infernal Wen'? The answer that the planners, both at County Hall and at Whitehall, would like to give is that they have gone as planned 'overspill' to the New and Expanding Towns — the New Towns established under Lord Silkin's New Towns Act of 1946 and the Expanding Towns developed by the GLC under the Town Development Act of 1952. These planned settlements, the final fruit of Ebenezer Howard's campaign for decentralisation, have certainly attracted an unusually large proportion of both the young and the skilled, the industries which have moved to them being predominantly modern and science-based. They have always been intended to be entirely self-sufficient, with their own industry and offices, and to a remarkable extent they still are, in spite of a gradually increasing groundswell of commuting to London from some of them, such as Stevenage and Harlow.

Yet in the last five years, the annual contribution of these model settlements, New Towns and Expanded Towns, cannot have amounted to more than a quarter of the total exodus from the Greater London Council area. Abercrombie in his Greater London Plan of 1945 had after all calculated that London needed one new town of 60—80,000 people every year. Seven were started in 1946—51, but then there was a disastrous hiatus, apart from the much smaller expanded towns, until Milton Keynes, Northampton and Peterborough were designated in 1967—9. Meanwhile, instead of the level or even decreasing birthrate that Abercrombie foresaw, the slackening of the New Town programme in the fifties coincided, as we have seen with a temporary, but very considerable, rise in the birth-rate. The population of London therefore declined very little until after 1961, by which time there were already enormous pressures for uncontrolled development in the countryside beyond the Metropolitan Green Belt — pressures which the exodus since 1965 has merely exacerbated.

The Green Belt has certainly been successful in lifting threats of urban development off the countryside immediately outside the built-up area. It is true that it is not a continuous belt, being broken up by the corridors of development spreading radially out from Central London along the commuter railway lines of the Victorian period: substantial bites out of the greenery are taken by places such as Redhill on the Brighton line, Woking on the Portsmouth line, Slough on the Great Western to Reading, Watford on the way to the Midlands, Hoddesdon on the Cambridge line and Brentwood on the Great Eastern in Essex.

It was the logical existence of these railway corridors from London that led the South-East Economic Planning Council to propose in its *Strategy for the South-East* that growth should continue to be promoted along the same radial lines. But the Planning Council also proposed that between the radials there should be substantial tracts of sacrosanct countryside — some of it protected by subsidy against mechanised farming as well. This would be a logical extension outwards of what the Green Belt has already so astonishingly achieved: the existence of wedges of greenery, far into the outskirts of London, of relatively unspoilt villages and farms along relatively remote hedge-lined lanes — Buckland and Betchworth west of Redhill, Wisley and Pyrford east of Woking, Dorney on the Thames near Slough. Immediately out of the large suburban shopping centre of Bromley are the unspoilt downland villages of Knockholt, Cudham and Downe. The only blots are the throw-ups of the thirties such as Biggin Hill and Pratts Bottom, where speculators threw up shanties on unadopted roads in the confident expectation of the civic amenities which Green Belt preservation is now helping to keep out; in such places some new building is indeed justifiable, if only to clear up some of the decidedly ungreen waste land.

So the Metropolitan Green Belt has on the whole held tight and now provides a wonderful recreational opportunity for the Londoners who were supposed to have 'levelled off' in population within it. But the trouble is that, given the inadequate progress of the New and Expanded Towns in siphoning off the expansion of the capital, the other three-quarters of that recent exodus has had to go somewhere else — to wherever in the villages beyond the Green Belt people could find cheap houses to buy. The result, all too clear on the one-inch map of the Metropolitan area, is that the saucer shape of the Green Belt boundary has acquired a filthy dirty rim of housing estates erupting ad hoc in the fields around expanding villages just beyond the limit of the Green Belt restrictions. Places like Yateley in Hampshire, Crowthorne and Winnersh in Berkshire, Hildenborough in Kent, Tiptree in Essex and Hassocks in Sussex look as though they had been given a designation the opposite of 'conservation area' — 'disaster area', perhaps. Some county planning officers have artfully disguised their lamentable unpreparedness by talking about 'areas of opportunity', which is a euphemistic way of saying the same thing — not so much 'no-go' areas as 'let-'em-all-come' areas.

It was precisely to try to encourage better standards of design in such places that in 1964 Richard Crossman stuck his neck out and gave permission on appeal to the new village of New Ash Green which Span and Eric Lyons had planned for a site in Kent, just within the proposed extension of the Metropolitan Green Belt and close to the 'disaster' villages of Hartley and Longfield. Not that the local authorities had ever objected to village expansions of that deplorable kind, in the way that they howled outrage at Span. As blood money for their permission Span went on to spend £25,000 on research at the University of Kent under Ray Pahl on the whole question of villages in Kent: and the conclusion which stared them in the face was that the vast majority of the immigrants from London had not selected their new homes for any idealistic love of birds and flowers or village life, but purely and simply on price. This is specially so because the failure to siphon off sufficient growth into New Towns has led to a drastic increase of land prices and house prices within London itself — hence the dilemma of the young couple on whether to go on pouring their money down the drain of rising rentals conveniently close to their work or whether to invest their savings in some remote rural semi-detached with the burden of steeply rising rail fares or long-distance car commuting attached.

Rural district councils with delegated planning powers have felt powerless to prevent farmers selling off plots for development to builders — farmers and builders not infrequently being councillors themselves — and even the more idealistically preservation-minded planning committees have frequently made matters far worse for themselves by trying to make the new houses more 'in character' by insisting on lower densities. It is this which has been the real 'sprawl'. By building at 20 to the acre rather than 50, the gross increase in land take may be proportionately only as great as it is when 50 is preferred to 125; but the effect on the environment is incomparably worse, as bungalows at such low densities are still normally built to the edict of local officials on the same broad road widths as in the towns, with standard pavements and a standard 70ft gap between frontages — all this despite Unwin's victory for narrow cul-de-sac driveways at Hampstead 66 years ago. The resulting rural environment is not the bosky Arcadia of 'roads unadopted' and 'woodlanded ways' which delighted Betjeman in outer Camberley, but blue tarmac and concrete lamp-posts everywhere. Yet the traditional built-up character of village streets, as everyone from Unwin to Gibberd to Lyons has emphasised, is in fact traditionally a quite dense type of development (50—70 to the acre) with continuously built-up terrace houses and connecting walls. In spite of this, Governments who have presided over the destruction of so many village environments by the adoption of unrealistically low densities have been equally quick to recommend that people left in Central London should be rehoused at the unrealistically high densities of 136 to the acre or more.

There has certainly been a deplorable lack of leadership by the Government to local authorities on appropriate forms of village conservation. Buckinghamshire, with Fred Pooley as architect/planner and Ralph Verney as chairman of the planning committee, was for long a lone pioneer in preparing village plans

169

and also in promoting the idea of the new city which became Milton Keynes, as a means of relieving pressure on the rest of the county. But the really major failure of the Government, from the time that building licences came off in 1954, has lain in its total lack of firmness in relocating the main employers, particularly of white-collar workers, away from Central London and towards the New and Expanding Towns. Only in 1963 was the Location of Offices Bureau set up as an advisory service, followed a year later by the Labour Government's total ban on more offices in London, unless the developer had an exceptional case.

Faced with such restrictions, every big bank and insurance company and finance house has insisted the country's economic future will go to the dogs unless all their staff without exception are accommodated on the doorstep of the Bank of England and the Stock Exchange. It is indeed obvious that the directors and strategic staff of such businesses do have to be as far as possible within walking distance of each other; I remember Vincent Ponte, the co-ordinating planner of the new city centre of Montreal and now of Houston, pointing out to me that, in spite of all the marvels of telecommunication, the actual size of the business cores of metropolitan cities has remained totally unchanged from the Middle Ages, being based on the distance of the ten-minute walk. This is because business 'confidence' still depends upon two men being able at the drop of a hat to lay aside the telephone, walk across to each other, and bargain eyebrow-to-eyebrow across the table. But this does not mean that every uttermost clerk and typist has to bill and coo across the same table too. In the fast-growing suburban business centre of Croydon the high tower at the south end of the new Whitgift Centre shopping precinct is called Rothschild House, and it accommodates about three-quarters of the staff of the famous merchant bank, the other quarter naturally remaining where they have always been, at New Square just round the corner from the Bank of England. Surely the Government should be able to assert that what is good enough for Rothschild's should be good enough for the City in general. As it is, although the Conservatives since 1970 have maintained the machinery of the office ban in terms of Office Development Permits, they have been tempted to make more and more exceptions, permitting for example the grandiose Seifert-designed 600 ft skyscraper for the National Westminster Bank's headquarters in Bishopsgate, and even offering an outrageous 832,000 square feet for the Piccadilly Circus scheme which Westminster City Council has since been forced by public opinion to drop.

The danger is that the inner-city authorities take fright at loss of rateable value from decentralisation; the GLC itself came forward in 1971 with a scandalous proposal to permit nearly twice as much new office space in Greater London in the next five years (29 million square feet, most of it in the traditional centre) as in the past five years (16 million, much of it the result of pre-1964 planning permissions and thus unaffected by the office ban). Yet the GLC were suggesting this just at the moment when at last the decentralisation policies pursued ever since Abercrombie seemed about to bite. The first effect of the office ban had admittedly been to stimulate new office rentals but, as more and more businesses decided to move out, the rentals in 1971 began to show the first unmistakable signs of levelling out around £10 per square foot — the revamped Cunard building in Leadenhall Street was actually offered at £8. One can understand the GLC's reluctance to be faced with maintaining the same nineteenth century network of main roads and sewers on a diminishing income, yet this is where the lesson of Rothschild's is so significant, in that the mighty new complex of office blocks in Croydon — as many built there in the last ten years as in the centre of Birmingham — is still within the Greater London boundary and is thus economically no loss to the metropolis. Socially such decentralisation to the suburbs has involved nothing but gain, bringing people's work-life into a closer dramatic unity with their home-life, while at the same time spreading more evenly the load of commuting on the transport system — and above all, involving the minimal uprooting of traditional communities.

But the mad rush to villages beyond the Green Belt will assuredly continue until there is more positive discrimination in favour of the inner-city areas. It was the Plowden Report on primary education in 1968 that first drew to public notice the blindingly obvious fact (muttered about darkly for years by Professor Titmuss and his colleagues at the London School of Economics) that the majority of public investment since the war had gone not to the old deprived areas of the city centres but to the new well-built estates of the outskirts. The New Towns and new estates had been given the majority of the new schools, new hospitals, new roads, new sewers, new playing fields — purely as a pragmatic response by Government to an expanding population — whereas the older areas of declining population were left to sweat it out in whatever they happened to have inherited. In this way the Welfare State actually discriminated in favour of the middle classes. The Educational Priority Areas, the Urban Aid Programme and the Home Office's Community Development Projects are the first faltering steps in the reverse direction — although Mrs Thatcher's much-proclaimed assault on the older primary schools has turned out disappointingly to be little more than a book-keeping exercise involving parallel cutbacks in the programme for secondary schools, and her policy of nursery-schools-on-demand seems once again guaranteed to do best by the articulate and demanding middle classes. No one has yet dared to suggest that the correct price in priorities to pay for a really whole-hearted rehabilitation of all the inner-city schools might be that some of the new schools in the more affluent suburbs would have to start off in temporary buildings until there was money available to build them properly.

The legalising of unfairness between the inner and outer areas owes a great deal to the rigid 'zoning bands' of density in Abercrombie's County of London Plan and its official successor, the LCC

Development Plan confirmed in 1952. To be fair to Abercrombie, he did recognise the diffuse character of London's growth as a federation of villages, at least in terms of the medieval villages which gave their names to the smaller pre-1965 Metropolitan Boroughs — village cores such as Hampstead or Islington or Paddington Green; but he had no such sensitivity towards the late Victorian villages of the 'monotonous sprawl' type which often paradoxically have a less shifting and more deeply rooted local community. The great mass of London suburbs was classified in the Development Plan into a rigid series of concentric zones with arbitrary boundaries, each of a different density and slowly stepping down from 136 to the acre (with occasional pockets of 200) at the centre, via 100 in the inner suburbs, to 70 in the outer and then 50 on the edge.

Why were these rings of density laid down? When all is said and done, they were nothing more than a pragmatic rationalisation of the desire to be 'realistic' about 'overspill' — the desire not to build in the inner areas at densities which meant too great a displacement of the existing population. (It is interesting, however, that in Stepney, which has since been redeveloped throughout at an absolutely uniform 136, the displacement by the blitz had already pulled the population down from 299,000 in 1931 to 97,000 in 1951, so the opportunity to adopt a lower density was there ready-made.) But the much more sinister implication of the zoning bands was that, by protecting the lower densities of the outer suburbs, they cemented the class distinctions between inner and outer areas for another hundred years — in Lewisham, for example, council tenants in Deptford were herded together at 100 and 136, while those lucky enough to be offered accommodation in Blackheath or Sydenham found themselves at a more spacious 70.

To be fair again to Abercrombie, he did not himself intend his zoned densities to be as rigid in practice as they were later interpreted to be. As a garden suburb graduate himself (Dormanstown at Middlesbrough) he preferred a *maximum* density of 100 persons per acre with half the families in houses-on-the-ground and another 15 per cent or more in ground-floor flats and maisonettes — very similar in fact to the *average* of 80 to the acre, with variations upwards to 110 and downwards to 50 which I am advocating in this book. But unfortunately 'realism' on the part of the LCC forced the adoption instead of a maximum of 136 to the acre, with only one third of the families in houses; further 'realism' made the inner boroughs in the 136 zone adopt that figure of 136 as minimum as well as maximum, regardless of site conditions; and supreme 'realism' succeeded in virtually eliminating houses-with-gardens altogether. In 1952 the Central Housing Advisory Committee's sub-committee on flats reported the appalling statistics that between 1945 and 1951 the LCC had built 13,012 flats and only 81 houses, while 15 of the 28 Metropolitan Boroughs had built nothing whatever but flats. These were certainly the blackest years of postwar housing design, with cut-price variants on the prewar five-storey walk-up brick tenement erected indiscriminately in the blitzed areas under the LCC Valuer and scores of borough engineers, but rarely under an architect. In Central Glasgow in fact, simply because the existing densities and hence the overspill problem were more than half as great to the acre as those of Central London, the standard minimum/maximum density adopted for comprehensive redevelopment areas was not 136 but 170.

In the early fifties, when 'modern' architects took control in all the major cities, although the password visually was 'mixed development', the density zoning was maintained rigidly. The mixture was seen at its most varied and refined at Roehampton: high towers and slabs of flats on the Corbusian model, 'releasing space on the ground', intermingled with four-storey terraces of maisonettes, two-storey terraces of individual houses, and even single-storey bungalows as well. But behind the varied and even picturesque silhouettes, thinking was brutally Benthamite, in that, within tight restraints of high density, the different types of building were used to segregate different types of family: the childless and the middle-aged in the tall blocks, the young families with children in the maisonettes, the big families in the houses, the elderly in the bungalows — each category marked off by broad swathes of grassland. In effect one could see, set out architecturally, a kind of built diagram of the housing manager's filing cabinet, with each particular size of family neatly classified under the same heading. It was a far cry from the easy mixing of different ages and sizes (and classes) which is characteristic of traditional communities; and in grouping the larger families all together, the housing manager automatically created severe problems of 'child density' of the kind identified on a typical mixed development estate in Liverpool by Shankland, Cox & Associates in their survey of Childwall Valley (1968). There the social problems of the estate were concentrated on one particular area which, just because the small families had all been extracted off into the tower blocks, had a 'child density' of larger families equivalent to 130 or 140 — the outward and visible signs being vandalised fences, graffiti-covered walls and grassed areas worn back to dust and mud. In my own ward at Lewisham there is a superficially attractive example of 'mixed development' where, after segregating the families of different sizes, the GLC proceeded to place the large houses with many children in a continuous line across the end of the three blocks of old people's flats; there is continuous friction as a result and little fences have had to be built across the open landscaping to protect the privacy of the old people's windows.

Mixed development theoretically provided the best of all worlds; all too often it teetered towards the worst. In 1943 Abercrombie was tentatively suggesting that 'a certain number' of tall blocks up to ten storeys high 'might prove popular' for the single and the childless, the very people anyway who came bottom of everyone's list of priorities for rehousing; whereas by 1954 Archibald Jury was accepting that in Glasgow there would definitely have to be families with children in blocks of up to twenty storeys. By

1959 Pearl Jephcott found in her first survey of Glasgow high-rise flats that a third of the families in such blocks had children under sixteen. In 1961 J. P. Macey, when housing manager at Birmingham, was talking in terms of all the families with one and two children being housed in tall blocks at densities of 100—130, with lower maisonettes and houses only for the families larger than that; and a similar policy was adopted by the GLC after Macey moved there. No one ever bothered to consider why a child in a small family might be supposed to enjoy the experience of living high-up, if a child in a large family did not.

This worst of all worlds was given a spurious justification when the sociologically semi-sophisticated attempted, even within such artificially distorted surroundings, to provide for a 'natural balance' of family sizes. The Central Housing Advisory Committee report *Living in Flats*, for example, suggested that, since it was unnatural to house the single and the childless in separate blocks, it would be better to introduce families of different sizes, even in high blocks, so as to secure 'a better understanding of each other's problems and a consequent readiness to give neighbourly help when needed'. The sociologist Margaret Willis, in a talk to the RIBA in 1954, satisfied herself that families with young children could be housed on the lower floors of tall blocks where they might be more tolerant of the noise from children playing underneath than the childless households on the upper floors would be. It is admittedly true that some elderly and/or childless couples do enjoy having a 'room at the top': it would be wrong to deny the potential advantages in tall blocks of quietness (so long as traffic noise is not funnelled up, as it can be, from a wide area), cleanliness (so long as the rubbish chutes work), privacy (so long as it does not degenerate into loneliness) and panoramic views (so long as the weather keeps fine and the wind does not buffet too much). At the same time one must beware of some much-quoted survey material alleging the popularity of the high life: a survey of high-rise blocks commissioned by Wates from a market research firm asked tenants the question: 'Would you prefer to live higher or lower?' When the majority of those questioned answered 'Higher', the interviewers triumphantly reported it as indicating that people liked living in high blocks; when in fact those particular tenants were all living in high blocks already and must have interpreted the question in that light, the majority on the lower floors no doubt taking the attitude that 'If we *have* to live in a block of this kind, we might at least live high enough up to get such advantages as it has to offer in terms of privacy and views.'

The perennial problem of mass-produced architecture is its tendency to react from one rigid orthodoxy into the grasp of another rigid orthodoxy. When the severe social problems of high-rise flats began to become apparent in the late fifties — although the taxpayer continued to promote them by means of a special High Buildings Subsidy until 1968 — the first reaction was largely nostalgic and narrowly visual. The bittiness of 'mixed development' had exacerbated the break-up of the kind of rooted 'urban village' of working-class families which Michael Young and Peter Willmott described vividly in their book about Bethnal Green, *Family and Kinship in East London* (1957). Richard Hoggart's account of his upbringing in the Hunslet part of Leeds in *The Uses of Literacy* also drew attention abruptly to the lost intricacy of an environment which, however slummy, had consisted of houses-on-the-ground with their intricate appurtenances: 'To the insider these are small worlds, each as homogeneous and well defined as a village.... They know it in infinite detail, automatically slipping up a snicket here or through a shared lavatory block there; they know it as a group of tribal areas.'

These profound truths or half-truths about community life will be discussed in the next chapter; but the immediate effect of such writings upon architects and planners was dubious, in that Hoggart in particular struck a chord of nostalgic fellow-feeling in those like himself who had escaped from their working-class background via the grammar school and were now trying romantically to recreate it as New Brutalists. In the Avenham housing scheme at Preston (1961—2) James Stirling and James Gowan ruthlessly styled up a trio of conventional pitch-roofed terraces of flats in a grubby garment of hard red Accrington engineering bricks — what Banham rightly denounced as 'sentimental Hoggartry'. There was something inherently absurd in trying to force the affluent aircraft workers of Preston to return to the back-to-back style of environment of their cotton-spinning ancestors, particularly as real squalor was kept at bay by denying to the tenants any private open space at all and isolating the blocks in the usual cordon sanitaire of municipal mown lawn. Michael Neylan's competition-winning design of 1962 (completed 1968) for the hilltop cluster of Bishopsfield at Harlow also has dark brickwork and grimy alleyways of self-consciously 'hill-city' origin; it was this more than any other scheme that made fashionable the idea of 'high density low rise' (as against high rise). It certainly does have genuine virtues of family feeling in its secluded courtyard-gardens, each of them enclosed on two sides by an L-shaped bungalow, some of which have an optional 'granny-flat' attached for the mother-in-law, who has her own front door. It was the old people's bungalows at Roehampton which had first revived this prewar idea of L-shaped patio houses at high density, an ingenious device for maximising private space while minimising the waste of land on access; and it is houses of this type which Chermayeff and Alexander have championed in their book *Community and Privacy*. Edinburgh University's Architecture Research Unit used patio houses of this kind for their pilot project at Prestonpans of 1964—5; but there the limitations of the idea became clearly apparent, particularly the maze-like lack of orientation when too many houses are grouped together, flat-roofed and on a flat site, in contrast to Neylan's pantiled monopitches on a steep slope.

That this lesson had not been learnt is all too

apparent from the neighbourhood immediately below Neylan's at Harlow: Clarkhill, designed in 1966—8 by Peter Rich. He has written excellently of his aims in adopting a high density low-rise layout, in this case of 88 to the acre, talking of 'maximum contact with the ground for the maximum number of people, and all that this implies in terms of home entry conditions, private outdoor (usable) space, supervision of pram, toddler and child, the revalidation of the house.... and street.... this form of development fits well with our social and political traditions and aspirations in that it lends itself to the establishment of a humane balance between the requirements of the individual and the community as a whole.' It is a pity that Clarkhill is such a chillingly diagrammatic attempt to realise this apparently near-perfect aim: dense carpets of patio houses and long terraces of peripheral flats are executed on a rigid grid in an industrialised system of storey-height precast concrete panels. There is a staggeringly inhuman lack of balance between the *scale* of the individual and the *scale* of the community, the overall tone being set by the hard clattery concrete surfaces of paths as well as walls.

What may not be grasped so quickly by those who have not read the largely unpublished volumes of layout studies by the Government's Housing Development Group, is that tenants themselves, far from being Philistines, care more passionately about the appearance of their houses than about anything else in them. What is objectionable about Clarkhill is not merely the absurdity in human scale of constructing bungalows out of megaliths, but even more the terrible *greyness* of it all — all very subjective, I know, yet 'tenants' perception' of this kind is going to be absolutely crucial to the future design and management of low-cost homes in this country. Clarkhill, Bishopsfield, Prestonpans, and the Stirling & Gowan part of Avenham are all at densities of between 70 and 100 to the acre; in their different modishly assertive ways they prove that the reasonable density, with a majority of homes at ground level, which I have been advocating, is not in itself a panacea.

179

Not that tenant opinion is necessarily reactionary — quite the contrary: in the Group's tape-recorded interview with half-a-dozen housewives of Bethnal Green, when the ladies commented very freely on six alternative elevations of the proposed Granby Street estate which were shown them, the most traditional ('Swedish-Georgian') was found excessively solemn and barrack-like, although it was infinitely preferable to the modish neo-slum alternative in dark brick. What the wives actually went for — with instinctive commonsense in view of the greyness of our climate — was an elevation which was 'mainly white, with splashes of orange and purple' — it had lightness and brightness, they thought, with something of the Costa Brava about it. This tends to confirm my suspicion that the continuing popularity of the postwar prefabs — or those few of the 156,667 built under the 1944 Housing (Temporary Accommodation) Act that still survive — is not due merely to their convenience as bungalows with gardens but also has something to do with their sunny holiday-chalet cheeriness of appearance. It is remarkable to see how beautifully such prefabs are looked after by their tenants compared with permanent flats in the same locality (compare, for example, the prefabs in Westbourne Drive at Forest Hill, with the Pikethorne flats across the road, or those in Barlow Street at Walworth, with the dreaded Aylesbury estate round the corner).

What tenants will tend to reject with scorn (if given the chance to comment) will be both the gloomy neo-slum romanticism of the Stirling & Gowan or Neylan type and also the contrasting but equally gloomy technological rationalism of the Clarkhill kind. The most popular of all estates in Lewisham, according to the housing lettings section, is Maxwell Fry's Passfields estate of 1948—9 — certainly not a thatched-roof or Georgian fanlight image but a Corbusian box-frame, which is clad in warm golden bricks and brightly painted. Peter Shepheard has always stressed the importance of contrast against the greyness of English weather, and in Deptford it is interesting to contrast his plum-coloured Tanners Hill houses, with their brilliantly white window reveals,, with the equally plum-coloured GLC-designed Pepys estate, where the window details are all in dark-stained wood (dark heaped upon dark). It is a pity that most architects have a puritanical hatred of the bright colours and varied textures which flourished briefly at the time of the Festival of Britain; although such things do survive delightfully in the wilds of South Norfolk, where for twenty years Herbert Tayler and David Green have been building nicely variegated terrace houses around village greens for Loddon Rural District Council.

These questions of colour and texture have nothing to do with actual density, but they have a great deal to do with *perceived* density: brown and purple brick and dark-stained wood *appear* more massive and intrusive than pink brick and tubular steel porches — and therefore, inasmuch as what we perceive is truly a higher reality, so one estate at 80 to the acre can be positively denser than another estate at 80 to the acre. It was, as we have seen, the thickets of semi-mature trees that made the tenants' response to the Winstanley estate in Battersea so much more favourable than to other 136-to-the-acre estates surveyed by the Housing Development Group.

But if one cautionary qualification on low-rise houses relates to perception, the other relates to deception — the attempt by so many housing authorities to kid themselves and their public that they have been converted to building low-rise when in fact they are building consistently at four, five, six or seven storeys. This kind of building, known in Government circles as 'medium-rise', means back-to-the-courtyard: and it means as many as three-quarters of the homes being consigned to an upper level — not very far off the ground, it is true, but far enough not to enjoy the human relationships, as between mothers and children and neighbours, which flow from being on it. The Childwall Valley Study was emphatic about the unhappiness of families living on the upper level of four-storey maisonettes, with their ambiguous reversal of front and back in having the access balcony at the rear, and with their tantalising allotment gardens just out of reach. The Government's study of *Families Living at High Density*, which reported 71 per cent of the families in multi-storey blocks as wishing to move down to ground level, also found that just over 50 per cent of those on the upper level of four-storey blocks wanted to move down too.

The pioneering design in 'medium-rise', Brutalist modern as against neo-Georgian, was John Darbourne's competition-winner of 1961 for Lillington Street (off Vauxhall Bridge Road) in Westminster, designed for 215 bed spaces per acre — a planning density of nearly 200. The first part of it, completed in 1968, has a jagged brown-brick profile, between four storeys and eight storeys high, which has an interesting relationship with G. E. Street's St James-the-Less Church; it also, by means of rather costly variations in section, succeeds in accommodating a full range of sizes of dwelling and ages of family in each block. But only a small fraction of the homes (4.4 per cent) are at ground level, although it would have been possible for as many as 26 per cent to have had this advantage, had it not been decided instead to go for the cavernously architectural feature of brick cloisters. In the redesigned Lillington 2, completed in 1972, Darbourne & Darke have developed a much tighter arrangement, in which a four-storey block has a pair of cross-over or back-to-back maisonettes on the first two levels, each having access to a garden on one side only; over the top a secluded central 'street', open to the sky, is flanked by the front doors of smaller maisonettes on each side. By those means, still at nearly 200 to the acre, as many as 60 per cent of the homes succeed in being at ground level, and the remainder have private thresholds at the upper level. It is a brilliantly ingenious solution, yet so much more so on paper than in reality, where the excessive density is apparent to both ear and eye. Lillington Street gives rise at an extreme to the criticism Shankland, Cox & Associates met when surveying Wates estates: 'There's too much brick about.'

This is even so at the Bonamy estate in Southwark,

which was in its time (1965—8) a remarkably clever demonstration that at 136 to the acre (173 bed spaces) it was quite unnecessary to go above four storeys. The families with children there, even the largest, were located rather strangely at the upper level, thus keeping the elderly and the childless on the ground, but these upper maisonettes were then provided with living-room-sized roof terraces, bedecked with flowers (as referred to earlier). All the same, however admirable the Bonamy's restrained vernacular detailing and its straightforward arrangement of car parking in two great flanking galleries at semi-basement level, it is still very dense, even claustrophobic, and thus to some extent it deserved the strictures of the Ministry of Housing's former chief planner, Professor J. R. James, who saw it only as a Charybdis to the tower block's Scylla; 'Either he [the designer] must build high and relatively expensive buildings in which mothers are likely to be unhappy and children not to get the kind of environment they really need, or on the other hand [as at Bonamy] he may, by racking his brains and producing a complex design which avoids this defect for people, run into all kinds of difficulties and incur even greater expense trying to cope with them.'

James recommended architects to study the principles of 'peripheral layout' which had been developed at Cambridge University by Sir Leslie Martin and Lionel March. Martin with his clear geometrical mind had created for the Caius College hostel of Harvey Court a kind of inverted ziggurat, brilliantly concise on plan but once again overwhelmingly dense to the eye; assisted by the mathematically trained March, he has demonstrated how the wrapping of buildings in a continuous band around a series of spaces can dramatically reduce the amount of space wasted on car access and garaging. Two of Sir Leslie's former students, Richard MacCormac and David Lea, when working with Mike Kitchen and Peter Bell in the Merton Borough Architect's Department, designed a peripheral paragon in the Pollards Hill estate (1968—71), where at 110 to the acre every family is given a three-storey house with a garden and an integral garage, plus groups of three-storey old-people's flats on the awkward corners. It seems to set unarguably an absolute upper limit of 110 to the densities feasible for suburban housebuilding; and certainly one could not do more than a small area at such a high density, without running the risk of burying the environment under brick (or in the case of Pollards Hill, the insensitively cerebral choice of white stove-enamelled steel sheeting).

Certainly Pollards Hill is much fairer and fuller in its satisfaction of family life than the Ministry of Housing Development Group's mixture of deck-access blocks and terrace houses at St Mary's, Oldham, where the sudden panic swing from 20 per cent car parking to 110 per cent has resulted in large areas being laid waste for parking and left unused. It is similarly excessive car provision which spoils the brave experiment of Burghley Road, Camden (by John Green of the borough architect's department) where the ground-level environment is dominated by yawning concrete parking bays; on the garage roofs, however, there are upper-level terrace houses which not only have proper front doors and even little front patios off upper-level 'street-decks', but also proper back gardens supported over the ground-level houses' roofs. The other possibility at these densities around 100 is to develop the site with terrace houses of very narrow frontage and very deep plan, as at Milton Road, Haringey (E. F. Jacob, borough architect) and Field End Road, Hillingdon (Austin-Smith, Lord Partnership). In the Hillingdon case the extra insulation of so much party wall has made it possible to provide whole-house central heating (not just living rooms only, which is the limit of Government insistence). But tenants generally dislike these narrow and deep plans, as to obtain sufficient natural lighting into the centre of the house an open-plan living room is usually necessary, with all the inflexibility of handling young children which that means.

On the whole, for all but the special sites and for
184 all but the most exceptional architects, we will be

investing our money sensibly as ratepayers, in terms of the future value of the houses we build, if we keep the density generally down to 80. Estates of this kind, such as John Stedman's Lincoln estate at Corby or the GLC's at Andover and Thetford have been triumphantly re-establishing in modern terms the egalitarian cottage ideal of Parker & Unwin. My own borough of Lewisham has been a late starter in this field — content for far too long to spawn four-storey maisonettes without gardens in the 70 zones — but there is a leafy Victorian avenue called Lee Park where, quite apart from a handsomely rehabilitated crescent of Italianate villas, there is now a substantial stretch where it is impossible at first sight to distinguish the private owner-occupier houses on one side of the road from the council houses on the other side. Neither lot of 70-to-the-acre terraces is first-rate architecture, but both succeed in partaking pleasantly in the vocabulary of crosswall-and-white-weatherboarding which is part of the first widely acceptable builders' vernacular since the turn of the century. The architect who has done more than any other to create it is Eric Lyons, with his Span estates; and, had the GLC not treacherously withdrawn at working drawing stage, it would have been at his hands, at his 'new village' of New Ash Green, that we would have been able now to enjoy the spectacle of owner-occupied and council-tenanted houses sitting side by side, identical in appearance externally even if marginally different inside, with more space in the council houses, but better finishes and fittings in the private ones.

In view of the quite extraordinary divergences in design between the estates of flats at the same density of 136 which the Housing Development Group have analysed — anything from all four storeys to all twenty-four storeys, from two-thirds open tarmac to two-thirds private garden — I have no fear that the adoption of a fairly standard density around 80 to the acre will lead to soulless monotony. We need simply to abolish all density bands and tell our architects that they can design as far in density on either

side of 80 to the acre as seems appropriate to the
brief and to the site. In effect the community and its
political representatives have to weigh up as carefully
as they can the right balance between, on the one
hand, the fair distribution of advantages in the different neighbourhoods and, on the other hand, the
cherishing of the identity and individuality of the
special communities, the urban villages, across which
and around which the municipal boundaries run so
arbitrarily. It is with these urban villages and their
self-government that this book must conclude.

The village street at 80 to the acre, with its paths and yards and comfortable
roofs, is convincingly revived in John Stedman's Lincoln estate at Corby New
Town. (Bill Toomey, Architects' Journal)

6

The Urban Village

But is this home-centred existence in the house-on-the-ground that I have been advocating — the cultivation of the front garden gnome and the back garden trellis, the easy arrangement of comfortable furniture in the lounge round the telly — is all this being bought, as many architects and planners and politicians seem to fear that it is, at the expense of the warmer human relationships of traditional communities? Michael Young and Peter Willmott made an apparently telling comparison between the 'Family and Kinship' of the densely packed East London borough of Bethnal Green and the disorienting experiences suffered by those Bethnal Greeners who had emigrated from it after the last war to the new out-of-town LCC estate of Debden (dubbed 'Greenleigh' in the book). They were suggesting, though perhaps from a narrow and romantic viewpoint, that the semi-detached existence of the suburban estate was almost wholly to be deplored socially as a disintegration of the cohesive values of previous generations, particularly in separating daughters from mothers and thus breaking up the 'network of kinship' upon which life in Bethnal Green depended.

Young and Willmott had the honesty to admit that the Greenleigh homes, at least as homes, were immeasurably superior to those left behind in Bethnal Green: 'Who can wonder', they asked, 'that people crowded into one or two poky rooms, carrying water up three flights of stairs, sharing a w.c. with other families, fighting against damp and grime and poor sanitation, should feel their hearts lift at the thought of a sparkling new house with a garden?' — and yet, even in the quizzical tone in which they asked that question one could begin to detect their own personal devaluation of the benefits of such a transformation. Throughout their fifty pages on Greenleigh there was in fact a constantly reiterated implication — accompanied by all the conventionally snide remarks about 'keeping up with the Joneses' and the 'status symbolism' of acquiring possessions — that there was somehow something rather wicked in so many of its inhabitants being individually house-proud, the implicit judgement being that they should not have bought so many more television sets and motor cars than their counterparts in Bethnal Green and that conversely they should not have attended so many fewer public houses and cinemas.

I believe we have got to be very careful indeed before assuming that a home-centred existence — 'keeping themselves to themselves' is the Young and Wilmott chapter heading, again meant pejoratively — is in itself necessarily socially destructive and that the close relationships of the traditional community of the Bethnal Green type are necessarily more desirable. There is just one sentence in which the authors allow themselves to admit that 'This moral code which surrounds kinship [in Bethnal Green's close-knit 'extended families'] is sometimes harsh, imprisoning the human spirit and stunting growth and self-expression'; but that is only a pause for breath before they launch off on the following page into a lyrical concluding coda about 'the dutiful parent [in Bethnal Green] not discarding the child born mentally defective' and 'the mother [who] does not inquire whether she will be repaid before she does the washing for her sick daughter' — all this without a murmur, without even the barest of statistics, about the number of children in Bethnal Green at that time who were 'in care' or 'on probation' or just simply beginning the process of 'dropping out' from the rigidly traditional working-class mores of their parents which had become intolerable for them. Rosy impressions about romantic 'low life' à la Mayhew are particularly tempting for middle-class sociologists who themselves have no qualms about living a home-centred 'nuclear' existence up in Hampstead or Dulwich. I know that Willmott himself was absolutely consistent: he actually did live in Bethnal Green and sent his children to a local primary school; but that has not stopped many of his sociological-architectural disciples from applauding enthusiastically at a distance a gritty working-class togetherness that they would not be seen dead living in themselves.

188 Even for Young and Wilmott their fascination

with the dominant Mum led them to describe a kind of 'family and kinship' in which teenagers, then on the brink of 'Rock and Roll', barely seemed to exist at all; and so obsessed were they in stressing the undoubted dominance in Bethnal Green of the mother-and-daughter relationship that they quite failed to give reasonable value at Greenleigh to the new role in the home of the husband, gradually emerging as he was from the shadows of his previous refuges at pubs and dogs to a more domestic concern with saucepans and nappies (as in that 1970 'Daddy National' advert of husbandly nappy-changing).

What shows up more than anything else the phoneyness of Young and Willmott's picture of Greenleigh is their attempt to demonstrate that wives who fell ill there fared so disastrously worse than they would have done had they stayed back in Bethnal Green: 'At Greenleigh there was, of course, less help from relatives. Of the twenty-four Bethnal Green wives who had been ill, twelve had been helped during their sickness by relatives, eight of them by their mothers; but of the twenty-two wives at Greenleigh who had been ill since going there, only four had help from relatives, two from their mothers.' So what about the other seventeen who fell sick at Greenleigh? The answer is that 'Four people.... had help from neighbours, six from husbands.' So the poor old husband is not in Young and Willmott's terms regarded as a 'relative'! Count him in as one, and you find that the figures for charitable relatives are twelve out of twenty-four at Bethnal Green and ten out of twenty-one at Greenleigh, not a statistically significant difference. It is interesting too that in Young and Willmott's table on 'Care of Children at Last Confinement', husbands and children are put into the same classification as 'neighbours', rather than included amongst 'relatives'. There may be some arcane sociological justification for this, but it seems to me to consort ill with Young and Willmott's remarks in their first chapter, (particularly perceptive for 1957) about the gradually changing roles of the sexes and the ever-increasing participation in the home of the husband, who had figured so largely in the Victorian and Edwardian 'social problem' literature of Booth and Bosanquet as an absentee wastrel.

The point is that in 1972 we have got to rethink very carefully what we do now mean by such words as 'community' or 'relative' or 'neighbour' or, for that matter 'husband' or 'wife'. I am not necessarily defending the Greenleighs of the municipal world: vast unified estates built at one instant flick of the administrative switch have clearly lacked the very indefiniteness of extent and uncertainty of evolution which in the traditional slow-growth suburb, with its elaborately overlapping social networks built over three or four generations, have been proving to be so much more expressive of the potential richness and variety of modern life. It is unfortunate that it is only the apparently finite settlements at either extreme, the overcrowded Bethnal Greens on the one hand and the sprawling Greenleighs on the other, that have so far captured the imagination of the social analysts sufficiently for detailed surveys about them to be written up — no doubt partly because they seem to conform so closely to the imperatives traditionally contained in that awkward word 'community'.

What we as planners and politicians desperately lack are the equivalent studies of the so much less finite suburban villages where most people actually live: the Penges and the Yardleys, the Moss Sides and the Chapel Allertons, the Longbentons and the Mossley Hills. What we surely need to know is the extent to which these typically mixed and multifarious Victorian and Edwardian suburbs of ordinary terrace houses with gardens are themselves capable, not perhaps of becoming 'communities', but at least of giving their inhabitants a satisfying and meaningful 'sense of identity'. I prefer on the whole to settle for the phrase 'sense of identity' rather than the higher emotional and moral intensity of the word 'community' (as in Ruth Glass's definition below). When G. A. Hillery back in 1955 studied no less than ninety-four different definitions of the word 'community', all he could report back was that 'beyond the concept that people are involved in community, there is no complete agreement as to the nature of community'.

That does not stop the word from having a seductive note of neatness and uplift, particularly for public schoolboys who have been uprooted from their families and reared on ideals of cloister and quad, and for certain ex-working class graduates, no less uprooted by the eighteen plus, who feel understandably nostalgic for 'the folks from whence they came' — the 'sentimental Hoggartry' we noted in Stirling and Gowan's hard red-brick terraces at Preston in the previous chapter. But I suspect that the over-concentration by sociologists on closed communities has been more than a little provoked by the anthropologists: just as G. K. Chesterton's rolling English high road went to Brighton Pier by way of John o' Groats, so the academic sociologist has found himself approaching the mysteries of family life in Bethnal Green via the huts of Samoa and Papua recorded by Mead and Malinowski. It is typical that as many as four of the first eight chapters of Ronald Frankenberg's book *Communities in Britain* are a précis of studies of remote country villages and he finds himself able to pause only long enough to report on studies of three small towns, also somewhat isolated, before plunging straight into the heart of the conurbations with Young and Willmott's guide to Bethnal Green. Nothing on the railway viaducts through suburban London or suburban Birmingham seems to have caught the eye of commuting sociologists as possible communities. Frankenberg himself admits that it is the uncommonness of Bethnal Green's homogeneity and isolation, socially and geographically, that has attracted sociologists to its corpse like flies: 'It has a rarity value. At least we think it does. We have not enough studies of other urban neighbourhoods to say how typical it is.'

All Mr Frankenberg could do to complete his Cook's tour of British communities was to take the commuter train out of Bethnal Green and into the countryside again, to half-a-dozen of those out-of-town council estates of the Greenleigh kind which are

191

equally exceptional in their homogeneity. In studying them the interviewing sociologist's primary interest has lain time and again in discovering what kind of 'communal facilities' the active minority of tenants' leaders might have succeeded in conjuring up, against the odds, out of the prevailing municipal 'monotony'. When Ruth Glass (then Ruth Durant) made her classic study of the LCC's Watling Estate in 1936—7, she specifically set herself the task of answering the question 'Has the new housing estate grown into a community?' by defining the nature of community as being 'a territorial group of people with a common mode of living striving for common objectives'; and with a definition as narrow-minded and dogmatic as that — common mode of living, common objectives — it is not surprising to find that she was pretty disappointed with what she found at Watling. The estate waited six years for its community centre, and when it did get it, it was in the wrong place and competed poorly with the rival facilities offered by the chapels.

It is true that the same grievances of centrelessness on the cottage estates can be heard today from an activist minority, which finds itself faced by an almost total apathy even over drastic rent increases. But the fact remains that on those estates the vast majority of the cottage gardens bloom; and at a time when local authorities are already scratching their heads as to how to rehabilitate the basic amenities of family life in the sky-high flats of the sixties — for which Ruth Glass herself, perhaps in revulsion from Watling, became one of the principal postwar propagandists — the prewar cottage estates of the Watling type, however superficially 'monotonous', continue to remain, by and large, extraordinarily contented places, as satisfying to grow old in as they are popular for younger tenants to move to (and, whatever my Labour colleagues may say, for them to buy their own houses in too). The one big problem, ironically in conflict with Ruth Glass's aims of a 'common mode of living' and 'common objectives', is that there has been just too much uniformity in terms of age group, with so many young families in 1930 become elderly in 1970, leading in turn to as much alienation amongst such minority groups as teenagers as there is in country villages where there is no particular place for them to go.

So we come back, in a state of genuine ignorance as far as the ordinary suburb is concerned, to this basic question of 'identity' or 'belonging' — the extent to which the home-centred nuclear family can have a feeling within itself that it belongs somewhere, in some definite place: unique people within a unique environment, with powers of real responsibility for ordering their own lives. As readers of this book will know by now, I profoundly disagree with all those superficial generalisations about 'monotonous suburban sprawl', which are made by those who pass aloft on railway viaducts on the way to country cottages; and just as the word 'community' has been used by sociologists in a highly subjective way about societies which are finite and remote, so I shall be equally subjective in defending what I call people's 'sense of identity' in societies which are open-ended and suburbanised. Even Frankenberg himself supports a subjectivist approach in defending his own choice of so many unrepresentative villages to describe as 'communities'. 'Firstly,' he says, 'there is a practical reason. Writers and politicians from Feargus O'Connor, the Chartist, to Chesterton and Belloc have sought to lead us back to the countryside. The desire for a semi-detached in its own garden, and the summer weekend trek out of the towns are part of the national stereotype of ourselves as longing to get back to the country life. What has been lost by urbanisation and what gained?'

Now this seems to me the right kind of question to ask, a question of values in fact — not just the objective measurable statistics about traffic and trade and disease and how many people make use of certain 'communal facilities' on certain days, but the fundamentally immeasurable, and therefore so much more human, impressions or fantasies or ideas which are tied up in people's minds into that 'national

G

stereotype' of a longing for country life. Frankenberg concludes his book with a simplistic double-entry tabulation of contrasting differences of community behaviour between one sort of people, headed 'RURAL' and another sort headed 'URBAN' — although even he has had a moment's quasi-suburban doubt about the latter and has inserted in small letters, after the word 'URBAN', the words 'less rural'. Now this begs the whole question which I am trying to ask in this book: what is the nature of that 'less rural', and for that matter 'less urban', kind of life, which lies somewhere between these two contrasting lists, where most of us in fact actually live, and prefer to live. In particular, what kind of restructuring of politics and planning should we people of these places demand? It is these questions which underlie my very tentative attempts in this last chapter to try to define something called an 'urban village' — even if that definition relates possibly more to what is in the mind than to what is on the ground.

The phrase 'urban village' has unfortunately been used previously to describe something much more finite: it was Professor Herbert Gans who used *The Urban Villagers* as the title of his book in 1962 on the close-knit community of immigrant Italians in Boston. Ray Pahl in 1965 identified as 'metropolitan villages' those previously agricultural settlements in Hertfordshire which have now been almost wholly taken over by commuters to London. As John Connell suggests in a recent paper on 'Urban Villages and Social Networks', the 'new villages' built by Span at New Ash Green and Cubitts at Bar Hill are of a similar kind — 'an experiment in late twentieth century living' as Span's advertisements put it. Other definitions we can put on one side include the 'industrial villages' of the nineteenth century — although we have noted earlier, from Owen at New Lanark to Unwin at Barrow Hill, that they were important links historically in the transition between the rural 'model village' and the planned 'garden suburb'. There is also the specially American phenomenon, recorded by the Chicago School of sociologists, years before Gans, of previously rural groups of ethnic immigrants who had established themselves as distinct social entities in an urban setting — their equivalents in England ranging from Huguenot weavers in Bethnal Green (1690) to Russian Jews in Whitechapel (1880) and to West Indians in Brixton and Pakistanis in Bradford (1970). Connell suggests that 'the recognition of "urban villages" has been largely a result of wishful thinking in an attempt to glamorise the situation of often deprived urban communities.'

More relevant to my theme, though sometimes less important than it thinks itself to be, is the intellectually glamorous 'urban village' of the Left Bank or Greenwich Village kind which in Britain has become the seedbed of protest by those who feel alienated from the norms of industrial society. The recurring emphasis in English literature, from Goldsmith's Sweet Auburn onwards, has been on the village as the ideal place to live; and it so happened that the philosophers who were to carry the voices of Rousseau and Wordsworth down from the lakes and the mountains, via the studio and common room, to the factory floor were themselves brought up in suburban villages which had so far kept their character: Ruskin's wine-merchant father moved the family out in 1825 to the leafy South London slopes of Herne Hill, while William Morris's bill-broker father purchased in 1840 a mansion at Wanstead on the edge of Epping Forest. Morris's famous letter about his early life to the Austrian socialist Andreas Scheu describes his birthplace, Walthamstow, as 'a suburban village on the edge of Epping Forest, and once a pleasant place enough, but now terribly cocknified and choked up by the jerry-builder.'

Most of the radical art movements in Ruskin's wake were clustered in those villages of London that did keep their character or even had it hotted up a little: Rossetti's and Whistler's sets in Chelsea, the Watts-Prinsep circle in Kensington, Alma-Tadema's friends in St John's Wood. Ford Madox Brown's superb painting, *An English Autumn Afternoon* (1852–4), depicting the panoramic back gardens of

Hampstead, perfectly epitomises the luxuriant arcadia, private and bosky, which as a setting for artistic experiment in England was so fundamentally different from the public pavement cafés of the *grands boulevards* of the Continent; though, in fact even in Paris much of the attraction of Montmartre lay in its peculiarity, to French eyes, of being a village within a city. The Impressionist painter Pissarro, as we have already noted, was thrilled by the quiet leafy atmosphere he found in 1870 in South London at what he called the 'charming suburb' of South Norwood: while his friend Monet was painting the Houses of Parliament, Pissarro was busy not only at South Norwood itself, with barge-boarded stucco villas and intricate gardens, but also at Penge Railway Station, and St Stephen's Sydenham Hill, and *La Route de Sydenham.*

For some of Morris's followers the pressures of uniformity in the Great Wen became just too much: they followed his own exodus to Kelmscott by setting up village colonies of artists at such places as Chipping Campden and Sapperton in the nearby Cotswolds, and Newlyn and Solva on the rocky coasts. The genius of Sir Raymond Unwin was that he took this Late Victorian 'vernacular' appeal of the artists' colony which was set amongst 'real' peasants and fishermen, and then united it in a most down-to-earth manner with the workaday demands of genuinely vernacular family life which he had met in the mining village — the synthesis of the 'garden suburb' which we have seen developing in full bloom in Chapter Two and blighted in Chapter Five. What was in fact lost in intensity on the cottage estates of the twenties, the Becontrees and the Watlings, was still being bottled up intellectually in the Bloomsbury of Roger Fry and the Bells; right through to the Kings Road pop culture of the last decade each successive radical and artistic circle has tended to identify itself with particular villages. In places such as Hampstead or Dulwich or Blackheath, the 'village atmosphere' — going 'down to the village' to shop or to have a drink — has undoubtedly become a reality of a kind

The surburban adventure of commuting from a railway village is captured in its infant freshness in Camille Pissarro's 1871 painting of Penge West Station. (Courtauld Institute of Art)

for those who enjoy it, even if it also has in certain lights an overtone of snobbery and preciosity.

The aspirations these exceptional villages incite have an enormous circulation through the Colour Supplements and the women's mags, and through the visual impressions puṭ about by Betjeman and Geoffrey Fletcher. I am much more interested in the mundane suburb, and by this I do not mean the kind of *nostalgie de la boue* — old-fashioned 'slumming it' — which is the reverse side of the coin of village preciosity and has made it rather fashionable to live beside the railway yards of Camden Town or at least attend entertainments at the Round House there. I am concerned on the contrary with the great majority of ordinary red-brick suburbs, which I happen to love and enjoy for their very ordinariness and comfiness. They are occupied not by artists or admen, but by present-day Mr Pooters: by minor civil servants, bank clerks, shopkeepers, insurance salesmen, skilled mechanics. The glamorous villages still continue to give a lead in suburban style and fashion, but it is about the ordinary mundane suburbs where the other ninety per cent of us live that we need to find out so much more before we put them at risk socially as well as visually. Hampstead and Blackheath can look after themselves — any proposal there for a motorway, or even for the felling of a tree, will bring out the big brigades of 'public participation' in a multitude of preservation and protection societies. When the same outrages have occurred in the ordinary places, the silent majority have tended all too often in the past merely to stay silent. Yet there have in the last five years been clear signs at every level of a fundamental change in public opinion from preservation of the special to conservation of the pleasant, paralleled by the political emergence, on the small-scale level of local identity, of an army of residents' associations and tenants' associations which now far outnumber the more narrowly architectural or amenity bodies under the wing of the Society for the Protection of Ancient Buildings or the Civic Trust.

But what kind of identity, what kind of neighbourliness, do people find in an ordinary forty-to-ninety-year-old suburb? It is the sheer remoteness from it of our political decision-making that I find worrying, in our big new local authorities. There is, I suppose, apart from national patriotism, a modicum of regional patriotism: there may not be much meaning in those pseudo-Cockney ballads about 'Maybe it's because I'm a Londoner' — and their Mancunian or Glaswegian equivalent — but certainly the fervour which erupts on the football terraces seems to indicate some kind of city-wide identification on a grand scale. But when we come to the bread-and-butter problems of local government, of houses and of schools, of roads and of parks, the pattern of representation imposed upon London in the Act of 1963 and upon the rest of the great conurbations in the Local Government Act of 1972 seems to bear no more relation, in terms of boundaries and responsibilities, to the people it is supposed to serve than do those arbitrary lines on the map of Africa, slicing across tribes, which the colonial conquerors left behind them as fixed national boundaries.

Not that one rejects the logic of the basic Maud Commission argument about larger units of local government — more professionally staffed, more corporately planned, more clearly directed towards strategic goals (by means of Planned Programme Budgeting Systems and all the rest of the managerial paraphernalia). They could even be directed politically by paid councillors (given far less than directors in civilian commerce of course, but nonetheless just sufficient to enable the recruitment of others besides the elderly and the mediocre). It would be fruitless to deny for certain levels of strategic planning a necessity for sub-regional or city-regional authorities; but it would be equally fruitless to deny the utter remoteness of the Greater London Council from the people it serves, and this acts as a dire warning for the new metropolitan authorities of 1973 too. Apart from the two local issues with which the GLC happen to deal, the cutting of new motorways across established 'urban villages' and the administration of large numbers of existing council housing estates, County Hall has become in London a totally remote place — a remoteness which makes it politically extremely unattractive to serve on.

Even the second-tier authorities, and some of those in the 1972 Act for the provinces are as large or even larger than those already established in London, are frighteningly remote: the sweeping influx of young councillors such as myself into the London boroughs in 1971 found they had suddenly from scratch to start making instant decisions affecting the lives of over 265,000 people, merely because they happened to be, in my case, within the unchanged boundaries of the medieval and Georgian parishes of Lewisham, Lee and St Paul's Deptford. Let no one confuse remoteness with indecisiveness: I was horrified to discover that on a planning sub-committee we would make fifty or more definite decisions affecting real people and their properties in barely a couple of hours. No one could say we were not being decisive, but how many members of the sub-committee who had received their agenda the previous Saturday morning had actually visited any of the sites under discussion, or were they simply taking the officers' recommendations on trust?

I suppose that when we councillors sit self-importantly in our spanking new civic suite dishing out these decisions, we do have a certain corporate sense of representing 'Lewisham'; but the utter spuriousness of this in real terms of local identity is shown merely by the fact that the council notepaper on which I am writing this sentence is headed 'Lewisham Town Hall, *Catford*, SE6 4RU' — that is to say, Lewisham Town Hall is not at Lewisham, but in fact at the traffic-torn hub of a very particular suburban village called Catford. The locals call it 'Catford Town Hall', just as in Lambeth, for similar reasons, they refer to 'Brixton Town Hall'. Where Lewisham, the real Lewisham, actually exists is a mile up the road: a big ugly shopping centre called Lewisham High Street, with the old village church at one end of it and the railway station at the other — and perhaps up to half-a-dozen residential streets on either side. It is only the 2,000 or so people who live in these streets who really have an identity with Lewisham — who, if you ask them, will say with any conviction 'I live in Lewisham'. It is a local loyalty which was tested to destruction in the spring of 1972 when 108 families were rehoused from four small streets to make way for a major extension to Lewisham shopping centre. Part of this loyalty was of course Young and Will-mott's 'network of kinship' — one clan based on a ninety-year-old lady and her four married daughters, a second clan on an eighty-three-year-old lady and her three daughters (one of them single). Several of them expressed an emphatic demand for the council to find them accommodation within those same dozen nearest streets that make up Lewisham and I had to harrass the housing department without mercy to make sure that this actually happened; but the interesting point in terms of Young and Willmott is that this sense of belonging was just as passionately felt by other folk who had no relatives left living in the area at all but had simply lived there for a long time themselves.

It is in doing detailed family casework with people like these that a second-tier authority of 265,000 people is peculiarly unsuitable. It has neither the strategic powers of the quasi-independent city region nor has it the truly human touch that a much more narrowly based parish council or neighbourhood council could offer. While Lewisham proper has only about 2,000 people actually resident within its identifiable 'village', the other 263,000 people in the borough are meanwhile making their homes in something like twenty-seven separate places, 'urban villages' like Grove Park and Brockley and Telegraph Hill and Ladywell, not all of them entirely within the borough and some, like Deptford and Blackheath and Downham, quite ludicrously divided by some arbitrary boundary line between us and the next-door boroughs of Greenwich or Bromley. Ask a Hither Green man where he lives, and he will not say 'Lewisham' — he will say 'Hither Green'. Ask a Deptford man whether he lives in Lewisham, and he may display active hostility towards you. (Many of the citizens of that historic borough — already a major shipbuilding town at the time of Pepys and Evelyn when Lewisham was a one-street village — have not yet after eight years forgiven the way they were forcibly 'taken over' by Lewisham under the 1963 Act.)

But what is the peculiar quality of Deptford for the Deptfordians, Hither Green for the Hither Greensmen and Grove Park for the Grove Parkers? — that is what I, as chairman of a planning committee, charged with the preparation over the next three years of a Borough Development Plan, desperately need to know.

Not that there is anything new about this idea of local loyalties to 'villages embedded in the town', as a group from the London School of Economics called them in evidence to the Royal Commission on Local Government in Greater London. Already in 1946, Ruth Glass and Maureen Frenkel had done a study of 'How they live in Bethnal Green', demonstrating clearly that the local people felt themselves divided into half-a-dozen distinct districts, even though five of them appeared at that time to the outsider to be almost identical in their ubiquitous two-storey terrace houses stretching away in all directions. Frankenberg comments that 'it is this differentiation, coupled with its "isolation", which, in my view, helps to keep Bethnal Green a community'. Certainly Glass and Frenkel were able, even in those days, to distinguish carefully between the differing prestige and reputation of these six suburban neighbourhoods of which it was made up — what Young and Willmott also, in a passing reference, called 'the villages of the borough'.

For example, the district of Bow was clearly marked out geographically from the rest of the borough by lying eastwards of the Regent's Canal: 'It is a highly respectable neighbourhood: the small houses are remarkably well kept, with gleaming windows, shining door knobs and whitened doorsteps' — not that that has stopped most of them from being bull-dozed since. Immediately across the canal by contrast was what Glass identified as the borough's 'black spot', rife with dilapidated houses, casual employment, and politically a breeding ground for prewar fascism; and yet northwards again, towards Victoria Park, was the much more respectable area largely owned by the Church Commissioners, 'the only one with middle class pretensions'.

Dyos has shown in his brilliant unfolding of the nineteenth century map of Camberwell how much these 'urban villages' depended upon chance for their foundation, upon a particular death or a particular bankruptcy releasing land for development. At the same time the rapid growth in transport carved up the map in strange diagonals of industrial growth along speculative canals and railway viaducts — the railway companies on occasions ruthlessly destroying existing 'villages' (such as Agar Town for St Pancras Station) by their policy of buying up the cheapest land for their developments. Dyos calculates that between 1859 and 1867 something like 37,000 Londoners were displaced by railway building, and a further 19,000 by 1886. The introduction of cheap workmen's tickets in the Cheap Trains Act of 1883 — a profoundly sensible Victorian commitment to public transport — set the seal on the far-spreading tentacles of the suburban dormitory.

It is remarkable how ruthlessly man-made physical barriers marked off neighbourhoods which nowadays to their inhabitants seem satisfying distinct, one from another. Admittedly development was extremely haphazard in its actual timing; in understanding the extent to which people do conceive of their neighbourhoods as 'villages embedded in a town', those of us born since 1939 tend to forget how intense a reality, and not merely a myth, the memory of the encircling farmland still is for our elders. Even in the centre of downtown Lewisham, between the back of the High Street shops and the railway embankment, 86-year-old Mrs Alice Abbey could remember clearly in 1972 how in the early nineties there were still green fields on the site of the house in Rhyme Road from which she was now being cleared out to make way for the new shopping precinct; she was born in Molesworth Street next door, on the edge of what was then to a significant extent outside London, a country village. Even the leader of our local Conservatives, Alderman Herbert Eames, tells me that he can remember, as late as the 1920s, how flocks of sheep were driven along the public highway to a slaughter house in Honor Oak Road, which now seems impossibly far into Inner London for such rural realities. The earlier volumes of Henry Williamson's autobiographical novel sequence, *A Chronicle of Ancient Sunlight*, set in Lewisham, sensitively describe this still-remembered rural mingling.

This much of this chapter I had written in draft, when, with the mingled thrill of jealousy and self-satisfaction one feels on such occasions, I discovered that almost all my views had already been set down by the political scientist William Hampton in his excellent study of local politics in Sheffield, *Community and Democracy* (1970), and also in the much more widely ranging national study commissioned by the Royal Commission on Local Government and published by them as *Research Study 9, Community Attitudes Survey: England*. Both Mr Hampton and the Government Social Survey team studied the extent to which people actually identify themselves with the place in which they live — the extent to which a village on the ground can be inferred from a village in the mind. They carefully avoided such emotive terms as 'community' or 'village' by referring interviewees simply to a thing called a 'home area'. From the replies the sociologists were then able to define three basic motives which people had for identifying with such an area: first of all, 'social attachment', meaning the networks of family and kinship (and length of residence) that Young and Willmott concentrated on; secondly, 'interest in local affairs' which bulks so large in studies of the Watling 'community facilities' kind; and thirdly, an interesting hybrid they entitled 'employment/convivialiity' — the point here being that the

Young and Willmott generation of interviewers, in

their understandable compassion for mothers and babies and grannies, paid scant attention to the accompanying men-folk and the vast proportion of their hours they spend with workmates and other mates, leading to a close sense of local identification not only with the places of employment, work bench and conveyor belt, but also with the pubs and clubs of after-hours. Brian Jackson's studies of Hudders-field, *Working Class Community* (1968), are excellent on such aspects as the brass band, the bowling green, the workmen's club and the finishing room in the mill. But we also need to be much more sensitive about providing for the less obvious and more mun-dane places of contact such as launderettes, corner shops, betting shops, prize bingo saloons, public con-veniences.

Hampton's crucial chapter is entitled 'Perceptions of Community'. It proves first that Sheffield does possess markedly the sub-regional patriotism of the football terraces — more strongly than almost any other major city in fact, because it is unusually iso-lated geographically and also unusually stable socially (very few immigrants, white or black). On the nar-rower definition of 'home area', two key questions were asked of the sample. First, could they say whether they had one and if so define it? Second, would they be sorry or not to leave it? In England as a whole (excluding Greater London) as many as 78 per cent of the people were able to 'conceptualise' a home area, and in Sheffield 85 per cent. Further-more, although the proportion naturally grew markedly accordingly to length of residence (94 per cent in England as a whole for those actually born in their area), the proportion of people resident in their present houses for less than five years — the kind who might on the face of it be expected to feel themselves footloose and rootless — who in fact could already 'conceptualise' themselves as forming part of a 'home area' was significantly as high as 68 per cent in England and 70 in Sheffield. Hampton, as we shall see, found in Sheffield that most people were able to give highly specific descriptions of the places they felt at home in; and similar local loyalties, no less passionately felt for being somewhat inarticulate, have been unearthed by Norman Dennis in Sunderland and by Jon Davies in Newcastle-upon-Tyne.

But significantly these local loyalties seem to vary very little in quantity or in quality from those found by Ray Pahl amidst the much more sophisticated commuter villages of Hertfordshire — or from those found by Professor Herbert Gans in his classic study of the social life of that apparent acme of American suburban 'monotony', *The Levittowners*. In fact, both in Sheffield and nationally, there was no correlation whatever between intensity of local loyalty and social class (a vital point for Ministers and councillors to remember, in that middle-class amenity societies tend to appear keener just because they are cleverer). The survey's second crucial question — about willingness or reluctance to move away from a home area — in fact produced its highest results in Sheffield in two totally different parliamentary constituencies: on the one hand the leafy middle-class Aves and Drives of Conservative Hallam, and on the other hand the allegedly 'monotonous' interwar council estates of Labour Brightside — just the sort of place, Brightside, which, like Watling or Becontree, has been consistently derided by community-minded sociologists since the thirties.

The trouble is that we, the politicians and planners and sociologists, have known so little in actual fact about the feelings of all those silent majorities in the suburbs where we live that we have put ourselves ever since the war at the mercy of perpetual shifts of over-emphasis based on inadequate data. A perpetual sociological-architectural by-election atmosphere has led us to vote for disastrously contradictory candidates of built form, in which ordinary families are then expected to live out their lives without complaint.

First we had the rigidly defined 'neighbourhood unit' in the New Towns of the forties, led off by the plan for Stevenage prepared under Professor Gordon Stephenson for the Ministry of Reconstruction its neatly segregated hierarchies of layout were based partly on such statistical parameters as the catchment area of a primary school but also on such technical points as the convenient size for a single building contract — with the introduction of industrialised building in the sixties, as we have seen, the smallest size of New Town estate suddenly shot up from 250 dwellings to 500 or 750, purely to satisfy the need for longer production runs. Sir Frederick Gibberd's plan for Harlow has always been the most consistently executed example of this 'neighbourhood unit' approach to community building, with its clear hierarchical pyramid of structures: first the 'housing group' of 200—250 houses, based on what Gibberd hoped would give a 'sense of place' (a different architect being employed for each group); then the 'neighbourhood' of two or three housing groups, centred on a primary school and a few small shops; then the 'cluster of neighbourhoods' with a population of 7,000 or so and a sizeable district shopping centre; and finally the 'town centre' for the full 80,000 population originally intended, with a market square and the major multiples, not to mention the commercial amusements that were so long in arriving.

In the hands of a man of Gibberd's sensitivity — particularly his response to local variety in landscape — such a hierarchy could be made to seem plausible; but in more doctrinaire minds there was an implicit attitude that, just because people at Becontree had been allowed to 'sprawl' so much that somehow they had not flocked to the meagre community centres provided, then at least in a New Town of the welfare state, the ungrateful so-and-sos could be forced into some kind of neighbourhood spirit simply by the neatness and clarity of a plan. What in fact happened, because the densities were fortunately kept down to 40—50 people to the acre, was that families stayed at home a good deal, cultivated their own gardens and began to watch television; and so architectural critics soon began to find endless rows of small postwar terrace houses just as boring as prewar cottages — as early as 1953 J. M. Richards was

207

slating the New Towns in the *Architectural Review* for their 'prairie planning'.

The pendulum therefore swung violently away from the greenways and copses of the out-of-town 'new town', and back to what was felt in Young and Willmott's book, as in so much social realist photography, to be an implicit cry of 'back to the slum', back to the gritty realities of kinship in downtown. Architects accordingly stressed what they felt to be the 'urbanity' of hard paved surfaces and densely packed dark brickwork, yet this was met head-on by the opposing centrifugal force of the motor-car. At high-rise Roehampton, where it had been assumed that barely ten per cent of tenants would ever need garages, visitors suddenly found their approach roads so blocked by parked vehicles that even the fire engines and ambulances could not fight their way through.

At this point, around 1965, professional schizophrenia ran amok. On the one hand there was the compulsively determinist belief which architects had inherited from Le Corbusier, that it was the shape of the structures they designed which was the primary influence on forming the personal and communal attitudes of people: one had only to build a 'neighbourhood unit' to create neighbourliness or to lay out a paved piazza to make everyone come out and start haggling for second-hand carpets beside pavement cafes. On the other hand there was first the panic-stricken practicality of coping with the car: acre after acre disappeared under blue tarmac as the edict went forth from Whitehall that 10 per cent parking should henceforth be 100 per cent — every single family, plus up to 50 per cent hard standings for visitors. The fact that the tenants refused to pay the extra rent for the garages, particularly the vandal-prone multi-storey car parks, and even grudged paying a few pence for a hardstanding with a lockable post, meant that the estate roads stayed just as blocked as before but that the environment around them had both hardened and disintegrated at the same time.

At this point the transatlantic breezes of urban

sociology wafted across a more subtle change of emphasis, diametrically opposed to 'urbanity' and even to 'neighbourhood units' too. This new theory was quite simply that the possession of the motor car meant that families could choose their friends from people living at any distance down the freeway — that in fact the old-style hugger-mugger sort of community was dying fast. The same Peter Willmott who in 1957 had preached the eternal verities of Family and Kinship, with Mum ever-present round the corner, was to be found in 1967 leading a discussion group at the RIBA's Brighton conference with a slogan on his lips of a very different kind: 'Community without Propinquity' — the title of a paper by the Californian Professor Melvin Webber, he who invented also that unlovely phrase 'the non-place urban realm' to describe the new kind of freebooting footloose friendship pattern without boundaries of the 'get-away people' in the car ads.

Architectural students in London meanwhile cast themselves under the spell of the mobile 'think-tanks' and 'fun palaces' of Cedric Price, and the more romantically ephemeral pop imagery of the kits and nodes put on sale in the form of comic-cut graphics through the magazine *Archigram*. The new heroes from history were the pioneers of the 'disposable' home such as Rudolph Schindler or Jean Prouvé or the inventors of the 'well-tempered environment' of air conditioning chronicled lyrically by Reyner Banham.

But how fickle is fashion; hardly had the multimedia dream worlds of rapid obsolescence been able to emerge outside the boundaries of the television studios with their insatiable demands for big-budget scenery (nothing new for architects in this anyway: Inigo Jones started off as court designer of masques) than the prophets of ecological doom consigned them all to the scrapheap — or rather tried to recycle them. The President of the RIBA, Alex Gordon, started a new campaign for buildings with Long-Life/Loose-Fit/Low Energy — just the kind of advantages, as he pointed out, that the brick Georgain terrace house had

had, with its infinitely amendable inside and back-side. It is indeed full circle back to the simple suburban cottage, with its gnome at the front, its vegetable garden at the back and (in my own case) its Moulton bicycle parked in the basement passage — full circle back to those earnest Fabian ladies who pedalled so furiously round the Edwardian garden suburbs. Even Le Corbusier after all designed a little garden suburb in the twenties for Monsieur Fruges's workers at Pessac near Bordeaux; and those who five years ago would have been shocked to the core by the philistine vandalism of its inhabitants, who have utterly transformed its white cubes with gay little awnings and shutters and porches and gables, were in fact last year just ready to begin to appreciate the justice of it all in the meticulously photographed account of its transfiguration written by Philippe Boudon. The point is that Pessac had been transformed from a set of white chess pieces by Corb (in one of his Bobby Fischer moods) into a living suburban place where each family had been able to make for itself its own little fragment of identity.

What Pessac teaches us is that, amidst all the shifting architectural-sociological fads and fancies about them, people remain surprisingly the same two-legged animals, responding much more emphatically to their own images of themselves and of each other than to any extraneous image forced down their throats in the name of 'community centre' or 'neighbourhood unit' or 'urban grain' or 'disposable kit' — or whatever else the current fantasy of planning ideology may prescribe. The Government Community Attitudes Survey emphasised in fact, as if it needed emphasising, that community feelings are primarily 'concerned with the interaction of the individual with other people — rather than with his relationship to his *physical* environment'; and it is true enough that in Sheffield, if interwar Brightside registered the highest 'community score', the equally interwar Park constituency registered the lowest — though one might add that it does include many flats (rather than cottages) as well as the famous high-rise estates of recent vintage at Park Hill and Hyde Park.

Even when Hodges and Smith were studying Park in the early fifties it was already an unpopular area — regarded in people's minds as 'rough' — and, as any housing manager will testify, one of the great mysteries of communal identity which the planning authorities urgently need to penetrate is exactly how in practical terms, the process gathers force of an area acquiring a 'rough' reputation and, conversely, how the vicious circle of deprivation can be reversed. Some estates start brightly and then mysteriously degenerate. Take Honor Oak in South London, a thousand dwellings in five-storey walk-up neo-Georgian flats set down in 1937—8 on the site of an orchard ringed round on three sides by railways and on the fourth by a cemetery: it was a fine estate at first, a credit to those who lived there, yet those who now live there find that they literally cannot get credit. After a mere thirty-four years, it is now having to be designated urgently as a General Improvement Area, in order to pick up the fifty per cent grants for 'environmental improvements' intended in the Housing Act primarily for terrace houses of 1880.

The irony is that, the more liberal an authority's housing policy is, the more difficult it is to break through the vicious spiral of social decay in such places: given that tenants can turn down 'offers' of accommodation that they do not wish to accept, Honor Oak inevitably tends to finish up with all the least discriminating tenants — the don't knows, the don't cares, and those who have already turned down three or four offers and feel they daren't turn down a fifth. In such a situation, it is not necessarily the 'obvious' environmental perceptions of middle-class professionals — traffic congestion, for instance, or an absence of trees — that reflect the real priorities of those who have to live amongst it all, day by day: at public meetings at Honor Oak more seems to have been said than on any other subject about dog shit. This is presumably because anyone's perceptions in such a situation tend naturally to become more and more focussed on the immediate foreground: what kind of muck do I find on my threshold, and why does the communal staircase reek?

All the same, Hampton found that only seven per cent of his sample restricted their sense of a home area to their immediate street only — not that the street (or, on new estates, the frequent absence of it) is not a vital part of anyone's sense of local identity. But nearly three-quarters of the Sheffield sample did extend their definition of 'home area' to several surrounding streets even if in a conurbation the area may not be particularly large and may not comprise anything like the whole of a geographical 'village' with a definite name. In an historic town of 10,000 people with a single market square and a single central parish church, the Government Survey naturally found a tendency to name the whole town as the 'home area', whereas within the major cities there is a psychologically understandable inclination for the individual to withdraw from the broad built-up mass into a group of half-a-dozen streets with a corner shop and a pub.

While accepting that it is 'the interaction of the individual with other people' that counts so much more in community attitudes than 'his relationship to his physical environment', it is notable how specific Hampton found most people were about the precise boundaries of each area: 'From Drummond Road, up to Sheffield Lane Top, then round to Lindsay Avenue shops, and back home' (this being a place called Parson Cross) or 'As far as Doves House at the top of the lane: down as far as Kitson's at the bottom of the lane: that's Whitley.'

Politically, Hampton points out that only one in five of his sample gave as their home area the name of their political ward; of the forty names most frequently given to home areas, only eleven were wards — although historically each name had a definite origin, as a hamlet or village absorbed from outside the built-up area or as an estate created with clear boundaries within it. Most politicians in conurbations know in their hearts that the areas they represent are meaningless in terms of local identity; it is a fortunate councillor who has a well-defined village or estate as his parish. In my own borough, with electoral rolls of between six and eleven thousand adults, there are the occasional well-defined wards, such as Bellingham, a prewar LCC estate between two railway lines; by contrast the geography of wards in Deptford is chaotic, with railway viaducts criss-crossing wantonly and extravagantly across what was once marshy meadowland, the cottage terraces (and now the high-rise flats) being slotted in between 'the arches' afterwards. My own ward of Ladywell (electoral roll of 10,761 in 1971) has at least eight geographically distinct areas which also have a high degree of social homogeneity within themselves, ranging from a group of 1870 slum cottages between railway embankments to an isolated 1964 LCC estate, also enclosed by a railway, in the backland behind a leasehold estate of some pretensions built in 1905.

Hampton reaches two contrasting conclusions: one that the very unreality of the wards as they are means that the creation of larger and more convenient administrative units of local government can at least politically be no worse than the present alienation between councillors and their public: on the other hand that, within the new super-authorities and even the over-large 'district authorities' on the second tier, we need to find ways of expressing and responding to the much smaller identity of the immediate 'home area'. He points to the relative success politically of one of his own research students, Geoffrey Green, who polled 773 votes in Walkley, an area which the city had been proposing to knock flat but where residents wished to retain and improve their own Victorian cottage homes. It was not enough to get him elected but it was enough to tip the political balance; more important, although himself an 'outsider' he was able to capitalise on local alienation by forming a residents' association called the Walkley Action Group, which subsequently was brought into direct negotiations with the city council about the improvement of the area. Similarly in my own borough Rodney Whitelock scored 597 votes in 1971, the highest by any independent candidate in the

London boroughs; a couple of years earlier he had formed the Grove Park Residents' Association, initially on the narrow but burning issue of opposition to the Ringway Two motorway — the one the GLC has now shelved. The tenants' and residents' associations, the community groups and action committees which are now at last changing political action for the better in the suburbs; and their rapidly increasing existence — and on many occasions, the need to stimulate their existence — is going to mean a radical change in the style and pattern of local government.

The fundamental problem which faces us is still that of basic democracy: whom do you represent? Who were the 777 people who voted for Mr Green or the 597 who voted for Mr Whitelock? What particular spectrum of society and opinion in Walkley and Grove Park did they represent? What kinds of loyalty breed in the suburbs?

The dramatic unities of Folk, Work and Place, as Sir Patrick Geddes saw them, have certainly tended to dissolve into patterns of ever-increasing commuting both to work and to shop; and the political solidarity of the London and Liverpool dockers or the St Helens glass-workers may in the end prove a losing wicket on which to fight. But it would be wrong to posit that kind of community, as Frankenberg tends to do, as an absolute criterion on which to base a swingeing condemnation of the new, more open, order of things: 'Separated from work and from play, from beer and from books, paved with good intentions, the social life of housing estates [the prewar cottage type] seems as far as it is possible to get from the utopian dreams of a village fellowship made urbane by town civilisation.'

Yet one could condemn just as vividly the claustrophobic uniformity of the old order — after all, why *have* the young people upped and gone from the old villages? Surely just because they want more work and more play, more beer and more books. J. H. Connell, who considers the phrase 'urban village' in the end worthy only of 'being consigned to the wastepaper basket of sociological jargon', points out

reasonably enough that 'in a locality which is entirely
residential only subsystems connected with family
and neighbouring can develop' — but why stress the
word 'only'? Are not family and neighbours important — even if workmates are scattered loosely down
the commuter lines? If the neighbours (wives as well
as husbands) are all doing different jobs in different
places, is it not just possible that this might enrich
their social intercourse with each other at evenings
and weekends rather than impoverish it? In fact the
very excitement of the Richmonds and the Black-
heaths, the Chelseas and the Hampsteads, with their
richness of leisure-time arts and entertainments and
'second jobs', has stemmed precisely from their cen-
turies-old absorption of the villas of Thames-side
commuters of all shapes and sizes.

Connell says scornfully: 'The middle-class urban
village is far from homogeneous and its culture is only
marginally distinct from the rest of the urban area. Its
focus is entirely spatial and its boundaries are subjective and indeterminate. It is a product of status symbolism and is not a real urban community. It may be
dismissed peremptorily.' How infuriating such richly
varied and elaborately active places must be to the
sociologist or planner who wants to keep his desk
tidy and his files neat: 'far from homogeneous',
culturally open-ended, 'subjective', 'indeterminate'.
How much more convenient for study it would be if
the inhabitants could agree to stay deprived, repetitive, dull-minded, lumpen, and easy to interview — in
the same way that housing managers have had a tendency to group together 'problem families' in single
blocks or estates so that welfare workers can attend
to them conveniently together.

What has to be faced, and reconciled, in the minds
of politicians and planners is that society in England
is undergoing an experience of galloping *pluralism*, by
which I mean not an increase in population, which as
we have seen is levelling off again, but an increase in
the variety of individual and social life.

I suspect that part of the sociological hatred of the
suburb, and particularly of the car-borne commuter,

lies in the guilt that sociologists and many other professionals feel for living in them themselves. Few
people have the honesty in these matters of Sir Colin
Buchanan, who tries sometimes almost to overcom-
pensate in the opposite direction: I well remember
just after his *Traffic in Towns* report was published
hearing him in the course of a single afternoon ad-
dress first a lunch-time meeting of the mechanistically
minded Design and Industries Association, at which
he tenderly stressed the need to preserve the handmade brickwork of Queen Anne's Gate houses from
traffic, and then a tea-time meeting of the Society for
the Protection of Ancient Buildings, at which he no
less tenderly pointed out that even if he ever were to
be deprived of the use of his car, he would still revel
in the pleasure simply of owning one, proudly protecting it in its garage and polishing it up on Sundays.

As planners we must examine our motives carefully, and try to cater for the full extent of our neighbours' lives. This is where in fact I find myself neither
in the Young and Willmott neo-slum camp nor in the
Melvin Webber non-place urban realm camp — nor for
that matter attached to Jane Jacobs's insistence on
high density as being a precondition of diversity.

The truth is surely that an increasing number of us
are playing out different roles at quite different scales
at different times of the day and week and at different times of our lives: when we walk down to the
corner shop for a packet of fags (or in my case, a bar
of chocolate) we are playing the Young and Willmott,
or Hampton, role of close attachment to a small
'home area' — we nod to Mr J next door, exchange a
word or two with Kenny's Mum down the road where
our children play, listen to the woes of Miss B about
the racket of the pop-group next door. Even if I were
not a councillor, I would now feel myself identified
closely with Tyrwhitt Road and the top of Loampit
Hill — and feel myself to be poised between the two
urban villages of Brockley and Ladywell. We have
friends in the immediate neighbourhood, fellow
parents and managers at our son's school, fellow
members of the local political party, fellow attenders

at the same church and so on. But put us behind the wheel of a car and we suddenly find ourselves faced with a wholly different scale of identity — a metropolitan scale: big shopping centres both for the 'weekly shop' and for specialities such as furniture and clothes (what the experts respectively call 'convenience shopping' and 'comparison shopping'); a network of friendship which stretches all over London of people we have got to know through college or through work; opportunities for entertainment that take us in to the bright lights of the city centre or out to the green fields of Kent.

This is the reflection of the differences we have already distinguished between the sub-regional loyalties of the football terrace and the convenience of big local government on the one hand, and the intensely local sense of identity with the immediate environment of neighbours and gardens and trees and corner shop on the other. It is not a question of 'either-or' — either mobility in the urban realm or close networks of friendship in the village — it is a question of 'both'. Political decision-making is now geared up for the sub-regional end of the scale; but can it also get to grips with the intensely local? And get to grips it must, if disasters are to be avoided of the kind that the sub-regional GLC and Westminster City Council have already landed themselves in at Covent Garden and at Piccadilly Circus, where slick PR-dominated exhibitions have been followed by rough locally led demonstrations. In those two cases the plans were of the old-fashioned knock-it-all-down kind beloved of developers, and deserved rough handling. But even where the plans are enlightened, the gap between planners and public remains — the gap which the Labour Government tried to close in 1968 through the Skeffington Report on *Public Participation in Planning*. Major reforms in planning practice, reflecting a new sensitivity to the local community as a whole and to the gradualness of its evolution, have in fact run far ahead of the reforms in political practice and sensitivity from which they cannot but be indivisible.

In planning practice there have been four principal advances, all stressing neighbourhoods rather than just buildings: first the concept of the 'environmental area', which Sir Colin Buchanan introduced in his *Traffic in Towns* report of 1963, as the idea of an 'urban room' within which residents would have priority over cars; then the concept of the 'conservation area' in the Civic Amenities Act of 1967 (promoted by the Civic Trust and helped along by the Labour Government) which goes beyond the idea of simply *preserving* individual historic buildings (on the 'lists' begun in 1947) by allowing local authorities to attempt *conserving* the character of whole areas of pleasant town or village or suburb; thirdly, there has been the revision of the system of development plans in the Planning Act of 1968, by which 'structure' plans for the overall strategy of a large local authority were distinguished from 'local plans' in detail for smaller areas, the idea being that at both levels, of principle and of detail, there should be 'public participation in the planning process'; and finally, there has been the concept of the 'improvement area' contained in the Housing Act of 1969, which, as we have already seen, has radically changed the emphasis of housing policy away from simply slum-clearing the worst areas, and towards achieving the best possible quality in the nation's housing stock as a whole by encouraging the improvement of older areas which would otherwise degenerate into slum. These four concepts — environmental area, conservation area, structure plan and local plan, and improvement area — were all enthusiastically endorsed or promoted by the Labour Government of 1964—70; yet that same Government, and even more the Labour councils of major cities, were simultaneously promoting monstrously inhumane high-rise barracks of the old kind, which involved not only a disregard for the elementary principles of conservation and improvement, but even more totally a disregard for 'public participation in the planning process'.

Behind such Jekyll-and-Hyde split-mindedness there lies a fundamental confusion of attitude in most councils, amongst both officials and councillors. Labour councillors in particular tend to have a curiously neurotic attitude towards the communities they are serving. On the one hand there is a clear tradition of Socialist belief which directly supports 'public participation': a belief that ordinary people have the right to have a say in the running of their own affairs and 'top people' do not have any monopoly of wisdom. In fact in the inner suburbs senior officials are often woefully ignorant of the areas they serve, simply because they commute in every day from the posher outer suburbs. The individual councillor in relation to his own ward, and the committee chairman in relation to the whole borough, have a fundamental responsibility to ensure that what people are saying is being heard. Yet what one finds in practice is that many councillors, particularly the more elderly, are fundamentally hostile to any idea of opening up their private discussions and private decision-making. They dislike attending public meetings and give as little as possible away when their turn comes to speak; they regard deputations and petitions and demonstrations as being the work of 'troublemakers', and often refuse to meet them; they even have a habit of passing individual letters of complaint straight on to the officers, without taking the trouble of personally investigating the case on the spot themselves, and without realising that only such clear personal intervention by the councillor himself can lead to the necessary sense of urgency, without any victimisation of the complainant. Above all, they have an absurdly over-sensitive and neurotic attitude towards the local press who, whatever their manifold failings of bias and inaccuracy, are still the only real medium of day-by-day communication behind a council and its wider public (a bi-monthly official newsletter, however desirable, is not the same kind of animal, when it comes to instant reaction and instant comment). The House of Lords were absolutely right, in their amendment to the Local Government Act on the admission of the public to council committee meetings, to insist on putting the onus of exclusion on the councillors — that is to say, the public will statutorily be admitted unless the committee in question specifically resolves to exclude them.

The press has, however, because of its self-interest, tended to overstress the importance of opening up committee meetings and simply listening to what councillors are saying. Experience seems to indicate that few people turn up after the first few weeks and local journalists soon get bored. The fundamental point in any case about public participation is that it is a two-way process. Most councillors see it in terms only of public *consultation*: the council brings its own preconceived plan out from behind the dust-sheets and, by means of a meeting or an exhibition, says: what do you think? The 150 or so who turn up to the meeting and the 500 who happen to be in the public library when the exhibition is on can make a suitable response — after which the councillors and officials go away and do what they were going to do anyway.

Public *participation* is quite different: it means that ordinary residents are drawn into the actual process of preparing the plan. Clearly this will mean other techniques than simply meetings and exhibitions: it can mean actual consultation of people on their doorsteps, whether in a full-scale social survey or in a small-scale random canvass; it can mean the appointment, suggested by Skeffington but rejected in Peter Walker's disappointing circular on the subject, of a community development officer, whose job it would be positively to encourage the formation of local associations and pressure groups; and it can mean the establishment in an area of a 'council corner shop', where a team of officials would get on with their ordinary work but would be available to discuss problems with anyone who dropped in. Particularly in the deprived inner suburbs which have, as we noticed in the last chapter, lost in recent years so many of their younger and more skilled residents, it will be necessary for councils positively to stimulate the formation of residents' groups, even if these groups became actively hostile to council policy and campaign against it.

The real trouble about Labour councils is that, in the bad old tradition of Herbert Morrison or Harry Watton, they have been obsessed by the 'grand slam' approach to local government symbolised by the vast flatted estates: a machine is set rolling which it is hard to stop and hard even for sensitive councillors to divert, let alone the general public. Civic dignitaries have seen their 'home areas' not in terms of a continually evolving way of life within distinctive local cultures and ecologies; they have seen them instead as economic systems which present a series of 'problems' to which have to be applied a set of 'solutions'. The fact that the solution of today may be the slum of tomorrow never occurs to these extrovert bureaucrats; and the fact that it may in any case not even be what the local people actually want today is treated as an irritation, a little local difficulty to be by-passed.

The contrary view of Socialism which I hold is that planning is only necessary in order to prevent the exploitation of man by man in the market, and its prime aim, in freeing people from exploitation, is to make them fully free to choose their own peculiar personal or family or community life-style. This is what Ruskin and Morris were aiming for in their desperate desire to release the creative powers of individuals from the bondage of mass-production — that bondage being culturally and personally as damaging today when the labour is well-paid as it was when the labour was cheap. As long ago as 1928 Harold Laski was putting forward a gospel of 'planning for freedom', which a generation of committee chairmen in the Morrison mould soon lost sight of. 'The reward each citizen earns', Laski insisted, 'must be his own to do with as he will. He may choose, as is so typical of America, to sacrifice the creature-comforts of his home to the possession of a motor-car; or he may wish, as in the case of many Londoners, to endure the discomfort of a long railway journey for the pleasure of cultivating his own garden. The more a man is tempted to experiment with his own standards of consumption, the better it is for society. The one thing we want to avoid are those long rows of villas with identical wallpaper, identical books and identical standards of pleasure. Life is an art which we can know only from experience. And the experiment must be fully our own, shot through with the texture of our unique personality, if we are to realise the things within us which make us different from our fellows.'

It is easy to see why, in the exigencies of slum clearance, uniformity has been thrust upon people instead; it goes back to the fact that, in Sidney Webb's words, 'the early Victorian community, bare of schools, or drains, or Factory Acts, had to get itself supplied with the common article of standard pattern.' It has been all too easy for the standard pattern to be provided simply because it is the easiest thing that can be managed in a crisis — the word 'crisis' then being used, as in wartime, to justify the most elementary suppression of personal liberties. Undoubtedly in most of the areas slum-cleared in the late fifties and early sixties, under the 1957 Housing Act, the majority of tenants were only too glad to get shot of the hovels they had been living in; but the fact that they may have since been less than perfectly happy in a standard municipal box of bliss in the sky, has led inevitably to a much less willing response to clearance from their former neighbours when their turn for 'decanting' has come. At the same time, the kind of houses 'represented' to the Minister for clearance in the 1965—70 programme tended by the very nature of things to be better dwellings than those cleared in the previous programme.

In his book *People and Planning* Norman Dennis has meticulously charted in one city, Sunderland, how this gradual change of attitude led to a hardening resistance to slum clearance amongst the slum dwellers themselves. Already in 1966 in the Ministry's own Deeplish Study of part of Rochdale, the surprising fact emerged that even in the poorest houses (in those less than 30 per cent as good, on an artificial index, as a new dwelling of the same size) there were as many as 28 per cent who were 'very well satisfied' with where they lived and 33 per cent more who 'found it all right'; in the higher category of houses which were over 61 per cent as good as new, as many as 77 per cent of the people there were 'very well satisfied'. Behind such satisfaction with the status quo lies among other things a substantial increase in home ownership amongst working-class families. From being a middle-class prerogative it has rapidly spread to those of lower income, often because landlords have given up the struggle to repair their property on controlled rents, and have sold the freeholds to sitting tenants for nominal sums. Dennis found in Sunderland that, in the clearance areas for 1965–70, as many as four out of ten families were 'very satisfied' where they were; and amongst the elderly and childless, seven out of ten did not expect to be better off on a council estate. Among owner-occupiers two-thirds were against demolition. So the question then arises: should they be coerced?

It is easy enough for officials to dismiss objections to clearance as coming simply from those who are trying to squeeze out more compensation, in that 'full market value' on borough valuer's terms is sometimes marginally behind full market value as the market sees it. But much more important is the growing discontent of families, at a time of rising living standards, with the kind of accommodation which councils have available to offer; almost every major housing authority has recently had to face a rising tide of 'refusals of offers'. A stock response is to say that this shows either the blank ingratitude of the working classes or alternatively that those who say they need council housing do not in fact mean it. But I can on the contrary see nothing but good in the development of an increasingly sensitive and discriminating attitude of people to their surroundings; people are supposed to be educated to be critical, and now that men are spending more time in the home and less in the pub, they are beginning to respect their wives' sensitivity rather more than in the past.

In Sunderland the council's answer in 1965 to the

rising tide of 'refusals', particularly of prewar flats and high-rise flats, was the brutal one of limiting the number of refusals to two. A 77-year-old owner-occupier widow for example was sent the following characteristic letter: 'You will be aware that the houses in the above area must be demolished as soon as possible because they are unfit to live in. To enable demolition to take place the Housing and Estates Manager has made you two offers of alternative suitable accommodation which I understand have been refused by you. I hereby give you notice that the offer will remain open for acceptance by you until... and if you do not accept by that date, no more offers of accommodation will be made and steps will be taken, without further notice to you, to have you evicted from the property to enable the same to be demolished as required by the Minister of Housing and Local Government. I will advise you in your own interest to accept this final offer immediately.'

It is not surprising that, under treatment of that kind, the worm has begun to turn. The 'evangelistic bureaucrat', as Jon Davies calls him, has for so long been able to tell people without question, like Don Carlos's executioner, 'I hang thee, but for thine own good', using the wholesale hypothetical argument that 'future generations' will suffer unless particular abuses can be rooted out. With all those letters after his name, lay councillors tend to feel that he must be right. Yet, as Norman Dennis points out, the knowledge of officials is sometimes far from detailed: areas in Sunderland were designated for clearance purely on the basis of what planning assistants could see on maps or, on occasions, from a moving vehicle, there being a shortage of public health inspectors at the time; and interviews with husbands or wives to ask them whether they were overcrowded or lacking in the 'standard amenities' took an average of two minutes and specifically, as the Council's letter put it, 'will not involve an inspection of the properties'.

Yet even careful lengthy examinations by fully trained public health inspectors are not an objective revelation of God's word, but only a statement of personal opinion. The 1954 Housing Repairs and Rent Act laid down a national definition of a slum: 'In determining for any of the purposes of this Act whether a house is unfit for human habitation regard shall be had to its condition in respect of the following matters, that is to say (a) repair; (b) stability; (c) freedom from damp; (d) natural lighting; (e) ventilation; (f) water supply; (g) drainage and sanitary conveniences; (h) facilities for the storage, preparation and cooking of food and the disposal of waste water; and the house shall be deemed to be unfit for human habitation if and only if it is so far defective in one or more of the said matters that it is not reasonably suitable for occupation in that condition.' But the word 'defective' is purely a statement of opinion. Who is to say what it means? The answer in practice is the Inspector who reports to the Minister; but at an earlier stage it is the Public Health Inspector who reports to councillors, and it would be quite wrong for councillors to rubber-stamp clearance areas purely on the grounds that a particular man happens not to think much of the houses in them. In particular, the first category of unfitness — 'repair' — is capable of the widest possible interpretation. We must also remember that different opinions on fitness may be held by a working-class housewife as against a middle-class professional: as many as 65 per cent of Dennis's sample, for example, far from considering an outside loo a disadvantage, actually thought it superior, and criticised inside loos by comparison: ' "It's not hygienic. It's not *polite*! A toilet *inside* the home? Oh, no, thank you!" It was felt "not nice" to bring the sound of, for example, the emptying cistern into the home.'

Now what is true of Sunderland may not be true of other places — those who were particularly unwilling to lose their homes there were admittedly those who lived in that city's special peculiarity of single-storey terrace houses. Each local authority has got to find out what the idiosyncrasies of its own citizens are, and what it is they hold dear in any particular neighbourhood. There has been far too much concentra-

H

tion in the past on the 'objective factors' such as loos and ventilators, and far too little on people's subjective amalgam of fears and fancies about what makes their area nice to live in or what makes it 'rough'. Norman Dennis tellingly compares two different perceptions of the same Sunderland 'slum', first of a professional, and then of a local: 'Within the first frame of reference, Millfield is a collection of shabby, mean and dreary houses, derelict back lanes, shoddy-fronted shops and broken pavements, the whole unsightly mess mercifully ill-lit. Within the second frame of reference, that, say, of a sixty-year-old woman who lives there, the same scene may convey messages of quite another kind... Millfield for her is Bob Smith's, which she thinks (probably correctly) is the best butcher's in the town; George McKeith's wet-fish shop and Peary's fried-fish shop...Maw's hot pies and peas prepared on the premises; the Willow Pond public house, in which her favourite nephew organises the darts and dominoes team; the Salvation Army band in a nearby street every Sunday and waking her with carols on Christmas morning; her special claim to attention in the grocer's because her niece worked there for several years; the spacious cottage in which she was born and brought up, which she now owns, has improved and which has not in her memory had defects which have caused her or her neighbours discernible inconvenience (but which has some damp patches which make it classifiable as a 'slum dwelling'); the short road to the cemetery where she cares for the graves of her mother, father and brother; her sister's cottage across the road — she knows that every weekday at 12.30 a hot dinner will be ready for her when she comes from work; the bus route which will take her to the town centre in a few minutes...' Need I go on: this is where we need either the assistance of the social psychologist, as Dennis suggests, or else just plain commonsense based on personal observation; and Sunderland, after all, is Dennis's home town, where he is now a Labour councillor (as well as commuting to his lectureship in sociology at Newcastle).

The problems of communication are not just those of language, but also those of professional training which reinforces contempt for people without technical knowledge. In presenting their grievances, working-class people, however vivid and accurate their observations of the life around them, often find it difficult to conceptualise overall problems, so that the solutions they offer appear half-brained to the expert. Yet the expert, in rejecting those 'solutions' with contempt, all too often rejects, or fails to explore, the direct and vital observations which gave rise to them — this being the great divide that Bernstein has discerned between the 'public' language of immediate response and the 'formal' language of trained analysis. Frequently the highly educated mind misses the point, and fails to see the real grievances about dogshit and rubbish through a haze of generalised jargon about 'social factors' (meaning people). Orwell rightly discerned (in his essay *Politics and the English Language*) that prefabricated panels of technical phraseology, far from being the product of thought, tend, as in the design of a tower block, to be the alibi for its absence.

Some politicians and some professionals may think that I am writing a mere prescription for anarchy, or advocating the kind of flabby populism — telling everyone that his grievance is justified — which was the political fallacy of George McGovern. Councillors must at all costs be honest: at a public meeting, in my experience, sincerity and openness are nine parts of the law, and, so long as he listens to what people have to say and meets the problems head-on, the councillor is fully entitled — indeed has the duty — to tell people when he does *not* consider their grievances justified. In the end the decision-making will still be made in the town hall, but as a result of proper public participation, it should be immeasurably better informed. The physical concepts still remain — the environmental area, the conservation area, the general improvement area (or GIA) — but by coming directly out of discussion with the residents, they have the chance of evolving from the start as part of the living 'sense of identity' of an urban village.

Mind you, 'We're implementing Skeffington' has now become as much of a defensive municipal reflex as 'We're implementing Buchanan' was five years ago: in the case of Buchanan, usually one measly pedestrian precinct resulting from a sell-out by the local council to a property developer, in the case of Skeffington, a few public relation hand-outs and the occasional exhibition or film-show. Just as few councils have faced up to the fundamental implication of Buchanan — that, if we are to protect those 'urban rooms', the necessary corridors of traffic, and those who live along them, have got to be safeguarded — equally few have faced up to the fundamental difference between public relations and public participation — between handing down the tablets from the mountain, however attractively packaged, and discussing in the first place what their content should be.

Take the case of public meetings when launching a General Improvement Area: at present many councils make the fatal mistake of not holding one until the officers have produced a scheme. What follows at the meeting is that (a) the council is rightly accused of having made up its collective mind in advance and (b) the meeting is constantly side-tracked by apparently 'irrelevant' complaints about why there is still a pile of rubbish on the waste ground behind number 36 — and what about the 'problem families' the council has been dumping in the area to 'drag it down'? Recent 'feedback' reports by outside consultants on their GIA experiences (such as J. L. Grove's at Caerphilly and Ronald Phillips's in the valleys of Ogmore and Garw) indicate the vital importance of holding *two* meetings, not one, with the crucial stage of making the design coming midway between the two. The first meeting is purely a 'gripe and grope' about the area, listening to the residents with no council proposals at all, except for explaining the idea of a GIA, possibly backed up by a hired film (such as the Department of the Environment's on Exeter). A first meeting of this kind not only allows the residents to say what *they* think is wrong with their area, but also gives the Councillors an opportunity, for example, of rejecting publicly the notion that there is some special category of family called a 'problem family' (with uniform and lapel badge to say so): there are only families with problems, yours as well as mine, some with bigger problems, some with smaller, all different.

Councillors should also make clear that if residents want to save their area from disintegration into slumdom, they must *organise* themselves into a residents' association — the vital point here being to ensure, by having a representative from each street, that the association fully reflects the area's different residents and different interests. J. L. Grove's wholly working-class residents' association at Caerphilly horrified his architectural sensibility by putting rightly as their first priority, and carrying out with their own bare hands, the clothing of a prominent wasteland slope in crazily ornate pattern of coloured bricks and stones — panoramic gnomery on a community scale. Up in the valleys Phillips and his multi-professional team grappled with such esoteric problems of the Welsh as the effect of wandering sheep on floral landscaping, and of miners' 'concessionary coal' dumped on neat pavements.

Outside consultants can be specially useful in GIAs, in that they act in an 'advocacy' role of independent mediation between residents and council; yet, as I know from experience, a good council architect at group leader level can consult just as well, if given the chance. In one area in my borough, after heated opposition to the original slum clearance proposals of the officers, which the councillors themselves rejected at the first opportunity, the residents have become so enthusiastic about the new improvement scheme that their committee members have actually been along, on their own initiative, to explain to the residents of the dozen or so houses that do have to be demolished exactly why it was necessary for the common good that they should. Here in fact is public participation acting not as a delaying factor — and every architect's and planning department will tell you how desperately time-consuming it all is — but instead promoting the agreed scheme positively, neighbour-to-neighbour.

There is a specially important role here for the local ward councillor, if only their calibre were not generally so poor, both main parties scraping the barrel for candidates. In the void left by the inactive or the incapable, it is not surprising that alternative democracies are beginning to arise in the form of the so-called Neighbourhood Councils (another Michael Young enterprise). The first of these, in the Golborne Ward of North Kensington, succeeded at least in attracting 27 per cent to the polls, as against 19 per cent for the previous ordinary borough council election. But such bodies soon run into difficulties of individual empire-building when they try to operate outside the normal party system; and, subsidised as they often are by borough councils, they lack the full political power of decision-making. Probably the most sensible kind of neighbourhood council is that which does not try to compete with the local government system, but complements it: Telegraph Hill Neighbourhood Council at New Cross, for example, is a straightforward federation of local residents' associations and community activities — the 'voluntary bodies' as against the council departments. It is this kind of organisation that is likely to be of most relevance in General Improvement Areas.

The most radical pioneers in this field have been the team under Des McConaghy, who in 1969—72 carried out as much as they could of the Shelter Neighbourhood Action Project (SNAP) in the exceptionally daunting environment of Granby Ward, Liverpool 8. Their special success lay, I think, in two simple things (which tend to be concealed beneath McConaghy's jargon-prone rhetoric): first, they established in an old fire station a clearly identifiable 'community corner shop' where everyone in the area could come for advice on all manner of problems which would (and could) never have been taken to the remote City Hall; secondly, their residents' association had, as in Leicester's successful Clarendon GIA, a clear hierarchy of team leadership, street by street — the street unquestionably being still the nearest and dearest of village foci.

The SNAP 'corner shop' has proved a prototype for more centralised Housing Advice Centres which have since sprung up all over the country under municipal authority, starting at Lambeth early in 1970 under their housing manager Harry Simpson (now grappling with the public housing of Ulster). Furthermore they can give (though not all do) a full range of legal and personal, and not just 'housing', advice — what in a sense the Citizen's Advice Bureaux have been doing for years in a less urgent and outgoing way. Such advice centres can thus become places where *all* residents feel they can come without stigma: tenants furnished or unfurnished, private or council, owner-occupiers, engaged couples. To this end Lambeth decked out their centre, within a modest converted warehouse, not only with the dishiest Scandinavian timberwork, but also with wall-to-wall carpeting, up-to-date magazines and background music — a spectacular departure from the municipal atmosphere of echoing lino and green tiles.

Simpson could justify the 'centrality' of his Centre at Brixton on the strong grounds that, being but three doors up the street from all the departments at the main Town Hall, a full range of municipal aid could be made available instantly for even the most esoteric client. The implication, however, is that the best of both worlds, SNAP and Lambeth, could be attempted if council departments, while keeping a strategic core at the centre, could otherwise be decentralised into multi-disciplinary teams working on a local area basis — not perhaps the extravagance of one for each single 'urban village' but certainly one for each group of urban villages. The more progressive council departments have already been decentralised in some places, but have then failed to liaise sufficiently with other departments when they have been decentralised too. In Camden the housing department set up district offices first, followed by the new (post-

Seebohm Report) social services department on a different geographical split; in Lewisham the reverse order was followed, first social services into district offices and then housing. But time and again the families with the most serious problems need answers which are spread across a number of different departments, and it is as wasteful as it is inhumane to shunt them from door to door. At the local level, as well as at the town hall, a full range of services should be available.

It all goes back to the evils I mentioned earlier of the division of responsibility between the rival empires of different council departments and committees — housing, highways, amenities, social services and so on — each soliciting its grants separately from different Ministries and each building its projects, even in Comprehensive Development Areas, on a separate programme. The adoption in 1971 of a 'block grant' system of 'locally determined expenditure' for some services has been less of a unifying influence than it might have been in some places because of the Government's exploitation of it as a means of providing less in toto. But certainly those local authorities who are adopting systems of Corporate Planning or Planned Programme Budgeting are at last giving themselves the opportunity of working out their priorities in a coordinated way, often through the 'cabinet' system of a central 'policy committee'. If this kind of coordination at the central Town Hall can then be translated into coordination at the local council corner shop — the village 'town hall' — there may be a chance of mere physical planning at last being transformed into community development.

Social services departments have tended to see the wider possibilities inherent in such coordination more clearly than those concerned with housing or planning; and this is, I think, because social workers have been forced, by the very nature of their jobs, to go out and find their clients, not merely respond to events. For too long the 'patients' who have been 'treated' by local authorities in housing and in welfare have been those who have been badly off, but not necessarily the *most* badly off, just because it has needed a considerable minimum of initiative on anyone's part to go out and search for the cure to his problems. The pitifully slow take-up of the Family Income Supplement, the widespread ignorance of the existence of rate rebates, the equally pitiful level of implementation of the 1970 Disablement Act — most authorities have no idea how many disabled people live within their boundaries — these will no doubt be followed by another sluggish response to the humiliating need for rebates and rent allowances under the 1972 Housing Finance Act. The fact that the average income of council tenants is rather higher than that of private tenants is not an argument for less council housebuilding; all it shows, as the rising tide of families actually homeless also does, is that many local authorities have not gone out of their way to make sure that their housing lists contain all those in greatest need.

The same applies with equal cogency to the process of 'public participation in planning'. The Skeffington Report devoted far too much of its space to the conventional methods of publicity — public meetings, exhibitions, press, radio and TV, movies — and to the conventional forms of environmental get-together among the professionally articulate — civic or preservation or amenity societies, chambers of trade, advisory panels of architects, culminating in its own idea of a portmanteau discussion group of like-minded folk called a 'community forum', in which architects and businessmen and churchmen would mingle. At a first glance the report, albeit under the chairmanship of a Labour Minister, would seem entirely to conform to those who think that 'the environment' or 'amenity' or 'ecology' are purely middle-class fads like stripped pine furniture or Habitat crockery. Not a mention, as far as one can see, of tenants' associations — and they did already exist in considerable numbers in 1969.

Just after I became a councillor in 1971, a local journalist suggested to me that 'the environment' was

233

only a middle-class fashion: my answer was that, although that word 'environment' may only be known in certain circles, he should go down to the newly built GLC housing estate at the bottom of the hill, and listen to what he heard: complaints about dangerous estate roads, complaints about heavy lorries revving up at 5 a.m., complaints about rubbish, complaints about rats, complaints about the lack of places for children to play. Are these matters not 'the environment'? Of course they are, and they concern the majority of people. But they are not necessarily the same concerns as those which motivate the minority of well-housed people who belong to civic societies or attend meetings and exhibitions.

This is where we come hard up against what Skeffington calls 'the non-joiners' and Norman Dennis (echoing many a local politician) calls 'the problem of public apathy'. When Sunderland Corporation first attempted participation in the proposed 'action area' of North-West Sunderland, a pamphlet and an exhibition elicited out of a population of 20,000 people a grand total of thirty-six written observations. Even the cases of 'successful participation' which the Skeffington Report chronicles in its appendices seem curiously unsuccessful: Coventry, for instance, held 28 ward meetings to discuss the First Review of its Development Plan, but attracted to them only 1,100 people, which means less than forty to each meeting. And then there is Appendix 10 of the report, on the Barnsbury Exhibition, which reveals that a superb Ministry-mounted display of improvement plans there succeeded in attracting just 3.15 per cent of the local families.

Barnsbury is in fact an important cautionary tale of community development and the rehabilitation of urban villages. The Government's previous pilot project, Deeplish, had been situated in a rooted working-class neighbourhood, in a town where few people were any longer on the move or on the make; so there were equally few ulterior motives at work as people bought their freeholds cheaply and set to work industriously to instal bathrooms and loos, while the

Ministry planted trees, equipped playgrounds, stopped up culs-de-sac and laid out parking bays. It is a process of renewal, particularly for areas of ageing population, which has since proved highly successful in the North, with Robert Matthew, Johnson-Marshall and Partners' studies of Nelson and Rawtenstall, *New Life in Old Towns,* as the official (Department of the Environment) bible. Barnsbury by contrast is an agitatedly mobile 'zone of transition', with landlords suddenly cashing in on the nearness of its decaying Regency houses to the City and tenants being turfed out, with enticements (£400 or £800 to go), in order to make way for immigrant admen and businessmen and architects.

The energetic immigrants, with the usual eagerness to 'put down roots', formed from the best of motives the Barnsbury Society, in order to fight a crass GLC compulsory purchase order on Regency cottages in Bewdley Street. It was the obvious good sense and expertise of their evidence that led Richard Crossman to choose Barnsbury as a southern companion piece to Deeplish; and in fact he specifically named the Barnsbury Society, without realising how narrowly based its membership was, as the one voluntary body which the joint Ministry-GLC-Islington study group would have to consult. But unfortunately the study was dominated by another mobile element — the long-distance lorry traffic ploughing through Islington on its way to warehouses and terminals in King's Cross and the City — and so the main emphasis of the study was not on rehabilitation of houses but on creating a Buchanan-type 'environmental area'. All would have been well if the GLC, as the primary roads authority, had been prepared, on the basis of 'restraint by congestion', to restrict lorry traffic to the obvious flanking commercial 'corridors' of Upper Street and Caledonian Road; but this, for crude reasons of maintaining traffic flow, they were not prepared to do. Accordingly the study group chose instead to divert lorry traffic from Thornhill Road and Cloudesley Way (where many of the 'new people' lived) to a couple of far-from-commercial thoroughfares within the environmental area, Liverpool Road and Copenhagen Street, where the working-class population of the area happened to be concentrated, in old multi-occupied houses and in prewar LCC flats. A roaring one-way road island was botched up around the local Victorian primary school.

Inevitably the crudest kind of class warfare broke out when this 'experimental traffic scheme' for Barnsbury was actually introduced by the Islington Conservatives in 1970; it was picked on as a nefarious attempt to create a precinct for the rich at the expense of the surrounding poor. Furthermore, following upon the 1969 Housing Act, it soon became apparent that Barnsbury was just the kind of area where property developers, taking 50 per cent of their rehabilitation money in grants from the public purse — up to a maximum of £1200 per house — were going to be able to make a quick killing in terms of profit margins.

The same 'gentrification' has tended to happen also in other exceptionally attractive yet exceptionally run-down areas of Inner London, in Camden and Hammersmith and Lambeth; and it is not surprising that this reluctance to line the pockets of developers had led to a situation by the spring of 1972 where only 12 per cent of the GIAs in the whole country had been designated in London. Certainly in designating GIAs local councils must insist and ensure that the rights of existing tenants are fully safeguarded, scrutinising carefully the credentials of applicants for grant, refusing to those on the make all but the £300 or so of 'standard' grants for loos and bathrooms that have to be paid by law and are not 'discretionary'.

But it must be emphasised, amidst media which tend to be dominated by propagandists who themselves live in these stressful parts of Inner London, that most GIAs, even in London, are unattractive to the trendy, and have a rooted local community of ordinary families. In the suburban terraces of South London, in the mining villages of South Wales, in the textile towns of Yorkshire and Lancashire, and in the industrial towns of the North-East — in all these parts of the country an encouraging picture is emerging of the improvement of the ordinary into the decent. It is all being done at bargain prices too, one of the great attractions of the 'drab' terrace house in the North being the value it gives for money in terms of space and flexibility compared with the modern flat. It was in their so-called 'impact study' on the effects on the surrounding region of the proposed Central Lancashire New City at Preston that Sir Robert Matthew's architect-planners first stumbled on the astonishing possibilities of all those houses which could be purchased for under £1000 in supposedly derelict cotton towns such as Nelson and Rawtenstall. Situated as they are in glorious Pennine scenery within easy commuting distance of Preston or Manchester — or even parts of Yorkshire, now that the motorways are being completed — these rehabilitated settlements in steep valleys can take on an enviable new life as, of all things, garden suburbs.

It is all a matter, as Raymond Unwin realised, of understanding and of sanctifying what 'culture' in its full sense is all about: the culture of the front garden and the back garden, the culture of the small church hall, the culture of the corner shop, the culture not of the arty 'play sculpture' for visiting councillors but of the school playground open after hours, the culture that Brian Jackson describes of the highly competitive brass band and bowling green. More and more people are taking on 'second jobs' in their spare time, while so-called 'leisure pursuits' are becoming increasingly professional: athletics, lawn tennis, ballroom dancing, even politics.

What we are seeing in fact is a great middlebrow explosion in the suburbs, with distinctions being broken down between the roles of men and women, of work and play, of amateur and professional, of High Art and Low Art. How well one can remember the sheer guilt, mingled with emotional panic, with which one used to listen with one's fellow Sixth Formers in the late fifties to Presley and Buddy Holly as well as Bach and Palestrina — and how dated such guilt seems today. The kind of community centre to

237

which people will be flocking in the next generation is foreshadowed on Teesside where first the Billingham Forum and then the Thornaby Pavilion have been developed as family centres: Billingham a fairly straightforward juxtaposition of swimming pool and gym and theatre, with a central creche; Thornaby a much more sophisticated mixture where the family can disperse, say, Dad to the gym and Mum to the bingo, girl to the pottery class and boy to the guitar recital, before they all come together again to feed in the common restaurant and share their experiences together. It is fascinating to see how, just as in a medieval university, the act of eating has become once more a moment of profound significance in community life; no new public library now should be without its coffee bar.

What is remarkable in the suburbs is the way in which the truly unexpected suddenly arises out of the very freedom and flexibility of the place. Here in my own borough the old derelict municipal baths have become the principal training ground for the British women's gymnastic team; meanwhile a mile or two away, in an ordinary Victorian terrace house, the two ex-actors Mander and Mitchenson have gathered together unobtrusively the finest collection of theatrical history outside the Victoria and Albert Museum; a mile further south, the Frank and Peggy Spencer formation dancing team from Penge are also supreme in their own field. We must in fact drop our inherited prejudices about the 'high' and 'low' in taste and ask ourselves more genuinely and unpuritanically whether or not the particular experience has been good of its kind.

I shall never forget the excitement of the opening sequence of Ian Engelmann's television film *The Wandsworth Sound*, with a long aerial tracking shot across the ordinary South-London-suburban rooftops and gardens of Putney and Southfields, as the famous Wandsworth comprehensive school choir, one of the finest and most professional in Europe, belted out 'Zadok the Priest and Nathan the Prophet'. What was fascinating in the interviews that followed was to see the classless singers, their sharp and vibrant timbre incidentally rather different from the effete hooting of the cathedral tradition, returning home in the evening to opulent Putney or decayed Battersea, to parents still rooted in divisions of class and culture, from which the boys themselves had been wonderfully liberated.

Other books in the series:

RACE, INTELLIGENCE AND EDUCATION
H.J. Eysenck

SEX, GENDER AND SOCIETY
Ann Oakley

STORIES FROM THE DOLE QUEUE
Tony Gould and Joe Kenyon

New Society comes out weekly, containing
articles by experts on sociology, anthropo-
logy, psychology, the social services, government, planning, education, and other matters
of social concern.

It always contains: social policy notes;
current research results; reviews of books;
and reviews of the arts.

The articles are written with intelligence,
concern and clarity about subjects that can
often be fogged by jargon.

New Society is available from newsagents
on Thursdays, or by direct subscription from
128 Long Acre, London WC2.

NEWsociety